# PHP and MySQL for Beginners

*PHP and MySQL for Beginners*

# PHP and MySQL for Beginners

Mark Lassoff

LearnToProgram, Inc.
Vernon, Connecticut

LearnToProgram.tv, Incorporated
27 Hartford Turnpike Suite 206
Vernon, CT06066
contact@learntoprogram.tv
(860) 840-7090

ISBN-13: 978-0-9904020-1-5
ISBN-10: 0-9904020-1-0

Mark Lassoff, Publisher
Kevin Hernandez, VP/ Production
Alison Downs, Copy Editor
Alexandria O'Brien, Book Layout
Jimda Mariano, Technical Writer
Niaz Makhdum, Technical Writer
Jeremias Jimenez, Technical Editor

Dedication

Dedicated to those who struggle to end bullying. If you have been
bullied, you are beautiful and we love you.

Courses Available from LearnToProgram, Inc.

3D Fundamentals with iOS
Advanced Javascript Development
AJAX Development
Android Development for Beginners
Become a Certified Web Developer (Level 1)
Become a Certified Web Developer (Level 2)
C Programming for Beginners
Creating a PHP Login Script
Creating an MP3 Player with HTML5
CSS Development (with CSS3!)
Design for Coders
Game Development Fundamentals with Python
HTML and CSS for Beginners (with HTML5)
HTML5 Mobile App Development with PhoneGap
Introduction to Web Development
iOS Development Code Camp
iOS Development for Beginners Featuring iOS6/7
Java Programming for Beginners
Javascript for Beginners
Joomla for Beginners
jQuery for Beginners
Mobile Game Development with iOS
Node.js for Beginners
Objective C for Beginners
Photoshop for Coders
PHP & MySQL for Beginners
Python for Beginners
SQL Database for Beginners
User Experience Design


Books from LearnToProgram, Inc.

HTML and CSS for Beginners
Create Your Own MP3 Player with HTML5
Javascript for Beginners
Python for Beginners
CSS for Beginners

# TABLE OF CONTENTS

About the Author:

Mark Lassoff

Mark Lassoff's parents frequently claim that Mark was born to be a programmer. In the mid-eighties when the neighborhood kids were outside playing kickball and throwing snowballs, Mark was hard at work on his Commodore 64 writing games in the BASIC programming language. Computers and programming continued to be a strong interest in college where Mark majored in communication and computer science. Upon completing his college career, Mark worked in the software and web development departments at several large corporations.

In 2001, on a whim, while his contemporaries were conquering the dot com world, Mark accepted a position training programmers in a technical training center in Austin, Texas. It was there that he fell in love with teaching programming.

Teaching programming has been Mark's passion for the last 10 years. Today, Mark is a top technical trainer, traveling the country providing leading courses for software and web developers. Mark's training clients include the Department of Defense, Lockheed Martin, Discover Card Services, and Kaiser Permanente. In addition to traditional classroom training, Mark releases courses on the web, which have been taken by programming students all over the world.

He lives near Hartford, Connecticut where he is in the process of redecorating his condominium.

About the Course Producer:

Kevin Hernandez

Kevin has worked at LearnToProgram since the company's formation in 2011. Kevin is responsible for the entire production process including video editing, distribution and testing of lab exercises. Kevin plays the French horn in multiple bands and orchestras throughout Connecticut.

*PHP and MySQL for Beginners*

# CHAPTER 1

## YOUR FIRST PHP SCRIPT

### CHAPTER OBJECTIVES:

- You will be able to define "PHP" and "PHP scripting".
- You will be able to identify and install the software development tools needed to create PHP scripts.
- You will learn how to set up the programming environment needed to work with PHP.
- You will be able to run your first PHP script.

## 1.1 SETTING UP YOUR DEVELOPMENT ENVIRONMENT

You might think that when learning **PHP** programming, you would be studying the PHP language in isolation. However, PHP is central to a suite of technologies used to develop PHP-based applications. Describing the technologies in that suite is a good place to begin.

PHP is a general purpose, open-source, server side scripting language designed for web development. It is used to produce dynamic web pages. It is a web scripting language used to add basic web features to a site. Examples of PHP's use are creating username and password login screens, checking form details, creating forum pages, picture galleries, surveys and many more. PHP is a powerful language that enables developers to create almost any type of application that they desire.

**PHP**

Unlike some web languages such as Javascript, PHP is not executed within your web browser but instead on the server—the computer that stores the page and makes it available to browsers on the internet. The server processes a request from a web browser and then returns the requested content—usually in HTML format. This is the reason that PHP is referred to as a "server side language."

PHP can be written in both an external document or embedded within the HTML document itself. The PHP code is interpreted by a web server (frequently an Apache server) that has a PHP processor module, which generates the resulting webpage. Other popular languages similar to PHP are ASP, Python, Perl, and Ruby.

One of the frequent uses of computer languages like PHP is to interface with a database or data source. Frequently, PHP is paired with the MySQL database. We'll talk about the interaction between PHP and MySQL towards the latter part of this book.

According to computer history, Rasmus Lerdorf developed the initial PHP specification. The term PHP is said to have evolved from his **P**ersonal **H**ome **P**age project into the open-source scripting language widely used and known today as Hypertext PreProcessor—a result of wide collaborative efforts by a pool of developers. However, it does not follow the original acronym PHP, thus, **P**re-**H**ypertext **P**rocessor. The scripting language itself was developed using the C language.

*As Rasmus Lerdorf puts it, PHP is not a new and revolutionary language as it borrows much of its syntax from languages such as C, Perl and Java. PHP is a very focused web design language. It is a language written for web developers.*

*PHP is perfectly suited for quickly creating web front-end and back-end systems—database creation and manipulation, direct access protocol for directory servers, simple network management protocol for directory servers or generating non-HTML dynamic content for the web such as images, flash or PDF documents.*

*An example of an easy PHP task is pulling up customer information from the database and dynamically generating a professional- looking PDF invoice. (www.computerworld.com, Interview with Rasmus Lerdorf, Feb 4, 2002)*

Many multiplayer online game servers are built using PHP.

MySQL is a free database management system based on standard SQL, which stands for Structured Query Language. SQL became a standard database language in 1986. It is used for accessing and manipulating databases. The SQL language is fairly consistent from database engine to database engine—meaning that moving from working with one database brand to another is fairly easy.

**MySQL** is an open-source relational database
management system (RDBMS) that runs on a server
that allows or provides multi-user access to several databases
simultaneously. The developer of MySQL is Oracle (formerly Sun

MySQL

Microsystems). It was named (according to Wikipedia) after the co-founder Michael Widenius', daughter, My, which was prefixed to SQL, thus MySQL.

MySQL is a popular database option for use in web applications. It is also a central component for the different open-source web language stacks, namely Linux, Apache, Perl, Python, etc. But the most common pairing is PHP and MySQL as they both tend to take minimalistic and very direct approaches to solving problems.

With MySQL you can create relationships between elements in the database so you don't have to repeat data whenever it is needed again for processing in web applications. MySQL will be discussed thoroughly at the latter part of the course.

The **Apache** web server application is available for **Apache** a wide variety of operating systems. It is an open-source (meaning non-proprietary) http server program developed and maintained under the auspices of the Apache Software Foundation. The application is available for a wide variety of operating systems including UNIX, Solaris, Novell Netware, Mac OS X, Microsoft Windows, OS/2, TPF, and eComStation. It is released under the Apache license. Legend has it that the origin of the name Apache came from the description of the software itself having many software patches—server software running full of patches = a patchy server = APACHE.

Another application that will complete the PHP **phpMyAdmin** programming environment is **phpMyAdmin**. It is an application written in the PHP language itself that provides a web-based interface for the administration of MySQL databases.

phpMyAdmin is a free and open-source tool intended to handle administration of MySQL with the aid of a web browser. It can perform various tasks such as creating, modifying, or deleting databases, tables, fields, or rows; executing MySQL statements or managing users and permissions.

## PREPARING YOUR TOOLKIT

To begin creating applications using PHP and MySQL, you will need several applications that will aid you in development. **Komodo Edit**

The first application needed is a text editor. In the examples in this book, I will be using Active State's **Komodo Edit** Freeware version, but other editors may be used as an alternative. Do not use word processors, as they add built in code that will interfere with the compiler.

You may download Komodo Edit for free and there are versions for Windows, Mac, and even Linux. This is what Komodo Edit looks like when run:

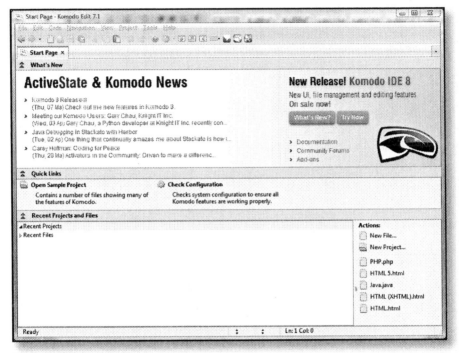

Figure 1.1: Komodo Edit's opening screen.

Komodo Edit comes with several templates for development, which can provide a good starting point.

Another application you will need is a web server environment. This is not separate computer hardware but a software application that lets your desktop computer act as a server for testing PHP scripts. This way you can test your PHP scripts without actually being online and connected to a live server on the internet. Your computer will be both client and server. For Windows and Linux users, the server software environment to be used is WAMP, while for Macintosh users it will be MAMP.

**WAMP** stands for **Windows, Apache, MySQL** and **PHP.** Once downloaded, it will put these tools in your tray: local host, phpMyAdmin, Apache, PHP, and MySQL, as shown in the following image:

Figure 1.2: WampServer's Main (or Control) Menu which can be activated by clicking on WampServer's Icon in the Icon Tray of Windows.

The URL for WAMP installation is: www.wampserver.com

For the Mac, MAMP is the environment to be set up. It stands for Macintosh, Apache, MySQL, and PHP. Its function is basically the same as the Windows version of the suite.

If you are working on a Windows machine, to begin setting up your working environment you need to make sure that the latest Visual C++ Service Pack is downloaded and installed for your system. This service pack should be readily available if you have the automatic updates set up on your PC. WAMP will also check if you have the latest version of the Visual C++ Service Pack and it will notify you accordingly.

You can now download WAMP by visiting www.wampserver.com/ en. WAMP is a free server software environment and everything is included in the package—Apache, PHP, MySQL and phpMyAdmin.

Figure 1.3: WampServer's Main Page at http://www.wampserver.com/en/.

You may check out the list of items included in the package–Apache, My SQL PHP and phpMyAdmin—in the download page.

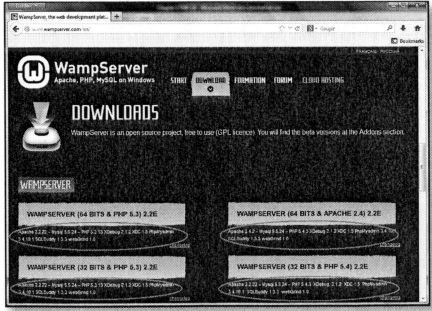

Figure 1.4: WampServer's download page also at http://www.wampserver.com/en/.

Take note of the directory in which you will extract the zip file of WAMP, as you will need to refer to it when you set up your Komodo Edit file path and your local server.

After extracting the WAMP folder into your local hard disk drive, launch Komodo Edit. Go to the menu bar and choose edit.

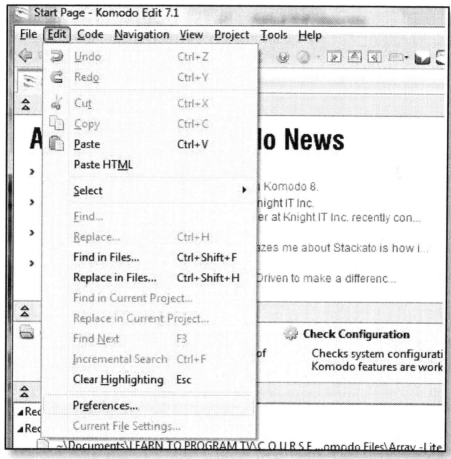

Figure 1.5: The dropdown menu of Komodo Edit's Edit option.

Under Edit choose Preferences. Then, under Languages Option, choose PHP.

If the directory for your PHP.ini is not yet set, do so by going into your WAMP folder and accessing the Apache 2.2.22 bin folder by going through folders in the following order: **WAMP>>bin>>Apache2.2.22>>bin**

Look for the text file named "PHP". This is your .ini file. Choose the PHP.ini configuration file and set it in your directory. This is done so that Komodo Edit can recognize PHP in its integrated development environment editor.

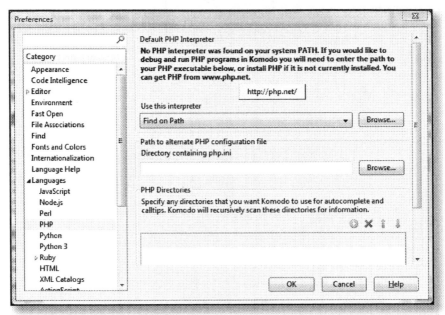

Figure 1.6: Selecting PHP as the language option in Komodo Edit's "Edit >> Preferences >> Language Option" menu path. In this screenshot, the path to the php.ini file still has to be set.

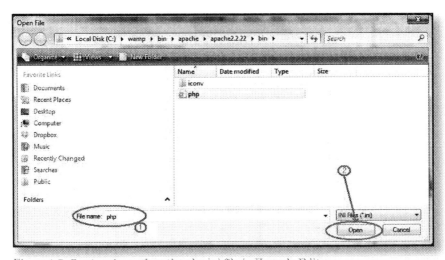

Figure 1.7: Setting the path to the php.ini file in Komodo Edit.

Once you have the language preferences set up, PHP is now recognized by Komodo Edit as the integrated development environment (IDE) language set.

## 1.2 UNDERSTANDING PHP DEVELOPMENT WORKFLOW

In this section, you will learn about PHP development workflow: how a PHP file is actually created and tested, what process it undergoes, and what happens during each phase of the process.

When creating PHP code, the first thing you do is launch your WAMP (or MAMP) environment.

**1** **Step 1:** If you're on a PC, you can find the WAMP icon either in the Windows Start Menu or in the Icon Tray at the bottom right side of the screen. If you are using a Mac you will find MAMP installed in your applications folder. Start it as you would start any other application.

**2** **Step 2:** When you launch your WAMP program, it automatically activates its server functions which will be indicated by the message "WAMPSERVER – server Online" when you hover your mouse over its icon in the Windows Icon Tray.

If you see the message "WAMPSERVER – server Offline" then you have to activate the server functions by clicking on the WAMP icon. This will bring up WAMPSERVER's Start Menu. Then, click on the last option on this menu "Put Online". This will then bring up WAMPSERVER and if you now hover your mouse over its icon, you should see the message "WAMPSERVER – server Online". WAMPSERVER is now ready to process your PHP scripts.

Figure 1.8: Selecting the WAMP icon (the green icon showing a fancy W within a rounded square) in Window's Icon Tray. WAMP is already up and running as indicated by the message "WAMPSERVER – server Online".

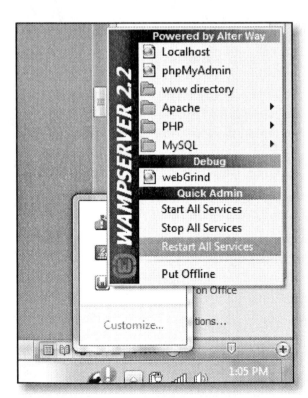

Figure 1.9: Launching WampServer from its Start Menu which is obtained by clicking on WampServer's icon in the Windows icon tray. Since WampServer is already running, the last option on the menu shows "Put Offline". If WampServer is not yet running, the last option would show "Put Online". Click this last option to put WampServer online.

**3** **Step 3:** To test if your server is really running, open your local browser and in the address or URL bar, type http://localhost. This should bring up a homepage generated by the Apache server.

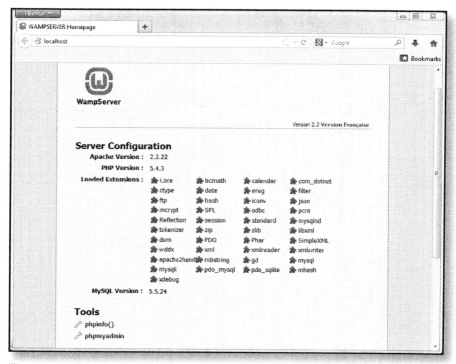

Figure 1.10. WampServer's opening page when you type http://localhost in the address or URL bar of your browser.

This is what the homepage of the WAMP server generated by Apache looks like. Feel free to browse through the page.

At this point, you can now start your first PHP script.

**4** **Step 4:** Switch to Komodo Edit and open a new HTML5 file.

Figure 1.11: HTML5 document with a simple structure.

**5** **Step 5:** Type the following code. It is the simplest (bare-bones) structure of a HTML5 document:

```
<!doctype html>
<html>
<head>
<title>Hello!</title>
</head>
<body>
    <h1>Hi There!</h1>
</body>
</html>
```

**6** **Step 6:** Now save your file as hello.html in a special folder called www which is found inside the WAMP folder. Make sure the file extension is .html. (If you're using a Mac, the path is Applications/MAMP/htdocs.) The www or htdocs folder is where all files that can be accessed through the server are placed.

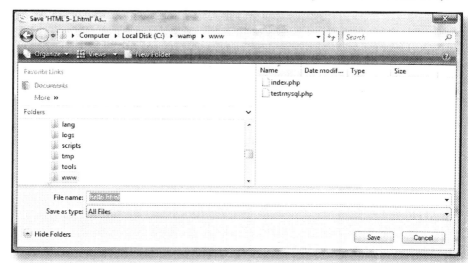

Figure 1.12: Save your HTML5 file to the c:\wamp\www folder. Make sure the file extension is .html.

**7**    **Step 7:** Open any browser of your choice.

**8**    **Step 8:** Make sure your server is online.

Figure 1.13: WampServer's Start Menu which indicates that WampServer is online by the last option which shows "Put Offline".

**9** **Step 9:** Type localhost/hello.html in the address or URL bar. You may have a different file name saved, so take note of that when typing in the address or URL bar.

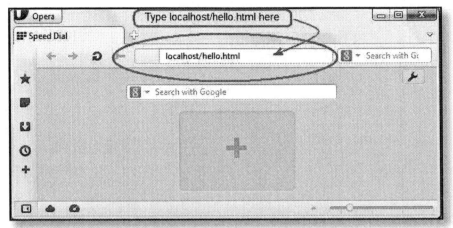

Figure 1.14: The address or URL bar of the Opera browser.

**10** **Step 10:** Click the "Go" icon/button in the browser and wait a few seconds. The Apache server software, during this brief moment, is processing any PHP scripts embedded in the file hello.html.

If you have previously learned Javascript or HTML, you will notice a difference in how the browser is launched to enable you to view the results of your code.

In PHP, the file is accessed by launching the browser first, then typing the file name in the address bar.

**11** **Step 11:** Wait a few more seconds, but don't blink. The browser is now interpreting the HTML file generated by the server.

**12** **Step 12:** This is how the output appears:

Figure 1.15: Output of Hello.html in the browser Opera.

Figure 1.16: Output of Hello.html in the browser Chrome.

There is an alternative if you want to call your browser from your local WAMP tray instead of directly launching the browser yourself. After saving your file in Komodo Edit, proceed to step 7.

**1-6** **Step 1-6:** Same as previous steps.

**7** **Step 7:** Click the WAMP icon from the tray and choose localhost.

**8** **Step 8:** The WAMP local server homepage launches. In the text found at the address bar, append the forward slash (/) followed by the html file name hello.html.

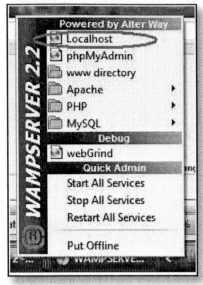

Figure 1.17: Launching localhost from WampServer's Start Menu.

Figure 1.18: Typing *localhost/hello.html* in the address or URL bar of Firefox.

**9-10** **Step 9-10:** The same as the previous steps.

**11-12** **Step 11-12:** This is the output.

From my PC's WAMP local server, it automatically launched the Firefox browser:

Figure 1.19. The result of typing *localhost/hello.html* in the address or URL bar of Firefox which then executes hello.html which simply displays "Hi There!"

If a webpage contains PHP, the server processes it then interprets it for the browser, since the browser can only interpret HTML, CSS and Javascript. This is the reason why the file has to be accessed through the server and not directly from the webpage browser.

**To recap the entire workflow:**

1. Set up the development environment—install WAMP (or MAMP) and the text editor. Here we used Komodo Edit.

2. Set up the default directory in the WAMP folder.

3. Put the PHP server online. Launch your text editor.

4. Encode your script.

5. Save your file to the folder specially assigned to the server.

6. Launch your preferred browser. Type in the script file to be processed.

7. The server processes any PHP scripts embedded in the file.

8. The browser interprets the HTML file generated by the server.

9. The webpage is loaded. That's it!

# 1.3 WRITING YOUR FIRST SCRIPT

PHP scripts are embedded in HTML documents. Therefore, the first thing you need to code in PHP scripts is the basic HTML structure.

This is a basic, bare-bones structure of an HTML document:

```
<html>
<head>
<title>First PHP Script</title>
</head>
<body>

</body>
</html>
```

To embed PHP code in this HTML document, you write the code between the opening, <?php, and closing, ?>, PHP tags inside the body element:

```
<html>
<head>
<title>First PHP Script</title>
</head>
<body>
    <?php

    ?>
</body>
</html>
```

These opening and closing PHP tags isolate the PHP code from the HTML code.

Now we can try adding more code by introducing the *echo()* command. This output command simply displays the text or values placed inside the quotes as shown in the following example.

*echo()* should be placed between the PHP script tags. Think of the command line being sandwiched between the opening and closing PHP script tags.

```
<html>
<head>
<title>First PHP Script</title>
</head>
<body>
    <?php
          echo("This is my first PHP
document");
    ?>
</body>
</html>
```

You should save your code in the www folder (for Windows) or in the htdocs folder (for Mac) as first_document.php. Take note that even if the document is made using HTML and PHP, the server will not be able to process the PHP scripts embedded in the file if the filename extension is not .php.

Open a local browser and type in the address bar: http://localhost/first_document.php

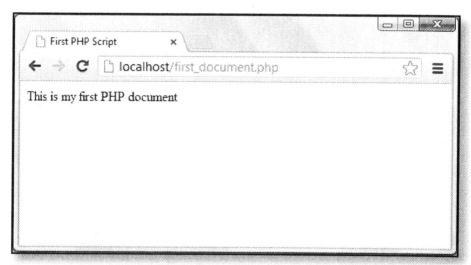

Figure 1.20: The output of executing your first PHP script, first_document.php.

You will see that the PHP script embedded in the HTML document has been processed and the echo command output the text (often called a string) to the browser window.

PHP also allows you to embed HTML tags inside the echo() command. This HTML will be processed as any other HTML would in the browser.

```
<html>
<head>
<title>Hello!</title>
</head>
<body>

<?php

echo("<h1><strong>This is my first PHP
document</h1></strong>");

    echo("</br>This is my second PHP
statement")

?>
</body>
</html>
```

Save the file with the changes under the same filename and refresh your browser.

Figure 1.21: The output of your modified PHP script, first_document.php.

You will notice that the HTML embedded within the echo() command has been processed and the string appears as large, bold text.

Remember that the browser does not process PHP scripts—the server does that. To confirm this process, view the source code of first_document.php in the browser.

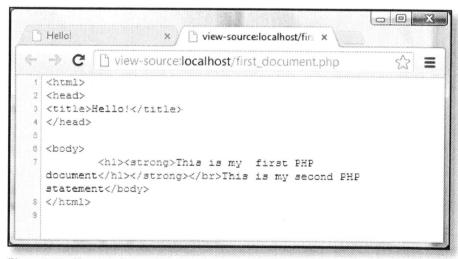

Figure 1.22: Viewing the source code of first_document.php in your browser. Only HTML5 code remains. All the PHP code has been executed and then stripped away.

Notice that all the PHP tags and commands have disappeared and what remained was the HTML tags. The reason for this is that the document was processed by the server which executed all the PHP scripts it found in the document, leaving only the HTML tag source code.

# 1.4 echo(), print() AND printf() COMMANDS

This section will discuss the basic commands for displaying content with PHP. By now, you are familiar with the *echo()* command. It is just one of the commands that can display text and also accommodate HTML tags within it.

The other commands that similarly display output to the computer screen are *print()* and *printf()*.

**print()** is the same as *echo()*. It displays the specified text in the browser. There isn't much difference between *echo()* and *print()*. Like the *echo()* command, *print()* may be used without the aid of parentheses, (). For example:

```
echo "Hello! "
```

will yield the same output as

```
echo ("Hello! ")
```

Now,

```
print "Hello";
```

will have the same result as

```
print("Hello! ");
```

**printf()** is different from *print()*. It also displays the output specified but uses a different format:

```
printf(format, arg1, arg2, argn)
```

*arg1*, *arg2* and argn are the parameters specified which will replace the % sign inserted in the format. For example:

```
printf("I am %d years old", 21);
```

*I am %d years old* is the format and *21* is the argument. This prints: I am 21 years old. "%d" is known as a signifier. This signifier is used in conjunction with an integer number—such as 21.

There are several different options for using *printf()*. For example a %f signifier represents a floating point number, which is a number that includes a decimal sign such as -32.454.

A wide range of signifiers are available for *printf* and can be viewed by visiting www.w3schools.com/php/func_string_printf.asp.

You implement these commands in PHP the same way you implement the *echo()* command.

Now let's construct a program that will use all three output commands at once so that we can see the differences.

**1** **Step 1:** Create a basic HTML document with a basic structure format and embed the PHP open and close tags. Use the new commands we have just learned following the presented format:

```
<html>
<head>
<title>output
</title>
<body>

    <?php
        echo "This is echoed out";
        echo ("</br>This is also echoed
out");
        print ("</br>This line was
displayed using print");
        print "</br>This line was
```

```
displayed using print without the ()";
        printf ("</br>Today is the year
%d.", 2013);
        printf ("</br>Five divided by two
is %f", 2.5);


    ?>
</body>
</html>
```

**2** **Step 2:** Save the file in the www (or htdocs) folder and name it output. Save it with the extension name .php.

**3** **Step 3:** Once you've saved your file, open your browser and type http://localhost/output.php in the address bar.

The output will appear like this:

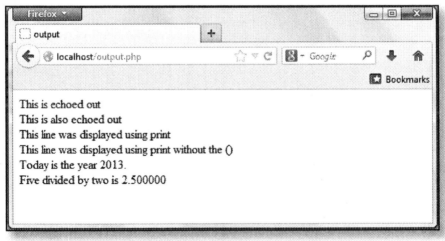

Figure 1.23: The result of executing output.php

*Printf()* has more features when compared to *print()* and it can make the content easier to comprehend because of the formatting.

That wraps up the three basic commands for displaying strings in PHP.

QUESTIONS FOR REVIEW

1. What does PHP stand for?
   a. Philadelphia Hyper People.
   b. Pre Hypertext Processor.
   c. Phenomenal Hilarious Panda.
   d. Post Hypertext Processing.

2. What does A in WAMP stand for?
   a. Apache.
   b. Analog.
   c. Algorithm.
   d. Asynchronous.

3. What address do you use to check the homepage generated by the Apache server for Windows?
   a. http://localhost
   b. https://localpage
   c. https://localhosts
   d. http://localhosts

4. What is the correct opening PHP tag?
   a. <php
   b.<?php?
   c. <??php
   d.<?php

5. Which command can display a formatted string output?
   a. echo( " ");
   b. print( " ");
   c. prints( " ");
   d. printf( " ");

# CHAPTER 1 LAB EXERCISE

1. Create a HTML document with a bare-bones, basic structure.

2. Insert the correct script tags so that PHP is recognized.

3. Create the necessary codes to display your name, interests or hobbies, age, and birthday. Use the <h1> tag for your name, <h2> for displaying your interests or hobbies, and use the printf() command to display your age and birthday with the date format dd/mm/yyyy.

4. Make sure that each piece of information is displayed in a new line. Use the break <br/> tags.

## CHAPTER 1 LAB SOLUTION:

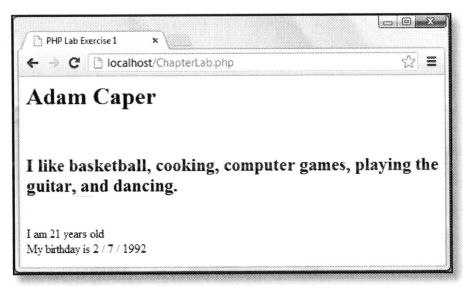

Figure 1.24: Lab solution output.

## CODE LISTING: CHAPTER 1 LAB SOLUTION

```
<html>
<head>
<title> PHP Lab Exercise 1</title>
</head>
```

```
<body>
    <?php
        echo("<h1> Adam Caper</h1>");
        echo("</br><h2>I like basketball,
cooking, computer games, playing the
guitar, and dancing.</h2>");
        printf ("</br>I am %d years old",
21);
        printf ("</br>My birthday is %d /
%d / %d", 2, 7, 1992);

    ?>
</body>
</html>
```

## CHAPTER SUMMARY:

In this chapter, you learned that PHP is a scripting language that is run on the server side. We also identified, downloaded and installed the software application packages needed to code and run PHP. We described the PHP workflow, and went into detail about how PHP codes are constructed, tested, and implemented.

We explained that PHP scripts are embedded inside an HTML document and that HTML tags can also be embedded within PHP scripts.

We also discussed three commands that are used to display text output, saw how PHP scripts are processed and explained why they disappear in the source code of the document.

In the next chapter, we will talk about variables: how to name them, assign values to them, and how to use variables with different operators.

# CHAPTER 2

## VARIABLES

### CHAPTER OBJECTIVES:

- You will be able to define PHP variables and operators.
- You will be able to describe the process of using variables and operators.
- You will learn how to properly code variable operations.
- You will be able to create and program PHP scripts involving variable operations.

## 2.1 INTRODUCING VARIABLES

**Variables** are memory units allocated to store the values of any of the eight PHP data types, namely: integers, floating-point numbers, strings, booleans, arrays, objects, resources (or handles) and null. (We will tackle these data types in the next chapters.)

**Variables**

Variables need to be given names. In PHP, variable names begin with the dollar ($) symbol followed by alphabetic and numeric characters and sometimes underscores. A rule of thumb in using underscores with variable names is that they may be placed anywhere in the name but never right after the $ sign. So, avoid variable names like *$_myvariable*.

PHP variable names are also case-sensitive and so *$MyVariable* and *$myvariable* are two distinct variables. There is no limit to the number of characters in a variable name, but keep in mind that variable names longer than 30 characters are impractical.

Some examples of acceptable PHP variable names are:

$no_of_students
$StudentNumber
$NumOfStudents
$customer_1

Variables are declared differently in PHP than in other programming languages. If you have encountered C, C++ or Java, you know that the declaration of a variable is usually accompanied by the declaration of its data type such as *string, int, float* or *double*. In PHP, the declaration of a variable does not need its data type to be declared. The only thing needed is for the variable name to be preceded by the "$" (dollar) sign. To illustrate, let's declare a variable called *age*.

In other languages, the declaration would be:

```
int age = 21;
```

But in PHP, the declaration is:

```
$age = 21;
```

Obviously, in PHP declarations the variable type is not required. This is the reason why PHP is called "a loosely typed language". PHP assumes, from the value of 21 that you are assigning, that *$age* will be a variable of type integer. What's more, in *loosely typed languages*, once you store a particular data type in a variable (for example, an integer) then you can later on store a float or a string to that same variable.

To test this loose variable data typing, let's declare different variables in PHP. Open your text editor and create a new file. On the starter page, look for the new file option at the bottom right portion of the screen. The location of the option is illustrated in the screenshot Figure 2.1.

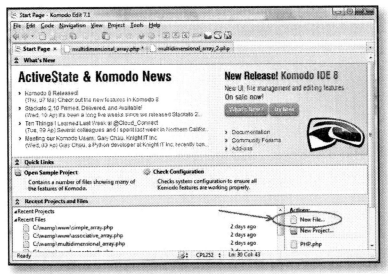

Figure 2.1: Start Page for Komodo Edit. This page is displayed when you open the text editor.

After clicking on *New File*, a pop-up window will display on your screen.

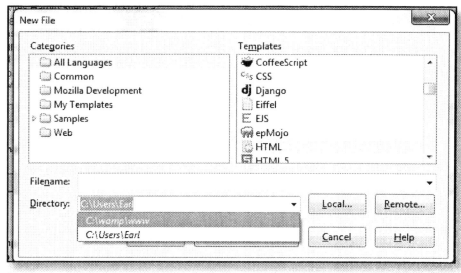

Figure 2.2: Creating a new file from a template using Komodo Edit.

Choose the HTML template option and then click the dropdown list for the directory and look for the \wamp\www folder option. For Mac users, look for the \MAMP\htdocs folder option. If you haven't used any of those directories before, you can locate either of them by clicking on the local button and manually specifying the location of the www or MAMP folder.

Save the file as *variable.php* and proceed with the new file creation.

Add the proper PHP script tags in the body of the HTML.

```
<!DOCTYPE>
<html lang="en">
<head>
    <title>Variables In PHP</title>
</head>
<body>
    <?php

    ?>
</body>
</html>
```

You are now ready to start declaring variables. Place your cursor between the opening and closing PHP tags.

```html
<!DOCTYPE>
<html lang="en">
<head>
    <title>Variables In PHP</title>
</head>
<body>
    <?php

    $name = "Adam";
    $age = 21;

    print($name);
    print("<br/>");
    print($age);
    ?>
</body>
</html>
```

Save the file as *variables.php*, and access it in the browser by typing in the address bar, for Windows:

**http://localhost/**variables.php

and for the Mac:

**localhost:8888/**variables.php

Your output should appear in the browser window like this:

In the coding example shown, the value "Adam" is the string value assigned to the variable *$name,* while "21" is the numeric value assigned to the variable *$age.*

Floating point numbers can also be stored in variables without having to declare their variable type. If you haven't worked with them before, floating point values (sometimes called "floats") are values that contain a decimal point.

Variables in PHP may be assigned a series of mathematical operations. The result of those operations are computed first, after which they are then stored to the variable they're assigned to.

---

**Tip:** I often tell my classroom students that when they encounter a variable assignment, always evaluate the right side of the assignment operator (=) first and then assign the result to the variable on the left side. For example, if you have the code:

```
$x = 2 * 5;
```

Two is multiplied by five and the result of the arithmetic, ten, is assigned to the variable $x.

---

Let's tweak the previous example and introduce the use of floating point number.

Open the file *variable.php* and add the line of code found inside the PHP script tags from the following code listing:

```
<!DOCTYPE>
<html lang="en">
<head>
    <title>Variables In PHP</title>
</head>
<body>
    <?php

    $name = "Adam";
    $age = 21;
    $height = 165.1;
    print($name);
    print("<br/>");
    print($age);
    print("<br/>");
    print($height);
    ?>
</body>
</html>
```

Save the file under the same filename *variables.php,* and access it in the browser by typing in the address bar, for Windows:

**http://localhost/**variables.php

and for the Mac:

**localhost:8888/**variables.php

Your output should look like this:

Figure 2.4: Outputting declared variables in the browser, including a floating point number.

Why don't we try adjusting the output a little so that it makes more sense? Labeling each output value will certainly make more sense to the user. Modify your code listing as follows, save under the same file name, *variables.php,* and display the output:

```
<!DOCTYPE>
<html lang="en">
<head>
    <title>Variables In PHP</title>
</head>
<body>
    <?php

    $name = "Adam";
    $age = 21;
    $height = 165.1;
    print("First Name: ");
        print($name);
    print("<br/>");
    print("Age: ");
        print($age);
```

```
      print("<br/>");
      print("Height: ");
          print($height);
      ?>
  </body>
  </html>
```

Now, access *variables.php* in the browser by typing in the address bar as we did previously: http://localhost/variables.php, for Windows, or localhost:8888/variables.php for Mac.

Your output should look like the following screenshot:

Figure 2.5: Labeling each output value.

We were able to successfully place some text labels in front of our values using the *print* command. However, there is another process called concatenation which will enable us to accomplish the same task with more ease. **Concatenation** is the process of joining several distinct things or objects into one whole unit. In this example, we will concatenate each text label and its associated value into a single unit and display this unit on a line.

Concatenation

The concatenation process in PHP is unique compared to other programming languages. If you are familiar with Javascript or HTML, you likely remember that the plus sign (+) is the concatenation operator. In PHP it is the period or **dot** (.) that is used for concatenation.

If we change the previous code listing to employ concatenation, the code is shorter and more efficient:

```
<!DOCTYPE>
<html lang="en">
<head>
    <title>Variables In PHP</title>
</head>
<body>
    <?php

  $name = "Adam";
  $age = 21;
  $height = 165.1;
  print("First Name: ".$name);
  print("<br/>");
  print("Age: ".$age);
  print("<br/>");
  print("Height: ".$height);
    ?>
</body>
</html>
```

When viewed in the web browser, the result should appear like this:

Figure 2.6: Labeling each output value using the concatenation process.

This example demonstrated a very simple case of concatenation. The following HTML document shows more examples of concatenation in PHP.

```
<!DOCTYPE>
<html lang="en">
<head>
    <title>Variables and Concatenation in
PHP</title>
</head>
<body>
    <?php

    $name = "Adam";
    $age = 21;
    $taxRate = 0.12;

    print($name);
    print("<br/>");
    print($age);
    print("</br> </br>");
    print($name . " is " . $age . " years
old.");
print("</br> </br>");
printf("The tax rate in Guacamole Island
is %0.2f", $taxRate);
        print("</br>");

        $value = 25*62/72+42-51+101*2;
print("The final value of "."(25*62/72+42-
51+101*2) "."is ". $value);
    ?>
</body>
</html>
```

When viewed in the browser, the output will appear like this:

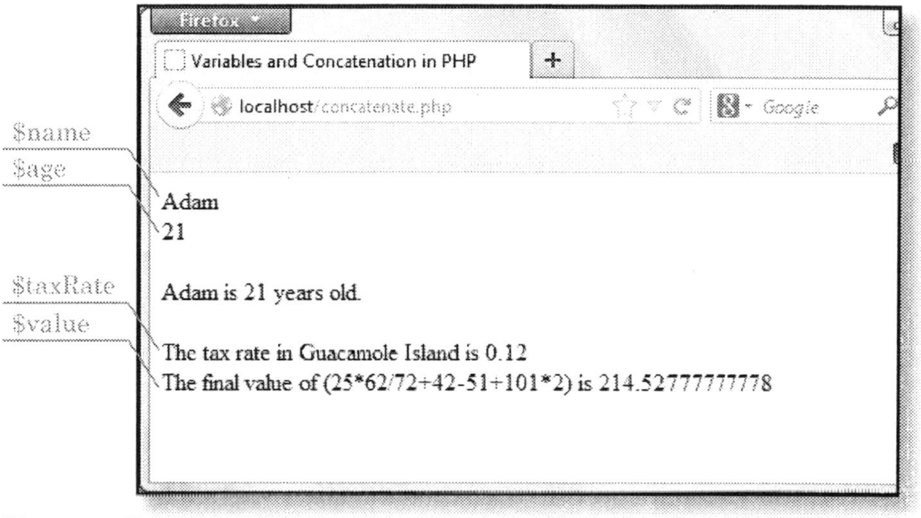

Figure 2.7: Using the concatenation process in more complex cases.

Keep in mind that when assigning variable names, you may use either alphabetic characters (A-Z, a-z), numbers, (0-9) or combinations of both, as well as the underscore character. While the underscore character can be used in any position after the $ sign, by convention it is not placed immediately after the $ sign. Lastly, variable names are case sensitive.

It is a good practice to adopt a consistent style in naming variables. One such style requires that the underscore is used to separate whole words in variable names, such as $tax_Rate. Note also that the first letter of the first word is not capitalized but the first letter of succeeding words are capitalized, such as $pending_Tax_Payments.

Whatever style or rules you adopt in naming your variables, they must be applied consistently.

## 2.2 Variable Operators

The math **operators** in PHP are the same as your everyday basic arithmetic operators: addition, subtraction, multiplication and division. Aside from these four basic operations, there are also **special operators** such as *increment, decrement, modulus* and the *combined operators*.

| Operators | |
|---|---|
| + | Addition |
| – | Subtraction |
| * | Mutiplication |
| / | Division |

The **addition** operation calculates the sum of its operands (values stored in variables), the **subtraction** operation calculates the difference, **multiplication** computes the product, and **division** computes the quotient.

The **increment** operator adds 1 to the value of the variable, the **decrement** operator subtracts 1, **modulus** gets the resulting remainder after a division operation between two values, and a **combined operation** is a combination of a variable operator and the

| Special Operators | |
|---|---|
| ++ | Increment |
| – – | Decrement |
| % | Modulus |
| = | Combine |

equal (=) sign. This operation processes the first operation then stores it to the variable to the left of the combined operator sign.

Take a look at the following examples:

Two variables $x and $y are to be added and the result is to be stored in $x. This is easily done using the *combined operator*:

```
$x += $y;
```

The expression $x += $y would add the values of $x and $y and then store the value to $x, overwriting its original value.

It is a good idea to familiarize yourself with these PHP variable operators. It is also expected that by this time you are already familiar with the process of creating new PHP files.

Let's brush up on the basic PHP program creation skills that you already learned and at the same time practice arithmetic operations.

First, create a basic HTML document.

```
<!DOCTYPE>
<html>
<head>
    <title>Addition Operation in PHP</
title>
</head>
```

Next, in the document body, include the PHP script tags. Assign two variables, *$x* and *$y*, that will hold two numeric values, 110 for *$x* and 52 for *$y*. Inside the PHP script tags, process the addition operation of the two variables.

```
<body>

    <?php

        $x = 110;
        $y = 52;

        print($x." + ".$y." = ". ($x +
$y));

    ?>

</body>
</html>
```

Save your file as *addOperation.php*. The output should display as shown:

110 + 52 = 162
110 - 52 = 58
110 * 52 = 5720
110 / 52 = 2.1153846153846

Figure 2.8: Processing the addition operation of two variables.

Let's include the remaining three basic operations in the program code. You may copy and paste the lines of code adding *$x* and *$y* three times and then change the addition operator to subtraction (-), then to multiplication (*), and finally, to division (/). Save your file as *operators. php* and then refresh your browser.

> **Tip:** I am a big advocate of using copy and paste when writing program code. If you retype a line you increase the chance that you will inadvertantly introduce errors.

The complete code listing for this example follows:

```
<!DOCTYPE>
<html lang="en">
<head>
    <title>Operators in PHP</title>
</head>
<body>

    <?php

        $x = 110;
        $y = 52;
```

```
        print($x . " + " . $y . " = " .
($x + $y));
        print("</br>");
        print($x . " - " . $y . " = " .
($x - $y));
        print("</br>");
        print($x . " * " . $y . " = " .
($x * $y));
        print("</br>");
        print($x . " / " . $y . " = " .
($x / $y));
        print("</br>");
    ?>
</body>
</html>
```

Your output should display as shown:

Figure 2.9: Processing the basic arithmetic operations of two variables.

Obviously, you should expect a different result if you assigned different values for *$x* and *$y*.

As you can see, the basic arithmatic operations are fairly easy to code. We will now discuss how the other special operators are implemented.

In the following table, the special operators are listed along with the brief description of what they accomplish:

| Operator | Description |
|---|---|
| increment      x++ | Increases the value of x by 1. |
| decrement      x-- | Decreases the value of x by 1. |
| modulus        x % y | Returns the remainder after dividing x by y. |
| **Combined Operators:** | |
| concatenate then return  .= | Concatenate then return the result in the expression on the left side of the operator. |
| add then return           += | Add the value of the expression on the left side of the operator to the expression on the right side of the operator. |
| subtract then return      -= | Subtract the value of the expression on the left side of the operator from the expression on the right side of the operator. |
| multiply then return      *= | Multiply the value of the expression on the left side of the operator to the expression on the right side of the operator. |
| divide then return        /= | Divide the value of the expression on the left side of the operator to the expression on the right side of the operator. |

Let's expand on the operations shown in the previous example. We will include incrementing and decrementing values, obtaining the remainder of a division operation (modulus), and using the different combined operators.

Continue with your PHP document *operators.php*.

Change the document title to

```
<title>"All PHP Operators"</title>
```

Then save as another file using the filename *alloperators.php*.

Add the following lines of code

```
$x++;
$y--;
```

**$x++ will increment $x.**

**$y-- will decrement $y.**

to your original code listing:

```
<!DOCTYPE>
<html>
<head>
    <title>Operators in PHP</title>
</head>
<body>

    <?php

        $x = 110;
        $y = 52;

        print($x . " + " . $y . " = " .
($x + $y));
        print("</br>");
        print($x . " - " . $y . " = " .
($x - $y));
        print("</br>");
        print($x . " * " . $y . " = " .
($x * $y));
        print("</br>");
        print($x . " / " . $y . " = " .
($x / $y));
        print("</br>");
```

Append the following lines for an aesthetic output:

```
print("</br>");
print("Incrementing x = " . $x);
print("</br>");
print("Decrementing y = " . $y);
print("</br>");
print("Modulus of x and y = " . ($x%$y));
print("</br>");
```

Next, we'll introduce more variables with the following names and values:

```
$first = 10;
$second = 3;
$third = 20;
$fourth = 4;
$fifth = 30;
$sixth = 7;
$seventh = 50;
$eighth = 6;
```

Using these new variables, perform a combined addition with the *$first* and *$second* variables, combined subtraction with *$third* and *$fourth*, combined multiplication with *$fifth* and *$sixth*, and combined division with *$seventh* (dividend) and *$eighth* (divisor) variables:

```
$first += $second;
$third -+ $fourth;
$fifth *= $sixth;
$seventh /= $eighth;
```

Using the *echo()* command, display the values for *$first, $third, $fifth* and *$seventh*. Remember that the echo command works identically to the print() command:

```
echo($first);
echo("</br>");
echo($third);
echo("</br>");
echo($fifth);
echo("</br>");
echo($seventh);
echo("</br>");
```

On the next two lines, use the combined operator *concatenate then return* (.=) to display the result of a concatenation.

```
$line = ("Hello this is a test for
concatenation and then...");
$line .= ("</br> Connect this next
phrase and place it on the next line");
echo($line);
```

Close the script and the entire document:

```
?>

</body>
</html>
```

This is the result when the code is run:

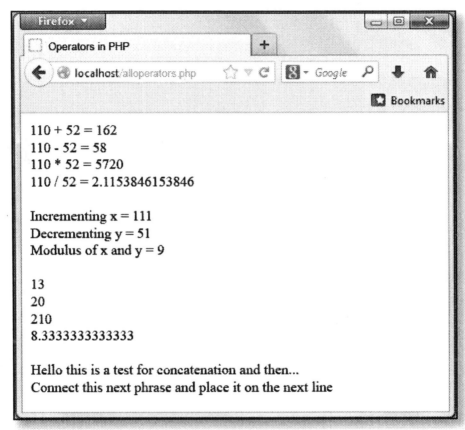

Figure 2.10: Using combined operators to output numbers and strings.

Following is the entire code listing:

```
<!DOCTYPE>
<html lang="en">
<head>
    <title>Operators in PHP</title>
</head>
<body>

    <?php

        $x = 110;
        $y = 52;

        print($x . " + " . $y . " = " .
($x + $y));
        print("</br>");
        print($x . " - " . $y . " = " .
($x - $y));
        print("</br>");
        print($x . " * " . $y . " = " .
($x * $y));
        print("</br>");
        print($x . " / " . $y . " = " .
($x / $y));
        print("</br>");

        $x++;
        $y--;

        print("</br>");
        print("Incrementing x = " . $x);
        print("</br>");
        print("Decrementing y = " . $y);
        print("</br>");
        print("Modulus of x and y = " .
($x%$y));
```

```php
        print("</br>");

        $first = 10;
        $second = 3;
        $third = 20;
        $fourth = 4;
        $fifth = 30;
        $sixth = 7;
        $seventh = 50;
        $eight = 6;

        $first += $second;
        $third -+ $fourth;
        $fifth *= $sixth;
        $seventh /= $eight;

        echo("</br>");
        echo($first);
        echo("</br>");
        echo($third);
        echo("</br>");
        echo($fifth);
        echo("</br>");
        echo($seventh);
        echo("</br></br>");

        $line = ("Hello this is a test for
concatenation and then...");
        $line .= ("</br> Connect this next
phrase and place it on the next line");
        echo($line);
    ?>
</body>
</html>
```

1. What are variables?
   a. Variables are containers for strings and numbers.
   b. Variables are containers for food.
   c. Variables vary with respect to time.
   d. Variables are processes that store values.

2. What are the operations of the common arithmetic operators?
   a. Addition, subtraction, concatenation, division.
   b. Addition, subtraction, multiplication, division.
   c. Concatenation, decrement, increment, addition.
   d. Increment, decrement, addition, subtraction.

3. What is the correct syntax for the combined operation concatenate then return in PHP?
   a. +=
   b. -=
   c. .=
   d. ==

4. Instead of writing a routine that adds 1 to a certain variable, what operator can be used instead?
   a. increment
   b. decrement
   c. subtraction of -1
   d. both a and c

# CHAPTER 2 LAB EXERCISE:

1. Create a HTML document with the simplest basic structure.

2. Add the appropriate tags to include PHP scripts.

3. Declare four variables. Name them *$w, $x, $y,* and *$z* and assign each of them the following integer values:

```
$w = 5;
$x = 25;
$y = 13;
$z = 101;
```

4. Using *echo()* or *print()*, display the initial values assigned to the variables *$w, $x, $y,* and *$z.*

5. Apply a line break. Add codes that will do the four basic mathematical operations to the four variables as follows:

$$\begin{array}{l} \$w + \$x \\ \$z - \$y \\ \$z\ /\ \$w \\ \$y\ *\ \$x \end{array}$$

6. Display the answer for each mathematical operation but format the answer with one decimal place value. Store each of the results in a new variable. Assign the results to the following new variables:

> the sum of *$w + $x* to variable $a ,
> the difference of *$z − $y* to variable $b,
> the quotient of $z / $w to variable $c, and
> the product of y * x to variable $d.

7. On the next line, display the results as follows—increment *$a* and *$b* displaying each of their results on separate lines, decrement *$c* and *$d* displaying each of their results on separate lines.

8. On the next line, display the result of the following combined operation +=:

> $wxyz = ($a+= ($b+=($c+=$d)))

# CHAPTER LAB SOLUTION

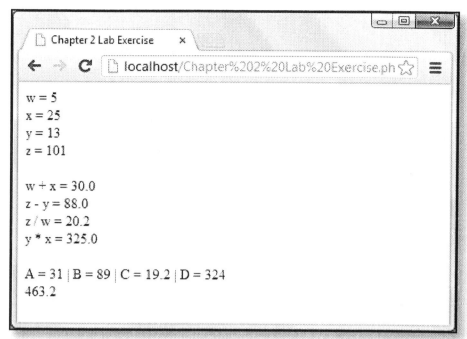

## CODE LISTING: CHAPTER 2 LAB SOLUTION

```
<!DOCTYPE>
<html lang="en">
<head>
    <title>Chapter 2 Lab Exercise</title>
</head>
<body>
    <?php

        $w = 5;
        $x = 25;
        $y = 13;
        $z = 101;

    //display values of w, x, y, z
```

```php
        echo("w = " . $w);
        echo("</br>");
        echo("x = " . $x);
        echo("</br>");
        echo("y = " . $y);
        echo("</br>");
        echo("z = " . $z);
        echo("</br>");

        $a = ($w + $x);
        $b = ($z - $y);
        $c = ($z / $w);
        $d = ($y * $x);

    //display result of basic operation
    //formatted with one decimal place
value
        printf("w + x = %0.1f", $a);
        echo("</br>");
        printf("z - y = %0.1f", $b);
        echo("</br>");
        printf("z / w = %0.1f", $c);
        echo("</br>");
        printf("y * x = %0.1f", $d);
        echo("</br>");

    //increment a and b, decrement c and d
        $a++; $b++; $c--; $d--;

    //concatenate A, B, C and D values
        echo("A = " . $a . " | B = " . $b
. " | C = " . $c . " | D = " .$d);
        echo("</br>");

    //display value of $wxyz
        $wxyz = ($a+= ($b+=($c+=$d)));
        echo($wxyz);
```

```
    ?>
</body>
</html>
```

# CHAPTER SUMMARY

In this chapter, you learned about variables in PHP and how they differ from other languages when being declared and implemented.

We discussed the different operators in PHP and how each of them is used. Also covered in this chapter were combined operators and concatenations in PHP and how they were implemented in actual program routines.

In the next chapter we will discuss arrays—simple, associative, multidimensional and global arrays.

# CHAPTER 3
## ARRAYS

### CHAPTER OBJECTIVES:

- You will be able to define arrays.
- You will be able to describe the two types of PHP arrays: indexed and associative.
- You will learn how to declare and instantiate arrays in PHP.
- You will be introduced to some of PHP's superglobal arrays.

## 3.1 SIMPLE OR INDEXED ARRAYS

Arrays are variables that can store more than one value. Each value of an array is called an element (or member) and each element is referenced by its own integer index 0,1,2,3, and so on. The index also identifies the position of the element in the array. (An index of 0 identifies the first element, an index of 1, the second element, and so on.) Elements can be added, removed, modified and rearranged (sorted) within the array.

Values stored in arrays can be any of the eight PHP data types: integer, floating point, string, boolean, object, resources, null and arrays. Yes, you read that correctly—arrays! Arrays can be stored within arrays!

Arrays are widely used for storing values for lists. For example, if you wanted to store all of the names of the members of a team, an array is perfect.

In PHP, the function used to create an array is *array()*.  **array()**

 **Simple arrays** (or **indexed arrays**) are arrays that use numeric indexing **Simple Array** of members or elements. This numerical indexing is usually sequential but random or skipped indexing is allowed.

Declaring arrays in PHP is similar to declaring variables in PHP—the dollar sign ($) is affixed before the variable name. Arrays are zero-indexed, meaning that indexes start from zero (0) – and that the zero index always points to the first member of the array.

Declaring an array begins by stating the name of the array followed by the equal sign (=), and then the values to be stored in the array enclosed in parentheses. In the following example, we have an array declaration consisting of four elements of the datatype string:

```
$names = array ("John", "Larry", "Jane",
"Lily");
```

If we look closely at the array presented, we'll see that the first element is *$names[0]* and has the value "John", the second element is *$names[1]* and has the value "Larry", the third is *$names[2]* and has the value "Jane" and last is *$names[3]*, and has the value "Lily".

The array can also be defined as:

```
$names[0] = "John";
$names[1] = "Larry";
$names[2] = "Jane";
$names[3] = "Lily";
```

Operations or commands that can be executed on variables can also be performed on each member of an array, such as *print()*, *echo()*, concatenations, *mathematical* and *special operations*. We will demonstrate each one of these operations with coding exercises using arrays.

Create a new HTML template and save it in the www (for Windows) or htdocs (for Mac) folder using the filename *simple_array.php*. Place the proper opening and closing tags.

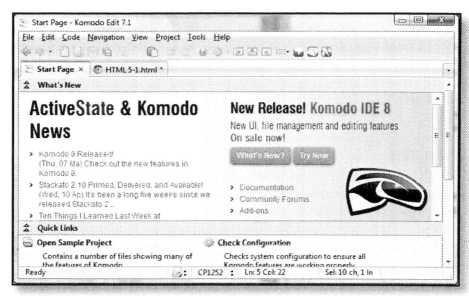

Figure 3.1: Komodo Edit start page.

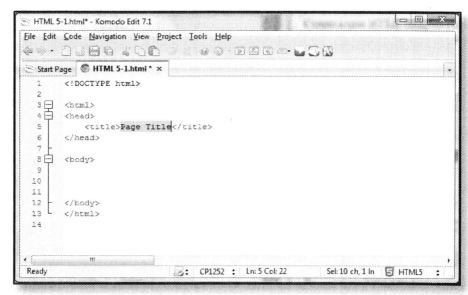

Figure 3.2: Creating a new HTML5 document in Komodo Edit.

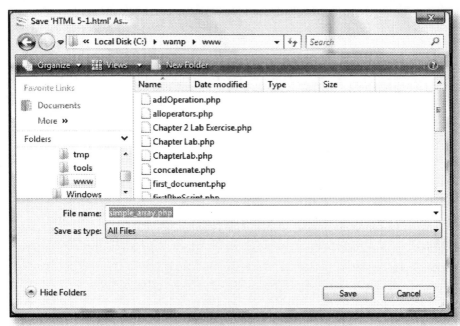

Figure 3.3: Saving the document as simple_array.php.

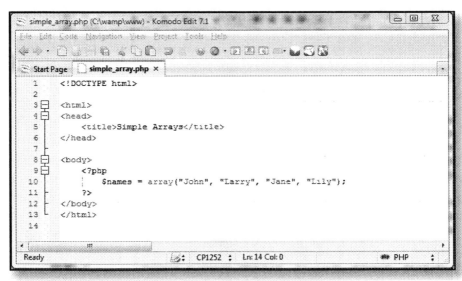

Figure 3.4: Declaring an array in PHP in line 10.

In the series of screenshots above, we have declared the array. Another way of declaring an array is the manual method where we assign the individual members of the arrays to their respective indeces.

We're going to declare the array using the array name *$fruit[ ]* and manually assign values to each element of the array by typing the following code:

```
$fruit[0] = "Berries";
$fruit[3] = "Mangoes";
$fruit[4] = "Apples";
$fruit[5] = "Grapes";
```

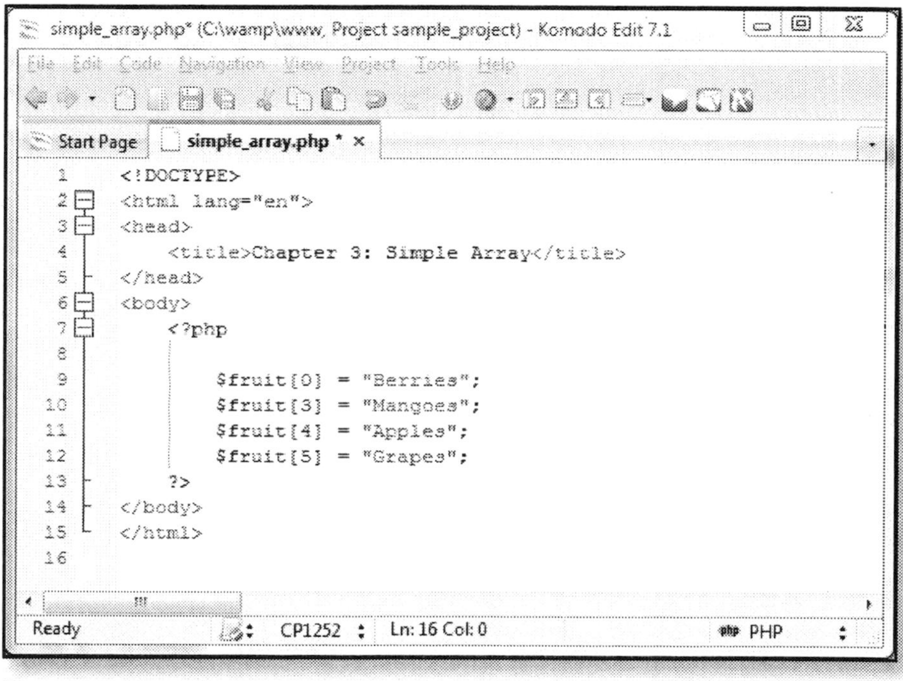

```
1   <!DOCTYPE>
2   <html lang="en">
3   <head>
4       <title>Chapter 3: Simple Array</title>
5   </head>
6   <body>
7       <?php
8
9           $fruit[0] = "Berries";
10          $fruit[3] = "Mangoes";
11          $fruit[4] = "Apples";
12          $fruit[5] = "Grapes";
13      ?>
14  </body>
15  </html>
16
```

Figure 3.5: Manually assigning values to members of an array. Lines 9 to 12.

Notice that we skipped the array indexes one and two while assigning values to the array.

When manually assigning elements of an array, it is possible to skip an index in the sequence. The previous *simple_array.php* example (which skipped a member index during array member assignment) was shown for illustration purposes only. This assignment method could prove useful in some instances, but does not imply the standard process of numbering array indexes. The best and standard practice is to store elements of an array sequentially.

Once the array has been created and populated, we now retrieve and display the elements of the array. This can be done using either or in combination *echo()*, *print()* or *printf()*.

Remember, when retrieving or referencing a member of an array, we do so by referring to the array variable name together with the member or index number. For example, if we want to call the *$name* array member "John", we refer to this member as *$names[1]*, or if we want to call the *$fruit* array member "Apple", we refer to it as *$fruit[4]*.

We will now demonstrate how to retrieve members of an array and perform concatenation operations on them.

**PROBLEM:** Create a program routine that will display the output:

> "John likes to eat Grapes."
> "Larry likes to eat Mangoes."
> "Jane likes to eat Apples."
> "Lily likes to eat Berries."

**SOLUTION:**

**1** **Step 1:** Construct each of the sentences using a series of concatenations. Store the names John, Larry, Jane and Lily in the array *$names*. Store the fruits Grapes, Mangoes, Apples and Berries in another array *$fruit*. Concatenate each member of the array *$names* with the corresponding member (members of the same index) of array *$fruit* with the phrase "likes to eat " inserted between the pair.

We would like the array members to pair as:

"John" to "Grapes"
"Larry" to "Mangoes"
"Jane" to "Apples"
"Lily" to "Berries"

**2** **Step 2:** Use the *echo()* command to display the output.

**3** **Step 3:** The command line that will display this output is:

```
echo($names[1]. " likes to eat ".
$fruit[5]);
```

The preceding statement will display: "John likes to eat Grapes"

**4** **Step 4:** The complete code listing to display all four statements—pairing each of the *$name* array members to the *$fruit* array members, respectively—is as follows:

## CODE LISTING: SIMPLE_ARRAY.PHP

```php
<!DOCTYPE>
<html lang="en">
<head>
    <title>Chapter 3: Simple Array</title>
</head>
<body>
    <?php
        $first_names = array("John", "Larry",
"Jane", "Lily");

    //Assign the array members
        $fruit[0] = "Berries";
        $fruit[3] = "Mangoes";
        $fruit[4] = "Apples";
        $fruit[5] = "Grapes";

    //Display the array member pairing
        echo($first_names[0] . " likes to eat
" . $fruit[5]);
        echo("</br>");
        echo($first_names[1] . " likes to eat
" . $fruit[3]);
        echo("</br>");
        echo($first_names[2] . " likes to eat
" . $fruit[4]);
        echo("</br>");
        echo($first_names[3] . " likes to eat
" . $fruit[0]);
        echo("</br>");
    ?>
</body>
</html>
```

**5** **Step 5:** View your result. The output should appear as shown:

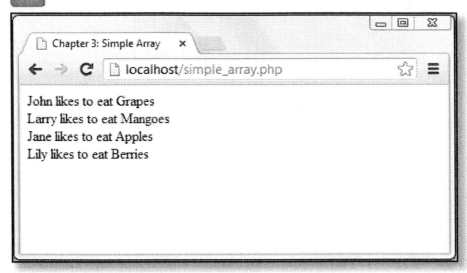

Figure 3.6: Constructing sentences by calling members of simple arrays.

# 3.2 ASSOCIATIVE ARRAYS

**Associative arrays** are arrays that assign a unique key value to each array member. These arrays use named keys to identify their members or elements as opposed to the numeric keys (indeces) used for simple arrays. Let's say you want to store employees' salaries in an array. Numerically indexed arrays will not be the best choice to store these values. In an associative array, the employee's name acts as the key and from their names, their salary rate is associated.

**Assoc. Array**

Declaring associative arrays is different compared to numerically indexed arrays. Numerically index arrays follow this array declaration format:

```
$variable name [index number] = value;
```

Associative arrays follow this declaration format:

```
$variable name = array(key name => value, )
```

Let's try this out.

**1** **Step 1:** Create a new HTML5 document in your text editor. Use the filename *associative_array.php*. Make sure you include the PHP opening and closing tags. Save your file.

**2** **Step 2:** Now let's create an array that contains four employees and their respective salaries.

We'll have the employees "Doe" with an annual salary of $30,000, "Smith" with an annual salary of $28,000, "Rogers" with an annual salary of $50,000,

The associative array declaration will be:

```
$salary = array("Doe" => 30000,
                "Smith" => 28000,
                "Rogers" => 50000,
                "Adam" => 120000,
                "Brown" => 60000);
```

"Adam" with an annual salary of $120,000, and "Brown" with annual salary of 60,000.

Note the use of whitespace and alignment to make the code more readable. We could have declared the array using one line, with minimal spacing, like this:

```php
$salary =
array("Doe"=>30000,"Smith"=>28000,"Rogers"=>
50000, Adam"=>120000,Brown"=>60000);
```

But this is not as readable as the previous declaration.

**3** **Step 3:** Then we'll have the output displayed using *echo()* or *print()* with the aid of concatenation stating "*Full name* has an annual salary of *$salary["Doe"]*." The command to display the intended output is:

```php
print("John Doe has an annual salary of "
. $salary["Doe"] . "<br/>");
```

The following code will display all of the values stored inside the array.

```php
    //Display the array members
        echo("John Doe has an annual
salary of $" . $salary["Doe"] . ".");
        echo("</br>");
        echo("Robert Smith has an annual
salary of $" . $salary["Smith"] . ".");
        echo("</br>");
        echo("Sam Rogers has an annual
salary of $" . $salary["Rogers"] . ".");
        echo("</br>");
        echo("Drei Adam has an annual
salary of $" . $salary["Adam"] . ".");
        echo("</br>");
        echo("Jim Brown has an annual
salary of $" . $salary["Brown"] . ".");
        echo("</br>");
```

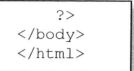

**4** **Step 4:** Close the PHP script, making sure you have the appropriate HTML closing tags. Save the file again.

```
        ?>
    </body>
    </html>
```

**5** **Step 5:** Compare your program with the following code listing.

## CODE LISTING: ASSOCIATIVE_ARRAY.PHP

```php
<!DOCTYPE>
<html lang="en">
<head>
    <title>Chapter 3: Associative Array</title>
</head>
<body>

    <?php

    //Declare the array
        $salary = array("Doe"=>"30,000",
"Smith"=>"28,000", "Rogers"=>"50,000",
"Adam"=>"120,000", "Brown"=>"75,000");

    //Display the array members
        echo("John Doe has an annual salary of
$" . $salary["Doe"] . ".");
        echo("</br>");
        echo("Robert Smith has an annual salary
of $" . $salary["Smith"] . ".");
        echo("</br>");
        echo("Sam Rogers has an annual salary
of $" . $salary["Rogers"] . ".");
        echo("</br>");
        echo("Drei Adam has an annual salary of
$" . $salary["Adam"] . ".");
        echo("</br>");
        echo("Jim Brown has an annual salary of
$" . $salary["Brown"] . ".");
        echo("</br>");
    ?>
</body>
</html>
```

**Step 6:** View your result in the browser. Don't forget to make sure you are viewing the results through the server using localhost. If you coded everything correctly, the output should look like this:

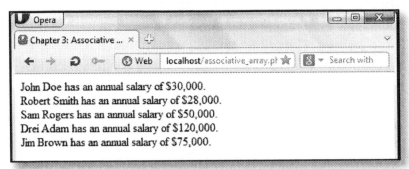

John Doe has an annual salary of $30,000.
Robert Smith has an annual salary of $28,000.
Sam Rogers has an annual salary of $50,000.
Drei Adam has an annual salary of $120,000.
Jim Brown has an annual salary of $75,000.

Figure 3.7: Outputting values stored inside associative arrays.

We could also use associative arrays to display a list of GPAs of several individuals and their courses. The complete code listing and the output are shown as follows:

```
<!DOCTYPE>
<html lang="en">
<head>
    <title>Multiple Associative Arrays</
title>
</head>
<body>
    <?php

   //Declare the GPA array.
        $gpa = array("Doe"=>3.0,
"Smith"=>3.0, "Rogers"=>3.5, "Adam"=>4.5,
"Brown"=>4.0);

   //Declare the COURSE array.
        $course = array("Doe"=>"Office
Management", "Smith"=>"Certified
Operator", "Rogers"=>"Office Management",
"Adam"=>"Electronics Engineering",
"Brown"=>"Information Technology");
```

```
    //Display the output for each array
member.
        echo("John Doe has a GPA of
" . $gpa["Doe"] . " and took up ".
$course["Doe"]. ".");
        echo("</br>");
        echo("Robert Smith has a GPA
of " . $gpa["Smith"] . " and is a
".$course["Smith"].".");
        echo("</br>");
        echo("Sam Rogers has a GPA of
" . $gpa["Rogers"] . " and took up
".$course["Rogers"].".");
        echo("</br>");
        echo("Drei Adam has a GPA of "
. $gpa["Adam"] . " and has a degree in
".$course["Adam"].".");
        echo("</br>");
        echo("Jim Brown has a GPA of "
. $gpa["Brown"] . " and has a degree in
".$course["Brown"].".");
        echo("</br>");
    ?>
</body>
</html>
```

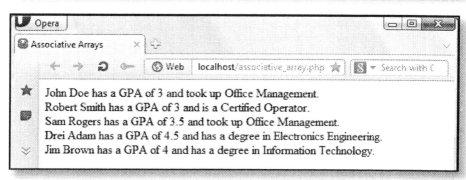

Figure 3.8: Using associative arrays to output a list of GPAs.

# 3.3 MULTIDIMENSIONAL ARRAYS

**Multidimensional arrays** are arrays whose elements or members are arrays. A multidimensional array is one main array containing several arrays called "sub-arrays". One common use of multi-dimensional arrays are in computer games. If you think of game "levels," typically, the information about these levels is held in one or more multidimensional arrays.

Declaring multidimensional arrays is similar to declaring associative arrays, but instead of having keys and their respective values, you would still have keys but each value would be an array.

**Multidimensional Array**

Let's work on an example. Let's open a new file and examine some coding samples to better understand the concept.

Create a new HTML5 document and save it in the www (for Windows, WAMP) or htdocs (for Mac, MAMP) folder under the filename *multidimensional_array.php*.

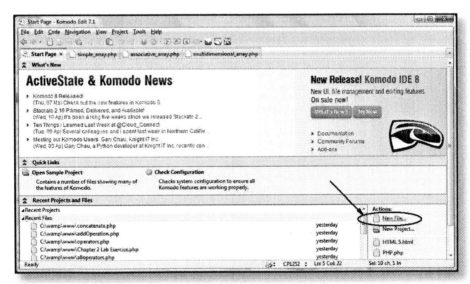

Figure 3.9: Komodo Edit start page.

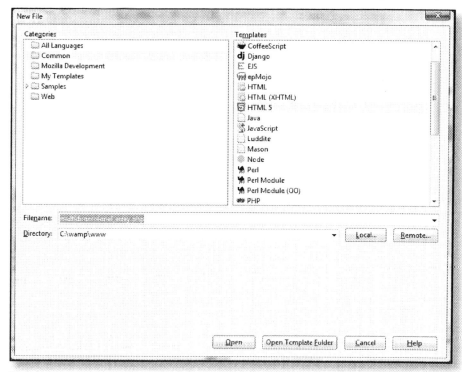

Figure 3.10: Saving a new document as a multidimensional_array.php.

Make sure you include the PHP opening and closing script tags in your file.

The following array content examples are from a popular online role-paying game. The main array is the *backpack* and the sub-arrays will be *Weapons, Armors, Useables, Key_Items* and *Magic_Items*. Each sub-array will be an associative array describing the contents of each division.

≫ *Weapons* will be a simple array consisting of the following members: *Krasnaya, Executioner, Violet Fear, Atroce's Blade*

```
"Weapon" => array
    (
        "Krasnaya",
            "Executioner",
            "Violet Fear",
            "Atroce's Blade"
),
```

➤ *Armors* array will consist of the following members:
*Lord Kaho's Horns, Megingjard, Sleipnir, Dragon Manteau, Ears of Ifrit*

```
"Armors" => array
    (
        "Lord Kaho's Horns",
        "Megingjard",
        "Sleipnir",
        "Dragon Manteau",
        "Ears of Ifrit"
    ),
```

➤ *Useables* will consist of the following members:
*Yggdrasil Berry, Berserk Potion, Authoritative Badge, Speed potion, Panacea, Cursed Water*

```
"Useables" => array
    (
        "Yggdrasil Berry",
        "Berserk Potion",
        "Authoritative Badge",
        "Speed Potion",
        "Panacea",
        "Cursed Water"
    ),
```

➤ *Key_Items* array will consist of the following members:
*Continental Guard Certificate, Ashes of Darkness, Dragon Tooth, Dragon Scale, Dragon Skin*

```
"Key_Items" => array
    (
        "Continental Guard Certificate",
        "Ashes of Darkness",
        "Dragon Tooth",
        "Dragon Scale",
        "Dragon Skin"
    ),
```

➤ *Magic_Items* array will consist of the following members: *Lvl10 Blessing Scroll, Lvl10 Increase AGI Scroll, Lvl 10 Assumptio Scroll*

```
"Magic_Items" => array
   (
        "Lvl10 Blessing Scroll",
        "Lvl10 Increase AGI Scroll",
        "Lvl10 Assumptio Scroll"
   ),
```

Now that the multidimensional array structure has been populated with elements, we can show you how to call each array member. The syntax used to reference a multidimensional array element would be:

```
$variablename[subarray1][subarray2]
[subarray...]
```

When implemented in the multidimensional array *$Backpack*, this would mean:

```
$Backpack = array ("Weapons" =>
array("Krasnaya", "Executioner", "Violet
Fear", "Atroce's Blade"),
                ("Armors" => array ("Lord
Kaho's Horns", "Megingjard", "Sleipnir",
"Dragon Manteau", "Ears of Ifrit"),
                ("Useables" =>
array("Yggdrasil Berry", "Berserk Potion",
"Authoritative Badge", "Speed Potion",
"Panacea", "Cursed Water"),
                ("Key_Items" =>
array("Continental Guard Certificate",
"Ashes of Darkness", "Dragon Tooth",
"Dragon Scale", "Dragon Skin"),
                ("Magic_Items" => array("Lvl10
Blessing Scroll", "Lvl10 Increase AGI
Scroll", "Lvl10 Assumptio Scroll"));
```

To make the above multidimensional array declaration easier to read, you might want to follow this format:

```php
$Backpack = array(
            "Weapons" => array
                 ("Krasnaya",
                  "Executioner",
                  "Violet Fear",
                  "Atroce's Blade"),
                      "Armors" => array
                 ("Lord Kaho's Horns",
                       "Megingjard",
                  "Sleipnir",
                  "Dragon Manteau",
                  "Ears of Ifrit"),
            "Useables" => array
                 ("Yggdrasil Berry",
                  "Berserk Potion",
                  "Authoritative Badge",
                  "Speed Potion",
                  "Panacea",
                  "Cursed Water"),
                  "Key_Items" => array
                 ("Continental Guard
Certificate",                "Ashes
of Darkness",
                  "Dragon Tooth",
                  "Dragon Scale",
                  "Dragon Skin"),
            "Magic_Items" => array
                 ("Lvl10 Blessing
Scroll",
                  "Lvl10 Increase AGI
Scroll",                "Lvl10
Assumptio Scroll")
            );
```

Tip: As experienced software engineers will tell you, you're writing code for multiple audiences. The first audience for PHP code is the server that will interpret it. The second audience is human beings (including yourself) that will have to read your code. Good software engineering practice demands that you write code that is readable by both audiences.

Now that each array is filled with members, we can try calling each member while inside the multidimensional array. To do this, we will follow the format:

```
$variablename[subarray1][subarray2]
[subarray...]
```

For example, let's say we want to call the *array member* "Executioner" (which belongs to the sub-array *Weapon*) and then display it. The correct code would be:

```
echo($backpack['Weapon'][1];
```

The same syntax is applied if you would want to access the other members in the array. Let's display the entire "backpack's inventory"— each division inside the backpack, then all the "items" in each division, after which we display a single item from each of the division in no particular order.

Display all "backpack" divisions and all the items in each "division":

```
echo("Backpack Contents for Weapons: </
br>");
echo($backpack['Weapons'][0] . "</br>");
echo($backpack['Weapons'][1] . "</br>");
echo($backpack['Weapons'][2] . "</br>");
echo($backpack['Weapons'][3] . "</br></
br>");

echo("Backpack Contents for Armors: </
br>");
```

```php
echo($backpack['Armors'][0] . "</br>");
echo($backpack['Armors'][1] . "</br>");
echo($backpack['Armors'][2] . "</br>");
echo($backpack['Armors'][3] . "</br>");
echo($backpack['Armors'][4] . "</br></
br>");

echo("Backpack Contents for Useables: </
br>");
echo($backpack['Useables'][0] . "</br>");
echo($backpack['Useables'][1] . "</br>");
echo($backpack['Useables'][2] . "</br>");
echo($backpack['Useables'][3] . "</br>");
echo($backpack['Useables'][4] . "</br>");
echo($backpack['Useables'][5] . "</br></
br>");

echo("Backpack Contents for Key Items: </
br>");
echo($backpack['Key Items'][0] . "</br>");
echo($backpack['Key Items'][1] . "</br>");
echo($backpack['Key Items'][2] . "</br>");
echo($backpack['Key Items'][3] . "</br>");
echo($backpack['Key Items'][4] . "</br></
br>");

echo("Backpack Contents for Magic Items:
</br>");
echo($backpack['Magic Items'][0] . "</
br>");
echo($backpack['Magic Items'][1] . "</
br>");
echo($backpack['Magic Items'][2] . "</
br></br>");
```

The complete code listing should now be:

```
<DOCTYPE!>
<html lang="en">
<head>
    <title>Multidimensional Arrays</title>
</head>
<body>
    <?php
        $backpack = array
            (
                "Weapons" => array
                    (
                        "Krasnaya",
                        "Executioner",
                        "Violet Fear",
                        "Atroce's
Blade",
                    ),
                "Armors" => array
                    (
                        "Lord Kaho's
Horns",
                        "Megingjard",
                        "Sleipnir",
                        "Dragon
Manteau",
                        "Ears of
Ifrit",
                    ),
                "Useables" => array
                    (
                        "Yggdrasil
Berry",
                        "Berserk
Potion",
                        "Authoritative
Badge",
                        "Speed Potion",
```

```php
                                "Panacea",
                                "Cursed Water",

                        ),
                "Key Items" => array
                        (
                                "Continental Guard
Certificate",
                                "Ashes of
Darkness",
                                "Dragon Tooth",
                                "Dragon Scale",
                                "Dragon Skin",

                        ),
                "Magic Items" => array
                        (
                                "Lvl 10
Blessing Scroll",
                                "Lvl 10
Increase AGI Scroll",
                                "Lvl 10
Assumptio Scroll",

                        ),
        );

    echo("Backpack Contents for Weapons: </
br>");
    echo($backpack['Weapons'][0] . "</
br>");
    echo($backpack['Weapons'][1] . "</
br>");
    echo($backpack['Weapons'][2] . "</
br>");
    echo($backpack['Weapons'][3] . "</br></
br>");

    echo("Backpack Contents for Armors: </
```

```
br>");
    echo($backpack['Armors'][0] . "</br>");
    echo($backpack['Armors'][1] . "</br>");
    echo($backpack['Armors'][2] . "</br>");
    echo($backpack['Armors'][3] . "</br>");
    echo($backpack['Armors'][4] . "</br></
br>");

    echo("Backpack Contents for Useables:
</br>");
    echo($backpack['Useables'][0] . "</
br>");
    echo($backpack['Useables'][1] . "</
br>");
    echo($backpack['Useables'][2] . "</
br>");
    echo($backpack['Useables'][3] . "</
br>");
    echo($backpack['Useables'][4] . "</
br>");
    echo($backpack['Useables'][5] . "</
br></br>");

    echo("Backpack Contents for Key Items:
</br>");
    echo($backpack['Key Items'][0] . "</
br>");
    echo($backpack['Key Items'][1] . "</
br>");
    echo($backpack['Key Items'][2] . "</
br>");
    echo($backpack['Key Items'][3] . "</
br>");
    echo($backpack['Key Items'][4] . "</
br></br>");

    echo("Backpack Contents for Magic
Items: </br>");
    echo($backpack['Magic Items'][0] . "</
```

```
br>");
    echo($backpack['Magic Items'][1] . "</
br>");
    echo($backpack['Magic Items'][2] . "</
br></br>");

    ?>
</body>
</html>
```

The output should look like this:

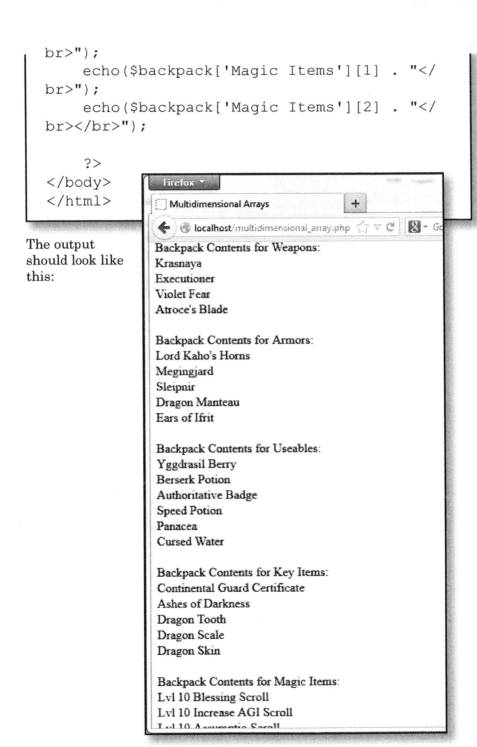

Figure 3.11: Outputting all members of a multidimensional
array.

92    *PHP and MySQL for Beginners*

If we just want the individual items displayed, then our code listing can be just as simple as:

```
<DOCTYPE!>
<html lang="en">
<head>
    <title>Multidimensional Arrays</title>
</head>
<body>
    <?php
        $backpack = array
            (
                "Weapons" => array
                    (
                        "Krasnaya",
                        "Executioner",
                        "Violet Fear",
                        "Atroce's
Blade",
                    ),
                "Armors" => array
                    (
                        "Lord Kaho's
Horns",
                        "Megingjard",
                        "Sleipnir",
                        "Dragon
Manteau",
                        "Ears of
Ifrit",
                    ),
                "Useables" => array
                    (
                        "Yggdrasil
Berry",
                        "Berserk
Potion",
                        "Authoritative
Badge",
```

```php
                                "Speed Potion",
                                "Panacea",
                                "Cursed Water",

                        ),
                "Key Items" => array
                        (
                                "Continental
Guard Certificate",
                                "Ashes of
Darkness",
                                "Dragon Tooth",
                                "Dragon Scale",
                                "Dragon Skin",

                        ),
                "Magic Items" => array
                        (
                                "Lvl 10
Blessing Scroll",
                                "Lvl 10
Increase AGI Scroll",
                                "Lvl 10
Assumptio Scroll",

                        ),
        );

    echo("Weapons[3]  :    ");
    echo($backpack['Weapons'][3] . "</br></
br>");

    echo("Armors[1]  :    ");
    echo($backpack['Armors'][1] . "</br></
br>");

    echo("Useables[5]  :    ");
    echo($backpack['Useables'][5] . "</
br></br>");
```

```
    echo("Key Items[0]   :    ");
    echo($backpack['Key Items'][0] . "</
br></br>");

    echo("Magic Items[2]   :    ");
    echo($backpack['Magic Items'][2] . "</
br></br>");

    ?>
</body>
</html>
```

The output should look like:

Let's do another example.

For this exercise, we will create the array *$teams* which contains three sub-arrays: *Yankees*, *Mets* and *Red Sox*. Each sub-array is an associative array whose elements are the *players' last names.*

Our program will complete a very simple task: display the first team's name together with its first member's name. On the next line, display the next team's name, and its first member. The program will do the same for the third team until all *teams* and *members'* names have been displayed.

Create a new HTML5 document and save it in the www (for Windows, WAMP) or htdocs (for Mac, MAMP) folder under the filename *multidimensional_array2.php*.

In your head element, type inside the &lt;title&gt; tag "Teams and Members". This will be your page's title.

```
<!DOCTYPE html>

<html>
<head>
    <title>Teams and Members</title>
</head>
```

Add the PHP tags in the &lt;body &gt; of the document:

```
<body>
    <?php

    ?>
```

Within the PHP tags, declare the main array *$teams*, whose members are *Yankees, Mets* and *Red Sox*. (These will be the keys to each element, which is itself an array, of the *$teams* array.) Fill in the members list accordingly by typing in the following:

```
        $teams = array
            (
                "Yankees" =>
                    (
                        "Rivera",
                        "Jeter",
                        "Granderson,
                        "Sabathia",
                        "Gradner"
                    ),
                "Mets" =>
                    (
```

```
                        "Dickey",
                        "Acosta",
                        "Pelfrey"
                ),
            "Red Sox" =>
                (
                        "Ortiz",
                        "Bard",
                        "Bucholz",
                        "Beckett"
                )
        );
```

While still within the PHP tags, add the command to display the name of the first *team* (as a string for now) followed by the *first member* of the *team* array. Use the *echo()* command:

```
echo("Yankees--1) " . $teams['Yankees']
[0]);
```

Display the name of the second *team* followed by the *second member* of that *team* array. Insert a break between the two output lines. The code should now progress as:

```
echo("Yankees--(1) " . $teams['Yankees']
[0]);
echo("<br/>");
echo("Mets------(1) " . $teams['Mets']
[0]);
```

Continue displaying the name of the *team* followed by the next *member* in succession until all *array members*, preceded by their team name, have been displayed:

```
echo("Yankees--(1) ".$teams['Yankees'][0]);
echo("<br/>");
echo("Mets------(1) ".$teams['Mets'][0]);
```

```php
echo("<br/>");
echo("Red Sox--(1) ".$teams['Red Sox'][0]);
echo("<br/><br/>");

echo("Yankees--(2) ".$teams['Yankees'][1]);
echo("<br/>");
echo("Mets------(2) ".$teams['Mets'][1]);
echo("<br/>");
echo("Red Sox--(2) ".$teams['Red Sox'][1]);
echo("<br/><br/>");

echo("Yankees--(3) ".$teams['Yankees'][2]);
echo("<br/>");
echo("Mets------(3) ".$teams['Mets'][2]);
echo("<br/>");
echo("Red Sox--(3) ".$teams['Red Sox'][2]);
echo("<br/><br/>");

echo("Yankees--(4) ".$teams['Yankees'][3]);
echo("<br/>");
echo("Mets------(4) ".$teams['Mets'][3]);
echo("<br/>");
echo("Red Sox--(4) ".$teams['Red Sox'][3]);
            echo("<br/><br/>");

echo("Yankees--(5) ".$teams['Yankees'][4]);
echo("<br/>");
echo("Mets------(5) ".$teams['Mets'][4]);
echo("<br/>");
echo("Red Sox--(5) ".$teams['Red Sox'][4]);
echo("<br/><br/>");
```

And then close the script and the document:

```
    ?>
</body>
</html>
```

Save the file and launch Firefox. In the URL or address bar, type localhost/multidimensional_array.php (for the Mac, type localhost/8888/ multidimensional_array.php) and view the output.

You will notice that the first three names displayed without any problem:

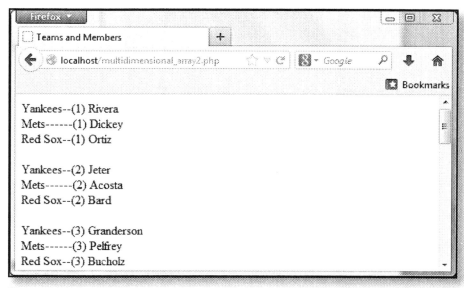

Figure 3.13: Outputting array members in the browser.

While the remaining array members displayed like this:

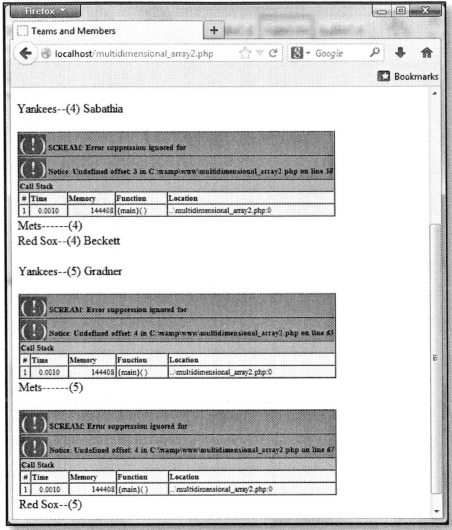

Figure 3.14: Calling undefined members of an array results in an error.

Array members that do not have an explicit assigned value were reported as "undefined offset". A good way to resolve this is to display spaces when there are no more names to display.

The routine should determine if the name read is the last member of the array, and, if it is, then it should just "print" spaces in place of the lacking array member until the task has finished displaying the names for all the teams. The commands that will help accomplish this are discussed in the next chapter—conditionals. We will reserve the discussion and presentation of the solution for the next chapter.

# 3.4 SUPER GLOBAL ARRAYS

**Superglobals** are built-in (pre-defined) associative array variables in PHP that were introduced in PHP version 4.1.0. These variables are automatically available to all PHP code, meaning there is no need to create an additional routine to make them publicly available to the entire PHP script.

**Super Global Array**

Superglobals represent data coming from URLs, HTML forms, cookies, sessions, and the web server itself. These arrays are also accessible within a function.

> For additional help and reference, you may visit the following URLs that provide friendly discussions on PHP:
>
> http://php.net/manual/en/index.php
> http://www.w3schools.com/php/default.asp

The most common uses of PHP superglobal arrays are in obtaining values from HTML forms. Here are nine superglobal arrays for the programmer to use. They are:

*$_GET*
*$_POST*
*$_REQUEST*
*$_COOKIE*
*$_SESSION*
*$_SERVER*
*$_ENV*
*$_FILES*
*$_GLOBAL*

Since we are operating on a local server in this book, our discussion will be limited to *$_GET, $_POST,* and *$_REQUEST* as we can easily demonstrate these three superglobals in the local sever context.

The superglobal *$_GET* represents data coming from a URL and sent to the PHP script via the get protocol. It is a pre-defined variable used to collect values from an HTML form using the method *get*. $_GET contains an associative array of variables passed to the current script through the URL parameters.

> **NOTE:** The GET method should not be used when sending passwords or other sensitive information because this information is then appended to the end of URLs and ends up being displayed in the URL's address bar and thus visible to the whole world. It is also not suitable for very large variable values and should not be used with values exceeding 2000 characters.

In the line below we use the *$_GET* superglobal to access a parameter called 'userName' that has been passed in from a form. We assign the value to a local variable called *$name*:

```
$name = $_GET['userName'];
```

The *$_POST* superglobal represents data from the hypertext transfer protocol (http) post protocol. It is a pre-defined variable used to collect values from an HTML form using the method *post*.

The *post* method is said to be more secure than the *get* method. This is because the *get* method passes values as a query string which is appended to the URL and thus visible in the address bar of the browser. There is no query string visible with the *post* method.

In the following line of code, the value of *$_POST* superglobal 'userName' is accessed and the value assigned to the local variable *$name*:

```
$name = $_POST['userName'];
```

The superglobal *$_COOKIE* represents an associative array of variables from the hypertext transfer protocol (http cookies) available to a PHP script. *$_REQUEST* represents an associative array of variables which by default contain the contents of *$_GET*, *$_POST* and *$_COOKIE* sent to the PHP script.

Following are the remaining six superglobals:

➤ *$_SESSION* represents data available to the current PHP script that has been previously stored in a session.

➤ *$_SERVER* represents data from the web server itself available to a PHP script. It is a special reserved PHP variable that contains all web information. It is an array containing information such as headers, paths and script locations. The entries in this array are created by the web server.

➤ *$_ENV* represents data available to a PHP script from the environment in which PHP is running. These variables are imported into PHP's global namespace from the environment under which the PHP parser is running.

> **NOTE**: Since PHP may run under different shells, a definite list of $_ENV global namespace is impossible.

**EXAMPLE:**

```php
<?php
echo 'My username is' . $_ENV[USER] . '!
';
?>
```

➤ *$_FILES* represents data available to a PHP script from http POST file uploads. *$_FILES* is the presently preferred method to handle uploaded files in PHP.

➤ *$_GLOBAL* represents associative array variables containing references to all variables currently defined in the global scope of the script. The variable names are the keys of the array.

Let's create a more extensive example that makes use of the superglobal variables *$_GET*, *$_POST*, and *$_REQUEST*. In particular, we will show the difference between using *$_GET* and *$_POST*.

The first step is to create a basic HTML5 form. In the form, we will ask for the name and age of the user. Then we retrieve that data, first from the superglobal variable *$_GET* and then from *$_POST*.

**1** **Step 1**: Create a fresh HTML5 document to come up with the form containing the following elements *userName* and *userAge*:

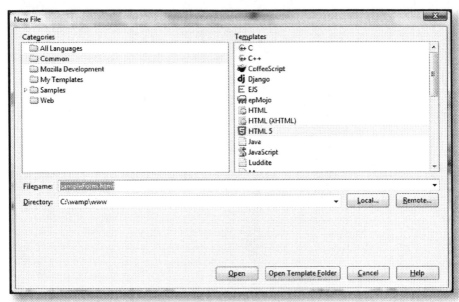

Figure 3.15: Creating a new document: sampleForm.html.

This is the resulting window after clicking Open:

Figure 3.16: Initial HTML code for sampleForm.html.

**2** **Step 2**: Type in the title tag "Sample Form".

In the document body, include a *form* tag with the *action* attribute equal to "superGlobals.php" and the *method* attribute equal to *post*, then close the tag.

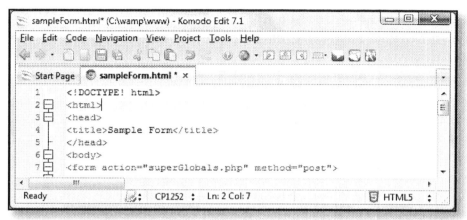

Figure 3.17: Adding a form tag to the document body. Note the attributes *action* and *method*.

**3** **Step 3**: Add a table. In the first table row <tr>, include a table data cell with the heading "Hello, this is our example." using <h1>.

```
<table>
    <tr>
        <td><h1>Hello,
this is our example</
h1></td>
    </tr>
```

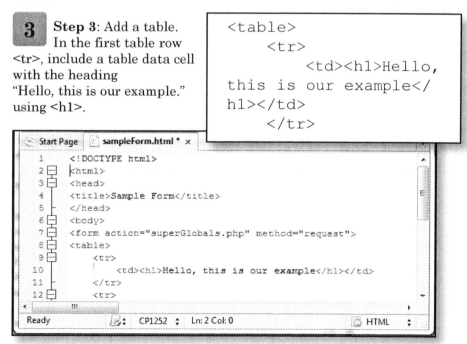

Figure 3.18: Adding table data cells to a table.

**4** **Step 4**: Add another table row with two table data <td> cells. The first table data cell will hold the text "Please Enter Your First Name:", while the second table data cell will contain the input form element to capture the user's first name, (userName).

```
<tr>
        <td>Please Enter Your First
Name:</td>
        <td><input name="userName" /></td>
        </tr>
```

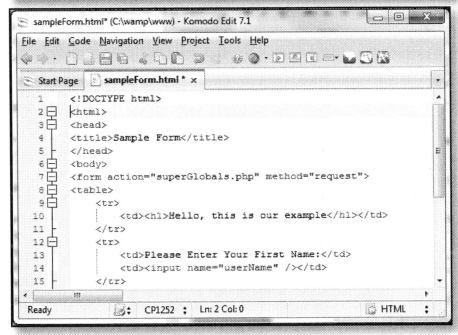

Figure 3.19: Adding an input form element (name="username") to a table data cell.

**5** **Step 5**: Add another table row with two table data <td> cells. The first table data cell will hold the text "Please Enter Your Age", while the second table data cell will contain the input form element to capture the user's age (userAge).

```
<tr>
    <td>Please Enter Your Age: </td>
    <td><input name="userAge" /></td>
</tr>
```

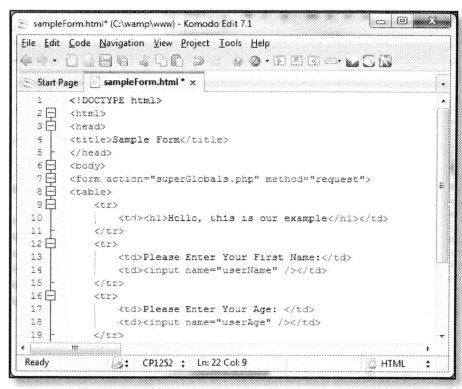

Figure 3.20: Adding a second input form element (name="userAge").

**6** **Step 6**: Lastly, add another table row that has one table data cell. This cell will contain the submit button:

```
<tr>
    <td><input type="submit"
value="Submit" /></td>
    </tr>
```

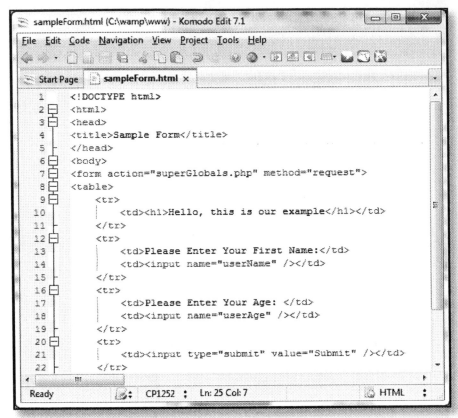

Figure 3.21: Adding a table data cell containing a submit button.

The complete code listing for *sampleForm.html is:*

## CODE LISTING: SAMPLEFORM.HTML

```
<!DOCTYPE! html>
<html>
<head>
<title>Sample Form</title>
</head>
<body>
<form action="superGlobals.php"
method="post">
<table>
    <tr>
        <td><h1>Hello, this is our
```

```
example</h1></td>
    </tr>
    <tr>
        <td>Please Enter Your First
Name:</td>
        <td><input name="userName" /></td>
    </tr>
    <tr>
        <td>Please Enter Your Age: </td>
        <td><input name="userAge" /></td>
    </tr>
    <tr>
        <td><input type="submit"
value="Submit" /></td>
    </tr>
</table>
</form>
</body>
</html>
```

**7** **Step 7**: View your output. This is how the form will look:

Figure 3.22: Viewing sampleForm.html in the browser.

Now that the form is ready, we can proceed with writing the PHP script document.

**1**   **Step 1**: Create a blank PHP document and save it under the filename *superGlobalsGet.php*.

We are now ready to proceed with the first superglobal variable *$_GET*.

**2**   **Step 2**: Type the following code in your *superGlobalsGet.php* document, then save:

```php
<?php
    $name=$_GET['userName'];
    $age=$_GET['userAge'];
?>
```

**3**   **Step 3**: Add the command to display the following output:

*userName* is *userAge* years old.

The code to do this is:

```php
echo($name . " is " . $age . " years old. ");
```

The complete PHP script should now look like this:

```php
<?php
    $name=$_GET['userName'];
    $age=$_GET['userAge'];

    echo($name . " is " . $age . " years old. ");
?>
```

**4**   **Step 4**: Save your *superGlobalsGet.php* file again.

With the *sampleForm.html* file open in your text editor, go to the document body element, and in the *<form>* tag, replace the *action* attribute's value with "superGlobalsGet.php" and the *method* attribute value with "get".

```
<body>
<form action="superGlobalsGet.php"
method="get">
```

**5** **Step 5**: Save the modifed file as *sampleFormGet.html*.

**6** **Step 6**: Launch your browser and call your *sampleFormGet.html* file and display the output.

**7** **Step 7**: View your output. This is how the result will look:

Figure 3.23: Viewing sampleFormGet.html in the browser. This form uses the "get" method attribute.

Type the values "John" in the user name textbox and "40" in the user age textbox. Click submit.

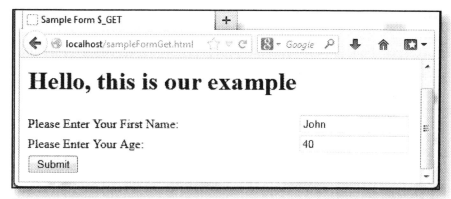

Figure 3.24: Inputting values into a form.

After clicking the submit button, this is how the output will look:

Figure 3.25: Viewing the output after clicking the submit button.

Notice the URL which displays the data the user entered. This string "?userName=John&userAge=40" is appended to the URL.

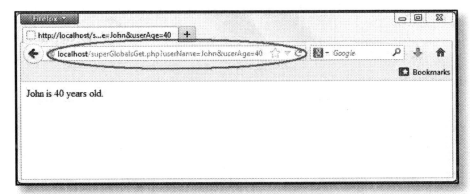

Figure 3.26: Displaying the user's information in the URL.

Let's go through the same process using the superglobal *$_POST*.

Type the following code in your *superGlobals.php* document then save:

```php
<?php
    $name=$_POST['userName'];
    $age=$_POST['userAge'];
?>
```

Add the command to display the following output:

```
userName is userAge years old.
```

The code to do this is:

```
echo($name . " is " . $age . " years old.
");
```

The complete code listing should now be:

```php
<?php
    $name=$_POST['userName'];
    $age=$_POST['userAge'];
    echo($name . " is " . $age . " years
old. ");
?>
```

Save your file as *superGlobalsPost.php*.

With the *sampleForm.html* file in your text editor open, go to the document body tag, and in the *<form> tag*, replace the *action* attribute with "superGlobalsPost.php" and the *method* attribute to "post".

```html
<body>
<form action="superGlobalsPost.php"
method="post">
```

Save the modifed file as *sampleFormPost.html*.

Launch your browser, call the *sampleFormPost.html* file and display the output.

Type the values "Fred" in the user name textbox and "20" in the user age textbox. Click submit.

Figure 3.27: Inputting values into sampleFormPost.html.

After clicking the submit button, the output should appear similar to the screenshot below:

Figure 3.28: Viewing the output after clicking the submit button.

Notice the URL is not displaying the information that the user typed in.

Figure 3.29: URL does not display the user's information.

The last superglobal we will discuss is *$_REQUEST*.

Type the following code in your *superGlobals.php* document:

```php
<?php
    $name=$_REQUEST['userName'];
    $age=$_REQUEST['userAge'];
?>
```

Add the command to display the following output:

*userName* is *userAge* years old.

The code to do this is:

```php
echo($name . " is " . $age . " years old.
");
```

The complete code listing should now be:

```php
<?php
    $name=$_REQUEST['userName'];
    $age=$_REQUEST['userAge'];
    echo($name . " is " . $age . " years
old. ");
?>
```

Save your file as *superGlobalsRequest.php*.

With the *sampleForm.html* file open in your text editor, go to the document body tag, and in the *<form>* tag, change the *action* attribute to "superGlobalsRequest.php". You may use "post" or "get" for the *method* attribute.

Either *method* can be assigned when used in conjunction with the action "request". For this example, we will pair "request" with "post". You may use either "get" or "post" as you type this example in to your text editor.

```
<body>
<form action="superGlobalsRequest.php"
method="post">
```

Save the modifed file as *sampleFormRequest.html*.

Launch your browser, call the *sampleFormRequest.html* file and display the output.

This is how the result will look when displayed in the browser window:

Figure 3.30: Viewing sampleFormRequest.html in the browser.

Type the value "Brandon" in the user name textbox and "30" in the user age textbox. Click submit.

Figure 3.31: Inputting values into sampleFormRequest.html.

After clicking the submit button, this is how the output will appear:

Figure 3.32: Viewing the output after clicking the submit button.

If you used the method 'get' you will notice that the URL displays the information that the user typed in. If you didn't, you will not see the query string in the URL window.

In our next example, to demonstrate that information taken from HTML forms can also be mathematically manipulated, we will modify our PHP script so that the value of the user's age will be increased by two.

**1** **Step 1**: Using the *sampleForm.html* and *superGlobals.php* files, modify the PHP script so that after the first echo statement the variable *$age* will be increased by two.

```php
<?php
    $name = $_POST['userName'];
    $age = $_POST['userAge'];

    echo($name . " is " . $age . " years old.");

    $age += 2;
    echo("</br>Two years from now " . $name . " will be " . $age . " years old.");
?>
```

**2** **Step 2**: Save the modified file.

**3** **Step 3**: Launch the browser and access *sampleForm.html* through the localhost.

**4** **Step 4**: View your output. This is how the result will look:

Figure 3.33: Inputting values into sampleForm.html.

After clicking the submit button, your browser should display a similar result to the following screenshot:

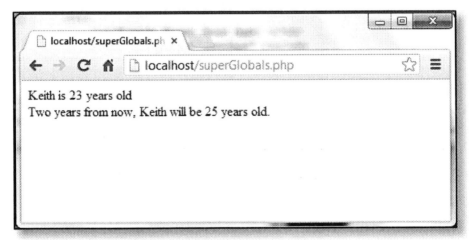

Figure 3.34: Viewing the output after clicking the submit button.

## QUESTIONS FOR REVIEW

1. What are arrays?
   a. Arrays are special variables that can store multiple types of homogeneous data.
   b. Arrays are containers for multiple variables.
   c. Arrays are special commands that get the values of many variables and store them.
   d. Arrays are special functions that create multiple data.

2. If a member of an array is to be assigned as the fourth member, what should the proper syntax be?
   a. $arrayName[3]=data;     c. $arrayNamc[4]=data;
   b. arrayName[3]=data;      d. arrayName[4]=data;

3. In the example,

```
$example = array(
"Cooper" => 25000,
"Oswald" => 23500);
```

which is/are the key's?
   a. Cooper, Oswald        c. $example
   b. 25000, 23500          d. array

4. What is the simplest explanation for multidimensional arrays?
   a. They are arrays that hold a particular key and associate value in each key.
   b. They are arrays within an array.
   c. They are arrays that have multiple members.
   d. They are arrays that have endless variables.

5. What is the difference between a simple array and a superglobal array?
   a. Normal arrays are larger than super global arrays.
   b. Superglobal arrays come from the user inputs from the web server, URLs, cookies, and HTML files, while normal arrays are declared by the programmer.
   c. Normal arrays use up less memory than superglobal arrays.
   d. Superglobal arrays are easier to process than normal arrays.

# CHAPTER 3 LAB EXERCISE

## LAB EXERCISE 1- SUPERGLOBAL SINGLE DATA SET

1. Create a PHP program that will display a form and ask for user information—name, age and the current year.

There must be a *submit* and a *reset* button in the form. Once the *submit* button is clicked, PHP must return a result reporting the approximate year the person was born.

2. Ensure that the WAMP or MAMP server stack is running.

3. Create an HTML5 document and save it as *yearOfBirth_prediction. html* inside the www or htdocs folder.

4. Adopt the following form layout and form fields: *userName, userAge* and *currentYear*. Place these elements in table form for a more organized layout.

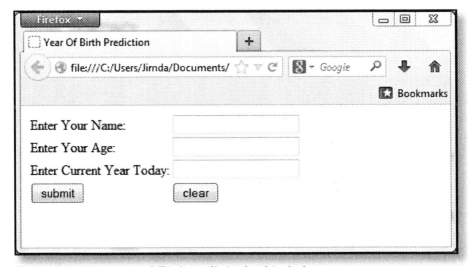

Figure 3.35: Viewing yearOfBirth_prediction.html in the browser.

Use the *maxlength* attribute to limit the number of characters of *userName* to ten, *userAge* to three, and *currentYear* to four.

```
<table>
   <tr>
      <td>Enter Your Name:</td>
      <td><input name="userName"
maxlength="10" /></td>
   </tr>
   <tr>
      <td>Enter Your Age:</td>
      <td><input name="userAge"
maxlength="3" /></td>
   </tr>
   <tr>
      <td>Enter the Current Year:</td>
      <td><input name="currentYear"
maxlength="4" /></td>
   </tr>
   <tr>
      <td><input type="submit"
value="submit" /></td>
      <td><input type="reset"
value="clear"</td>
   </tr>
</table>
```

5. Create a new text file and save it as *birthYear_calculator.php* under your www or htdocs folder.

6. Compute for the age and type in the codes in the *birthYear_calcucator.php* file.

We will use the *$_POST* superglobal variable here but feel free to tweak the code later using the other two superglobals, *$_GET* and *$_REQUEST*.

```
<?php
   $name = $_POST['userName'];
   $age = $_POST['userAge'];
   $year = $_POST['currentYear'];
```

```php
    $yob = $year - $age;

    echo($name . " was approximately born
in the year " . $yob. ".");
?>
```

This is how the output should look:

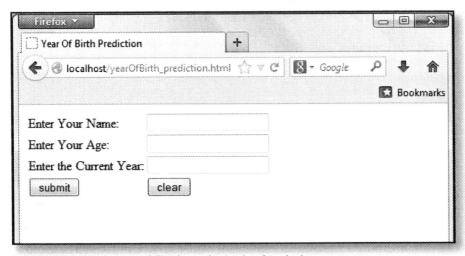

Figure 3.36: Viewing yearOfBirth_prediction.html in the browser.

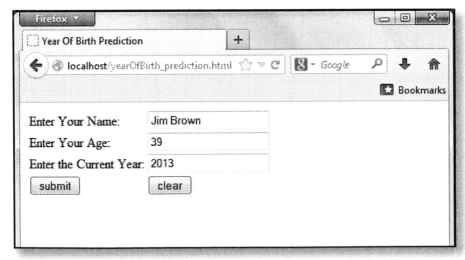

Figure 3.37: Inputting values into the form.

After clicking submit, this is how the output will look:

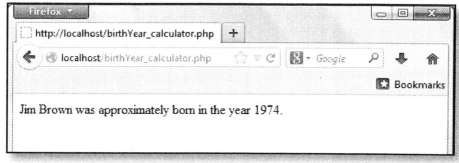

Figure 3.38: Viewing the output after clicking the submit button.

## LAB EXERCISE 2- SUPERGLOBAL MULTIPLE DATA SET

1. Create a PHP program that will display a form asking for data input from two individuals—the individuals' names, ages and then an entry for the current year.

There must be a submit and a reset button in the form. Once the submit button is clicked, PHP must return a result displaying a list of approximate years the individuals were born.

2. Use the same HTML5 document used in lab exercise 1 but update the codes in the in the HTML *yearOfBirth_prediction.html* as follows:

```
<table>
    <tr>
        <td>Enter First Person's Name:</td>
        <td><input name="userName1"
maxlength="10" /></td>
    </tr>
    <tr>
        <td>Enter First Person's Age:</td>
        <td><input name="userAge1"
maxlength="3" /></td>
    </tr>
    <tr>
        <td>Enter Second Person's Name:</td>
        <td><input name="userName2"
maxlength="10" /></td>
```

```
    </tr>
    <tr>
       <td>Enter Second Person's Age:</td>
       <td><input name="userAge2"
maxlength="3" /></td>
    </tr>
    <tr>
       <td>Enter the Current Year:</td>
       <td><input name="currentYear"
maxlength="4" /></td>
    </tr>
    <tr>
       <td><input type="submit"
value="submit" /></td>
       <td><input type="reset"
value="clear"</td>
    </tr>
    </table>
```

and in the PHP document *birthYear_calculator.php* as follows:

```
   <?php
      $name[0] = $_POST['userName1'];
      $name[1] = $_POST['userName2'];
      $age[0] = $_POST['userAge1'];
      $age[1] = $_POST['userAge2'];
      $year = $_POST['currentYear'];
      $yob[0] = $year - $age[0];
      $yob[1] = $year - $age[1];

      echo($name[0] . " was approximately
born in the year " . $yob[0]. ".");
      echo("</br>");
      echo($name[1] . " was approximately
born in the year " . $yob[1]. ".");
      echo("</br>");

   ?>
```

The output now should provide a form that allows you to enter information for two individuals:

Figure 3.39: Viewing yearOfBirth_prediction.html in the browser.

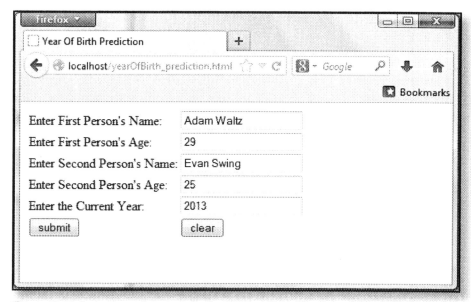

Figure 3.40: Inputting values into the form.

After clicking submit, this is how the output will look:

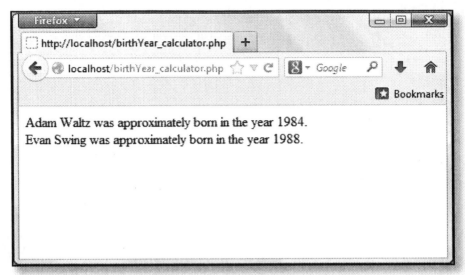

Figure 3.41: Viewing the output after clicking the submit button.

## CHAPTER 3 LAB SOLUTIONS:

### CODE LISTING: LAB 1 SOLUTION
#### *YEAROFBIRTH_PREDICTION.HTML*

```html
<!DOCTYPE html>

<html lang="en">
<head>
    <title>Year Of Birth Prediction</
title>
</head>
<body>
    <form action="birthYear_calculator.
php" method="post">
        <table>
            <tr>
                <td>Enter Your Name:</td>
                <td><input name="userName"
maxlength="10" /></td>
```

```
        </tr>
        <tr>
            <td>Enter Your Age:</td>
            <td><input name="userAge"
maxlength="3" /></td>
        </tr>
        <tr>
            <td>Enter the Current
Year:</td>
            <td><input
name="currentYear" maxlength="4" /></td>
        </tr>
        <tr>
            <td><input type="submit"
value="submit" /></td>
            <td><input type="reset"
value="clear"</td>
        </tr>
    </table>
</form>
</body>
</html>
```

## CODE LISTING: *BIRTHYEAR_CALCULATOR.PHP*

```php
<?php
    $name = $_POST['userName'];
    $age = $_POST['userAge'];
    $year = $_POST['currentYear'];
    $yob = $year - $age;

    echo($name . " was approximately born
in the year " . $yob. ".");
?>
```

```html
<!DOCTYPE html>

<html lang="en">
<head>
    <title>Year Of Birth Prediction</title>
</head>
<body>
  <form action="birthYear_calculator.php" method="post">
      <table>
        <tr>
          <td>Enter First Person's Name:</td>
          <td><input name="userName1" maxlength="10" /></td>
        </tr>
        <tr>
          <td>Enter First Person's Age:</td>
          <td><input name="userAge1" maxlength="3" /></td>
        </tr>
        <tr>
          <td>Enter Second Person's Name:</td>
          <td><input name="userName2" maxlength="10" /></td>
        </tr>
        <tr>
          <td>Enter Second Person's Age:</td>
          <td><input name="userAge2" maxlength="3" /></td>
```

```
        </tr>
        <tr>
          <td>Enter the Current Year:</td>
              <td><input name="currentYear"
maxlength="4" /></td>
          </tr>
          <tr>
            <td><input type="submit"
value="submit" /></td>
              <td><input type="reset"
value="clear"</td>
            </tr>
          </table>
      </form>
</body>
</html>
```

## CODE LISTING: *BIRTHYEAR_CALCULATOR.PHP*

```php
<?php
    $name[0] = $_POST['userName1'];
    $name[1] = $_POST['userName2'];
    $age[0] = $_POST['userAge1'];
    $age[1] = $_POST['userAge2'];
    $year = $_POST['currentYear'];
    $yob[0] = $year - $age[0];
    $yob[1] = $year - $age[1];

    echo($name[0] . " was approximately
born in the year " . $yob[0]."."");
    echo("</br>");
    echo($name[1] . " was approximately
born in the year " . $yob[1]."."");
    echo("</br>");
    ?>
```

# CHAPTER SUMMARY:

In this chapter we talked about arrays. You learned that there are two types of PHP arrays: simple or indexed arrays and associative arrays. You learned that multidimensional arrays are arrays within arrays and PHP provides access to globally scoped associative arrays named superglobal arrays.

We listed the nine immediately available superglobal variables and discussed three of them: *$_GET, $_REQUEST, and $_POST.* The other six superglobal variables can only be run and tested on a remote server.

In the next chapter, we will be discussing PHP conditionals.

# CHAPTER 4
## BRANCHING

### CHAPTER OBJECTIVES:

- You will learn the precise definitions of and study examples of **expressions**, **conditional expressions**, **operands**, **operators**, **comparison operators** and **logical operators**.
- You will be able to understand and analyze the branching control structures used in PHP.
- You will be able to understand the differences among the **conditional statements** used in PHP branching control structures.
- You will learn about the **ternary operator** and use it to write compact PHP code.
- You will apply the **conditional statements** and branching control structures in various PHP scripts.

## 4.1 SIMPLE CONTROL STRUCTURE—*IF* STATEMENT

In computer programming, a **control structure** allows you to alter the flow of execution of your program statements. Instead of a line after line, sequential flow of execution, you can have the program:

**Control Structure**

a. skip specific lines or blocks of code (**branching**), or
b. repeatedly execute a group of lines or blocks of code (**looping**).

The program performs these branching or looping actions by evaluating **conditional expressions** to either TRUE or FALSE.

We tackle **branching** control structures in this chapter while **looping** control structures will be the subject of Chapter 5.

A **branching control structure** consists of:

**Branching**

a. a **conditional expression** and a clearly defined block of code, or
b. several **conditional expressions** and several clearly defined

blocks of code.

Any of these blocks of code or none at all will be executed based on whether the **conditional expression** evaluates to TRUE or FALSE.

**TRUE or FALSE**

Conditional Expressions

> **TIP:** A block of code consists of one or any number of program statements delimited by curly brackets {}. If there is only one statement in the block of code, the curly brackets are not required. However, for the purposes of clarity and readability, curly brackets are always used.

Let's take the simplest branching control structure, the *if-statement*. Its syntax is:

```
If (conditional-expression) {
    statements . . .
}
Statements after if-statement. . .
```

If the *conditional-expression*, when evaluated, results in the Boolean value TRUE, then the block of statements enclosed by the curly brackets will be executed. Otherwise, (meaning if evaluating the *conditional-expression* resulted in the Boolean value FALSE) the block of statements will be ignored and program execution will skip to the *if-statement* right after the *if-statement's* code block.

**Expression**

Now, let's examine **conditional expressions.** First we must understand what an **expression** is.

In PHP, an **expression** is any valid combination of variables, constants, literals, operators, objects and even functions that can be evaluated to produce a value. This value can be any of the eight PHP data types: integers, floating-point numbers, strings, booleans, arrays, objects, resources (or handles) and null.

How do you evaluate an **expression?** The simplest and most used method is to place the expression on the right-hand side of an assignment statement:

```
$variable = expression
```

When this assignment statement is executed, the expression on the right-hand side will be evaluated and its value stored in *$variable* on the left-hand side. By using a variable to store the result of evaluating an expression, you can use that value later on at any point of your program.

Now, all **expressions** consist of at least one **operand** and one or more **operators**.

**Operator**

 An **operator** is a symbol that specifies a particular action to be performed. This action usually results in a new value.

 An **operand** is what receives the action of an **operator.** Most of the time, an **operand** is a variable but it could also be a literal, an object, a function or anything that an operator can validly perform its action on.

**Operand**

> **TIP:** PHP operators can be classified into ten groups, namely: arithmetic, array, assignment, bitwise, comparison, error control, execution, logical, string, and incrementing/decrementing.

The simplest expressions are *literal* values and *variables*. These are expressions that consist of only one **operand** and no **operators.** *Literal* values as expressions evaluate to themselves and *variables* evaluate to the values stored in them.

> **TIP:** A *literal value* is a single value expressed by its actual string value (i.e. not referenced by a variable). For example, 1, 1.414 and "string" are literal values.

Let's take the expression:

```
$days++
```

It consists of the increment **operator** ++ and the **operand** *$days* which is a variable. The increment operator adds 1 to its **operand**. So, if the value stored in *$days* is 7, then when you evaluate this expression, it will return 8 which is the value now stored in *$days*.

Here's another expression:

```
$cost + $margin
```

It consists of two **operands**: the variables *$cost* and *$margin* and the addition **operator**, +. This expression will add the values stored in the variables *$cost* and *$margin*. For this expression to be of any use, it has to be part of an assignment statement, such as:

```
$sellingPrice = $cost + $margin
```

Now, the result of evaluating the expression on the right-hand side of the preceding assignment statement is stored in the variable *$sellingPrice*.

Here is an example of an expression without an **operator**:

```
strtoupper($str)
```

This expression consists of the string function *strtoupper* and the variable *$str*. The function *strtoupper* converts all characters of a string to uppercase. If the value stored in *$str* were the string "LearnTo" then *strtoupper($str)* would return "LEARNTO". The original contents of *$str* would be unchanged, therefore if you want to make use of the modified string "LEARNTO" you would have to place the expression *strtoupper($str)* in an assignment statement:

```
$newstr = strtoupper($str)
```

Now, **expressions** that evaluate to either of the Boolean values TRUE and FALSE are known as **conditional expressions.** Moreover, **conditional expressions** specifically use the **comparison** and **logical operators**.

## Comparison Operators

**Comparison operators** let you compare

two operands in various ways in a **conditional expression**. If the comparison test is successful, the **conditional expression** evaluates to TRUE; otherwise, it evaluates to FALSE.

The following table lists the different PHP **comparison operators** and their descriptions when used in PHP.

| Operator | Example | Result |
|---|---|---|
| == (equal) | $LS == $RS | TRUE if the operand stored in $LS is equal to the operand stored in $RS; FALSE otherwise. |
| != or <> not equal to | $LS != $RS or $LS <> $RS | TRUE if the operand stored in $LS does not equal the operand stored in $RS; FALSE otherwise. |
| === ( identical) | $LS === $RS | TRUE if the operand stored in $LS is not only equal to the operand stored in $RS but also of the same type; FALSE otherwise. |
| !== ( identical) | $LS !== $RS | TRUE if the operand stored in $LS is not only equal to the operand stored in $RS but also of the same type; FALSE otherwise. |
| > (greater than) | $LS > $RS | Tests if the operand on the left side of the operator is greater than the operand on the right side of the operator. |
| less than < | $LS < $RS | Tests if the operand on the left side of the operator is less than the operand on the right side of the operator |
| greater than >= or equal to | $LS >= $RS | Tests if the operand on the left side of the operator is greater than or equal to the operand on the right side of the operator |
| less than <= or equal to | $LS <= $RS | Tests if the operand at the left side of the operator is less than or equal to the operand at the right side of the operator |

**Logical operators** allow you to combine **conditional expressions** to produce a Boolean result of either TRUE or FALSE.

**Logical Operators**

| Operator | Example | Result |
|----------|---------|--------|
| AND | exp1 AND exp2 | TRUE only if both exp1 and exp2 evaluate to TRUE; FALSE otherwise. |
| && | exp1 && exp2 | |
| OR | exp1 OR exp2 | TRUE if either exp1 and exp2 evaluate to TRUE or both exp1 and exp2 are TRUE; FALSE only if both exp1 and exp2 are FALSE. |
| \|\| | exp1 \|\| exp2 | |

Now let's examine some **conditional expressions**.

The first is a very simple PHP **conditional expression**:

```
$age <= 21.
```

It consists of the variable $age, the comparison operator <= (less than or equal to) and the integer value 21. This will yield TRUE if the value of the variable $age ranges from 21 to any values less than 21. If the value of the variable $age is greater than 21, then that conditional expression will yield FALSE.

The second example is not so simple:

```
$char >="A" and $char<="Z".
```

This will yield TRUE if the variable $char stores any of the uppercase characters from "A" to "Z".

The last is a complex conditional expression:

```
( ( ( $year % 4 == 0 ) && ( $year % 100
!= 0 ) ) || ( $year % 400 == 0 ) )
```

This will return true if the value stored in $year is a leap year, false if otherwise.

Now that we covered the definitions and studied examples of **expressions, conditional expressions, operands, operators, comparison operators** and **logical operators**, we look at PHP's **conditional statements**.

PHP has three basic **conditional statements** that you can use to create **branching control structures:**

  a. The *if-statement,*
  b. The *if-else-* and *if-elseif-statements,* and
  c. The *switch-statement.*

# 4.2 *IF*-STATEMENT

*If-statements* evaluate a conditional expression. If it is TRUE, the code block following the *if-statement* is executed. Otherwise, the code block is ignored. In both cases of either TRUE or FALSE, execution then proceeds to the statement right after the code block.

**If-Statement**

The syntax for the *if-statement* is:

```
if (conditional expression){
    code block of statements . . .
}
Statements after if
```

Let's work on an example.

**PROBLEM**: Create a short PHP program that will determine if a person is eligible to vote based on the following information.

| Variable Name | Value | Type |
|---|---|---|
| $age | 19 | Integer |
| $isCitizen | TRUE | Boolean |

**SOLUTION:**

**1** **Step 1:** Create a new HTML5 document. Include the opening and closing PHP tags in the document <body>. Name your document *conditionals.php*. Refer to the accompanying images for your guide.

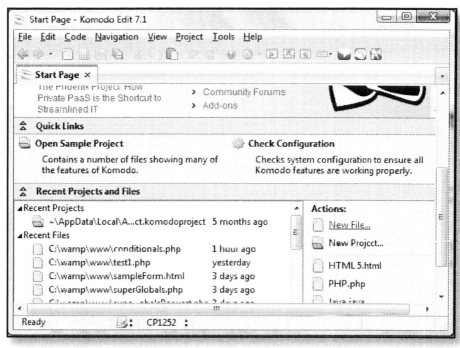

Figure 4.1: Komodo Edit start page.

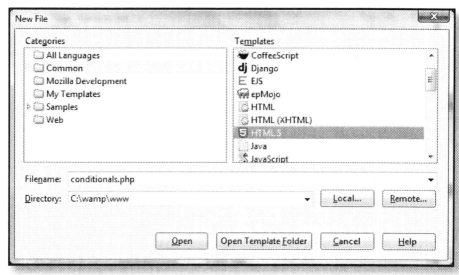

Figure 4.2: Opening a new HTML5 document.

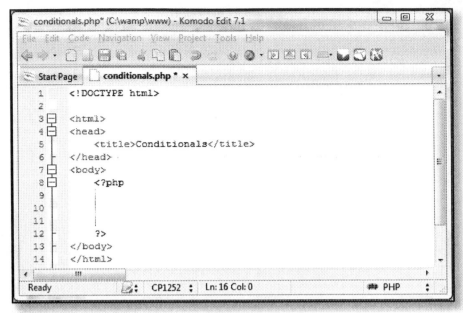

Figure 4.3: Adding opening and closing PHP tags to the document.

**2** **Step 2:** Declare and initialize the variables:

| Variable Name | Value | Data Type |
|---|---|---|
| $age | 19 | Integer |
| $isCitizen | TRUE | Boolean |

```php
<?php
   $age = 19;
   $isCitizen = TRUE;
?>
```

Refer to the variable assignment table given in Step 2. The third column indicates the "data type" of the values that will be assigned to variables *$age* and *$isCitizen*.

Variable *$age* is assigned an **integer** data type of 19.

Variable *$isCitizen* is assigned a **Boolean** data type of TRUE.

**3** **Step 3:** After declaring and assigning the variables, input the conditional expression of the *if-statement*, as follows:

```
If ($age>=18 && $isCitizen==TRUE)
```

Then the next statement that follows the *if-statement* is the code block that will execute if the **conditional expression** is evaluated as true:

```
{
    print ("You are eligible to vote");
}
```

**4** **Step 4:** Your final code listing should now be:

```
<!DOCTYPE html>

<html>
<head>
    <title>Conditionals</title>
</head>
<body>
    <?php
        $age = 19;
        $isCitizen = TRUE;

    if ($age >= 18 && $isCitizen == TRUE)
        {
            print("You are eligible to
vote.");
    }
    ?>
</body>
</html>
```

**5** **Step 5:** Save your file as *conditionals.php*.

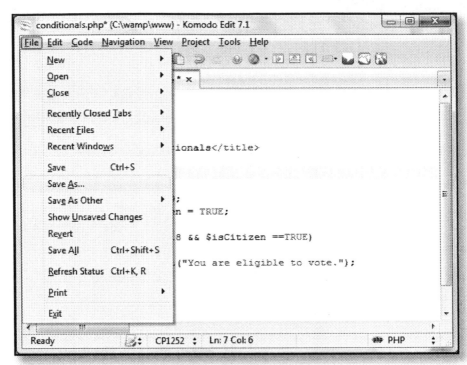

Figure 4.4: Saving a file in Komodo Edit.

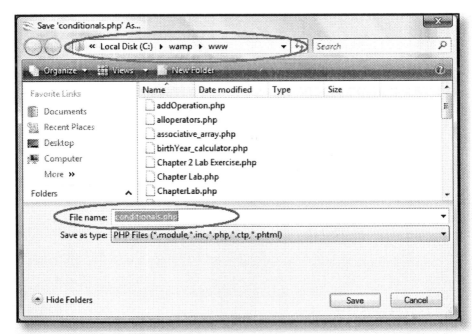

Figure 4.5: Saving conditionals.php to the www folder.

**6** **Step 6:** Make sure that WAMPServer is online and then launch your browser and type the URL http://localhost/conditionals.php in the address bar. Press the enter key so that the server may load and process the URL.

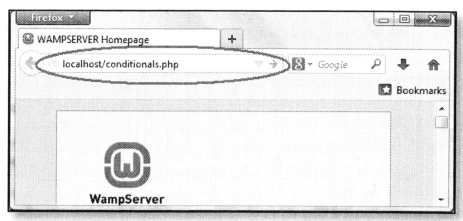

Figure 4.6: Accessing conditionals.php in the browser via localhost.

Now, let's analyze the execution of each line of the script.

The *if-statement* will evaluate two conditional expressions, namely:

(1) If the value stored in *$age* is greater than or equal to 18. Since the actual value stored is 19, the conditional expression *($age >=18)* yields a TRUE value.

(2) If the value stored in *$isCitizen* is TRUE. Since the actual value stored is TRUE, the conditional expression *($isCitizen ==TRUE)* also yields a TRUE value.

(3) The compound conditional returns TRUE when evaluated. Let's dissect the whole statement and see.

| Expression 1 | Compound Operator | Expression 2 | Value |
|---|---|---|---|
| if ($age >= 18) | && | if ($isCitizen ==TRUE) | TRUE && TRUE |
| TRUE | AND | TRUE | TRUE |

Since the conditional yielded TRUE when tested, then the next statement, which is:

```
{
    print ("You are eligible to vote");
}
```

is executed, and will display the output.

Figure 4.7: Outputting a compound conditional in the browser.

Let's see how the output will change if we store new values in the variables *$age* and *$isCitizen*.

**PROBLEM:** We change the values of the variables as follows:

| Variable Name | Value | Type |
|---|---|---|
| $age | 17 | Integer |
| $isCitizen | FALSE | Boolean |

## SOLUTION:

**1** **Step 1:** With your text editor still open, click on the *conditionals. php* document tab to reveal the previously encoded program.

Go to the PHP script portion of the document and change the assigned value of variable *$age* to 17 and the value of *$isCitizen* to FALSE. Your code should now look like this:

```php
<?php
    $age = 17;
    $isCitizen = FALSE;

if ($age >= 18 && $isCitizen == TRUE)
    {
        print("You are eligible to
vote.");
}
?>
```

**2** **Step 2:** Save your file. You may choose to overwrite the file by clicking *Save* or saving it under a different filename using *Save As.*

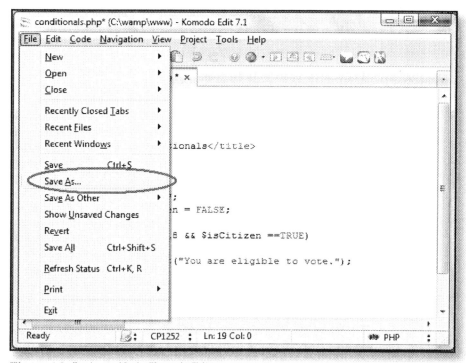

Figure 4.8: Saving a file in Komodo Edit.

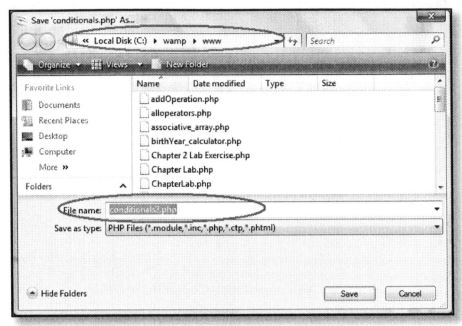

Figure 4.9: Saving the updated conditionals.php file in the www folder.

I chose to overwrite my existing file by choosing *Save* from the file menu.

**3** **Step 3:** Launch your browser and type in your file's name in the address bar (in my case, it's still *conditionals.php)* and press *enter*.

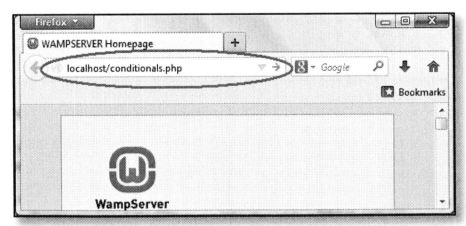

Figure 4.10: Accessing conditionals.php in the browser via localhost.

**Step 4:** View your output. This is how your output should look:

Figure 4.11: Viewing conditionals.php in the browser.

Notice that the browser displays a blank window. This occurs because the individual **conditional expressions** that make up the compound **conditional expression** both yielded FALSE, therefore it will not execute the code block that follows the *if-statement*. This resulted in a blank browser output.

Let's take a look at another example. This time, we will no longer embed the assigned values for *age* and *citizenship* inside the PHP code. Instead, the information will be derived from the user by means of a text box for the age, and radio buttons to state whether the user is a citizen or not.

**PROBLEM:** Create a simple HTML form that will ask the user to type in their age and will ask them to input their citizenship by clicking the appropriate radio button. Treat the variables as *superglobals* and use the pre-defined variable *$_POST*. Name your main HTML document as *votersForm.html* and the external PHP document as *votersEligibility. php*.

**SOLUTION:**

 **Step 1:** Create a new HTML5 document. Save the file as *votersForm.html*. Type in the <title> tag "Enter User Information", as shown here:

```
<title>Enter User Information</title>
```

The PHP script tags will not be included because the PHP script will be called externally—as a separate PHP document called by the "action" form attribute within this HTML document.

For your PHP action script file, assign the document name, *votersEligibility.php*.

In the <body> of the HTML document, include the form tag. Set the action attribute value to *votersEligibility.php* and the *method* attribute value to *post*.

```
<body>
    <form action="votersEligibility.php"
method="post">
```

**2** **Step 2:** Continue working on the HTML code. Lay out the form elements using tables. Using <table> will keep the form more organized and structured, and will prevent the code listing from having excessive <break> tags.

Your HTML form document will have the following elements in it:
*   an input element for age, with value "userAge"
*   two radio button input elements, one for "Yes" and one for "No"
*   a submit button element with value "Submit"

In the first table row, <tr>, we'll ask for the user's age. The first table data cell, <td>, should display the text "Enter Your Age".

```
<table>
    <tr>
        <td>Enter Your Age</td>
```

The second table data cell will contain the input tag with name attribute's value set to "userAge".

```
            <td><input name="userAge"
></td>
        </tr>
```

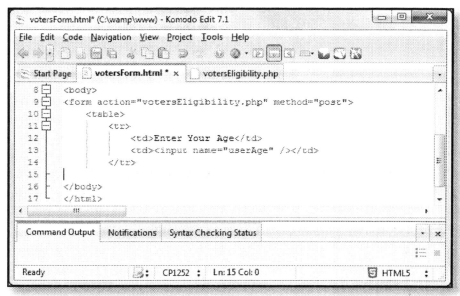

Figure 4.12: Creating a form using a table structure.

In the second table row, we'll place the radio buttons. The first table data cell should display the text "Are you a citizen?"

```
<tr>
        <td>Are you a citizen?</td>
```

The second table data cell will contain the two radio buttons for Yes and No responses.

```
<td>
<input type="radio" name="citizen"
value="true">Yes</input>
<input type="radio" name="citizen"
value="false">No</input>
</td>

</tr>
```

In the third table row, place the "submit" button in the only table data cell contained here.

```
     <tr>
          <td><input type="submit"
value="Submit" ></td>
          </tr>
```

**3** **Step 3:** Place the closing tags *</table>* and *</form>*, make sure there are the closing *</body>* and *</html>* tags as well, then save your document.

```
     </table>
     </form>
</body>
</html>

<!DOCTYPE html>

<html>
<head>
     <title>Enter User Information</title>
</head>

<body>
<form action="votersEligibility.php"
method="post">
     <table>
          <tr>
               <td>Enter Your Age</td>
               <td><input name="userAge" ></
td>
          </tr>
          <tr>
               <td>Are you a citizen?</td>
               <td><input type="radio"
name="citizen" value="true">Yes</input>
<input type="radio" name="citizen"
```

```
value="false">No</input></td>
        </tr>
        <tr>
            <td><input type="submit"
value="Submit" ></td>
        </tr>
    </table>
</form>
</body>
</html>
```

**4** **Step 4:** View your output. This is how your *votersForm.html* input page should look:

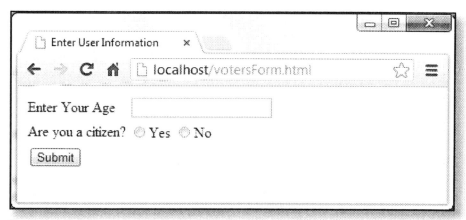

Figure 4.13: Viewing votersForm.html in the browser.

The page displayed is not yet functional. The PHP script will still have to be created to make the program display accordingly.

**5** **Step 5:** Create the *votersEligibility.php* document using your text editor. This is the complete code listing for our PHP script.

```php
<?php
    $age = $_POST['userAge'];
    $citizen = $_POST ['citizen'];

    if ($age >= 18 && $citizen == "true")
    {
```

```
            echo("You are eligible to vote");
        }
    ?>
```

Notice the conditional statement

```
    if ($age >= 18 && $citizen == "true")
```

*$citizen* is tested for the string value "true" and not the Boolean value TRUE. This is because information from the form page, *votersEligibiity. php* was sent as string data, in particular the Boolean TRUE was converted to the string "true".

```
<?php
    $age = $_POST['userAge'];
    $citizen = $_POST['citizen'];

    if ($age>=18 && $citizen=="true")
    {
            echo("You are eligible to vote");
    }
?>
```

Make sure you save your file.

**6** **Step 6:** Launch your browser and type in the address bar http:// localhost/votersForm.html. (Or, simply switch to your browser launched earlier in Step 4.)

**7** **Step 7:** In the displayed form, type in 18 for the age and select *Yes* for the citizen radio button. Click the *Submit* button. View your output.

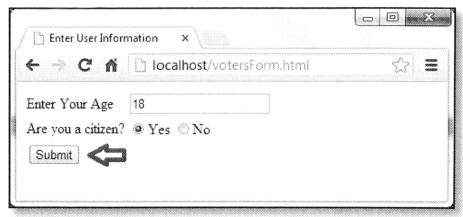

Figure 4.14: Clicking the submit button.

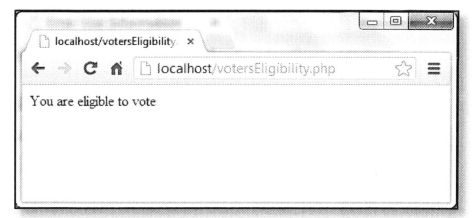

Figure 4.15: Submitting the form and viewing the output.

**8** **Step 8:** Reload the *votersForm.html* page and change the user information based on the following table. Observe the outputs.

| Age | Citizenship |
|-----|-------------|
| 25  | Yes         |
| 15  | Yes         |
| 25  | No          |
| 15  | No          |

Ensure the results you get are correct according to the program logic.

## 4.3 *IF-ELSE-* AND *IF-ELSEIF-* STATEMENTS

The simple *if-statement* provides one code block which is to be executed if the *if-statement's* **conditional expression** evaluates to TRUE. In contrast, the *if-else-statement* provides two code blocks. One is to be executed if the **conditional expression** returns TRUE, the other if the **conditional expression** returns FALSE. This is the structure and syntax of the *if-else-statement*.

**If-Else-Statement**

```
if (conditional expression){
    code block of statements for TRUE . . .
} else {
    code block of statements for FALSE . .
    .
}
Statements after if
```

Let's work on an example:

**PROBLEM:** Refer to the first version of our previous example, *conditionals.php,* where the PHP scripts were embedded in the HTML document. We will modify this to include an *else* statement that will state "You are not eligible to vote." when the condition yields FALSE.

Use the following default values for the variables *$age* and *$isCitizen*:

| Variable Name | Value | Type |
|---------------|-------|---------|
| $age | 19 | Numeric |
| $isCitizen | TRUE | Boolean |

**SOLUTION:**

**1** **Step 1:** Create a new HTML5 document.

Type in the basic HTML document structure and make sure you include the opening and closing PHP tags in the document *<body>*. Name your document *conditionals_ifElse.php*

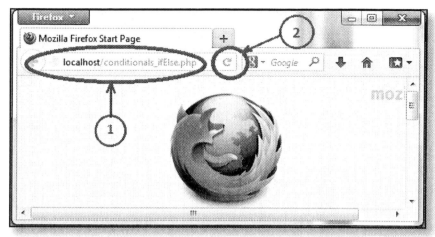

Figure 4.16: Basic HTML document structure, including PHP tags.

**2** Step 2: Place the text "Complex Conditionals" inside the title element and then complete the PHP code listing by including the *else* clause after the last command line of the *if-clause* as follows:

```php
<?php
$age = 21;
$iscitizen = false;

if ($age >= 18 && $citizen == true)
{
    print("<h1>You are eligible to vote</h1>");
}
else
{
    print("You are not eligible to vote");
}
?>
```

Close the PHP script tag and make sure the HTML closing tags are present in the document as well. Save your file.

**Step 3:** Launch your browser and type http://localhost/ conditionals_ifElse.php into the address bar. Click *Go to* or simply press the *Enter* key.

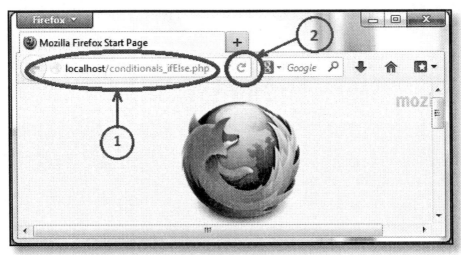

Figure 4.17: Accessing conditionals_ifElse.php in the browser via localhost.

**Step 4:** Wait a few seconds and view your output.

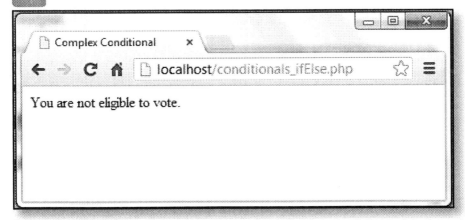

Figure 4.18: Outputting conditionals_ifElse.php in the browser.

You got the result "You are not eligible to vote." because the variable *$citizen* contains the Boolean value FALSE.

Here is the complete code listing for the example shown:

## CODE LISTING: SOLUTION FOR CONDITIONALS_IFELSE.PHP

```
<!DOCTYPE html>

<html>
<head>
    <title>Complex Conditional</title>
</head>

<body>
    <?php
        $age = 21;
        $citizen = true;

        if ($age >= 18 && $citizen ==
true)
        {
            print("<h1>You are eligible to
vote.</h1>");
        }
        else
        {
            print("You are not eligible to
vote.");
        }
    ?>
</body>
</html>
```

**5** **Step 5:** Reload the *conditionals_ifElse.php* and change the user information based on the following table.

| Age | Citizenship |
|-----|-------------|
| 21  | TRUE        |
| 16  | TRUE        |
| 21  | FALSE       |
| 16  | FALSE       |

**6** **Step 6:** View your output after each entry and ensure that the result is correct.

The *if-statement* and the *if-else-statement* test only one **conditional expression**. In contrast, the *if-elseif-statement* tests more than one **conditional** expression.

The *if-statement* has one code block, the *if-else-statement* has two code blocks while the *if-elseif-statement* has as many code blocks as it has **conditional expressions**.

This is the syntax for the *if-elseif-statement.*

```
if (condexpr0){
   code block for condexpr0 == TRUE . . .
} elseif (condexpr1) {
   code block for condexpr1 == TRUE . . .
} elseif (condexpr2) {
   code block for condexpr2 == TRUE . . .
} else {
   code block if all conditional
expressions are FALSE
}
Statements after if-elseif
```

Three things to note about the *if-elseif-statement:*

a. The *else* clause is optional.
b. If any of the evaluated **conditional expressions** are TRUE, the

code block for that **conditional expression** is executed and then
control jumps to the first statement after the *if-elseif-statement*.
c. If none of the *if-elseif-statement's* **conditional expressions**
evaluates to TRUE, then the code block associated with the *else*
clause (if present) is executed.

Let's work on an example.

> **If-ElseIf-Statement**

**PROBLEM:** Create a program routine that will display a description of
a numerical grade value based on the value identified. The PHP scripts
must be embedded within the HTML document. Use the variable name
*$grade* to hold the values for the numerical grades. Set the default
grade to 93.

Use the following grades description table. Save the document under
the filename *complexConditionals_2.php*.

| Condition | Message |
|---|---|
| $grade == 100 | Your grade is perfect! |
| $grade > 90 | Your grade is excellent! |
| $grade > 80 | Your grade is great! |
| $grade > 70 | Your grade is good! |
| $grade >= 60 | Your grade is average. |
| $grade <= 50 | Your grade is below average. |
| else | Either your grade is super low or you entered an invalid grade :( |

**SOLUTION:**

> **CODE LISTING: SOLUTION FOR**
> **COMPLEXCONDITIONALS_2.PHP**

```
<!DOCTYPE html>
<html>
<head>
    <title>Complex Conditionals 2</title>
</head>
```

```php
<body>
    <?php
        $grade = 93;
            if ($grade == 100)
            {
                echo("Your grade is
PERFECT!");
            }
            elseif($grade <=99 && $grade>=90)
            {
                echo("Your grade is
Excellent!");
            }
            elseif($grade <= 89 && $grade>=80)
            {
                echo("Your grade is Great!");
            }
            elseif($grade <= 79 && $grade>=70)
            {
                echo("Your grade is Good");
            }
            elseif($grade <= 69 && $grade>=60)
            {
                echo("Your grade is Average");
            }
            elseif($grade <= 59  &&
$grade>=50)
            {
                echo("Your grade is Below
Average");
            }
            else
            {
                echo("You entered an invalid
grade :( ");
            }
    ?>
</body>
</html>
```

**1** **Step 1:** Create a new HTML5 document. Save your document as *complexConditionals-2.php*.

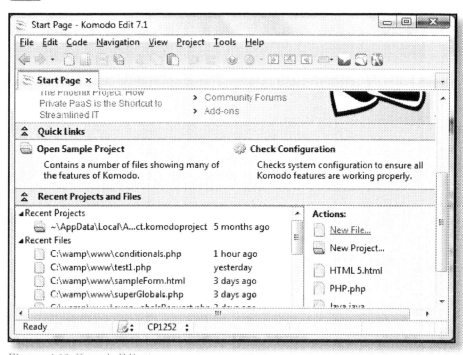

Figure 4.19: Komodo Edit start page.

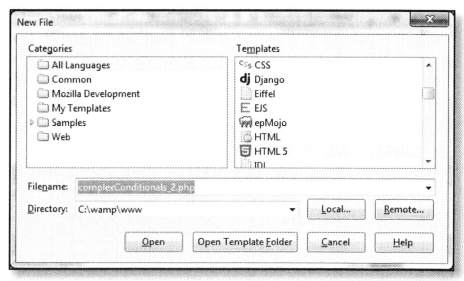

Figure 4.20: Saving a new document as complexConditionals_2.php.

Type in the <title> tag "Complex Conditionals 2". Include the opening and closing PHP tags in the document <body>.

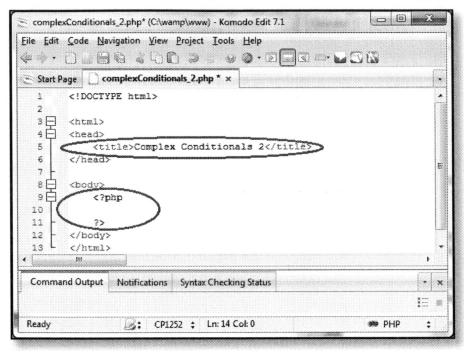

Figure 4.21: Adding a title and PHP tags to the document.

**2** **Step 2:** Assign the value 93 as the initial value for *$grade*. Encode the entire code solution and save your file again.

```
<!DOCTYPE html>
<html>
<head>
    <title>Complex Conditionals 2</title>
</head>

<body>
    <?php
        $grade = 93;
            if ($grade == 100)
            {
                echo("Your grade is
PERFECT!!!");
```

```
              }
              elseif($grade <=99 &&
$grade>=90)
              {
                   echo("Your grade is
Excellent!");
              }
              elseif($grade <= 89 &&
$grade>=80)
              {
                   echo("Your grade is
Great!");
              }
              elseif($grade <= 79 &&
$grade>=70)
              {
                   echo("Your grade is Good");
              }
              elseif($grade <= 69 &&
$grade>=60)
              {
                   echo("Your grade is
Average");
              }
              elseif($grade <= 59  &&
$grade>=50)
              {
                   echo("Your grade is Below
Average");
              }
              else
              {
                   echo("You entered an
invalid grade :( ");
              }
     ?>
</body>
</html>
```

**3** **Step 3:** Launch your browser, type the filename in the address bar and click *Go to* or press the *enter* key. Wait a second or two.

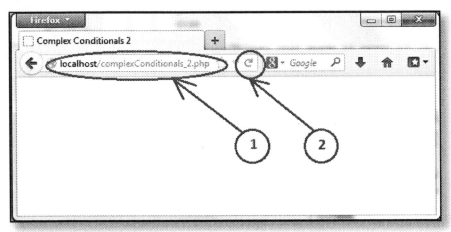

Figure 4.22: Accessing complexConditionals_2.php in the browser.

## OUTPUT:

**4** **Step 4:** View your output.

Figure 4.23: Viewing the output of complexConditionals_2.php.

## MODIFY THE GIVEN VALUE:

**5** **Step 5:** Changing the values of *$grade* will yield different results.

| Grade | Expected Output Message |
|-------|-------------------------|
| 95 | Your grade is excellent! |
| 100 | Your grade is perfect! |
| 72 | Your grade is good! |
| 45 | Your grade is below average. |
| 88 | Your grade is great! |
| 66 | Your grade is average. |
| A | You entered an invalid grade :( |

**Step 6:** View the output.

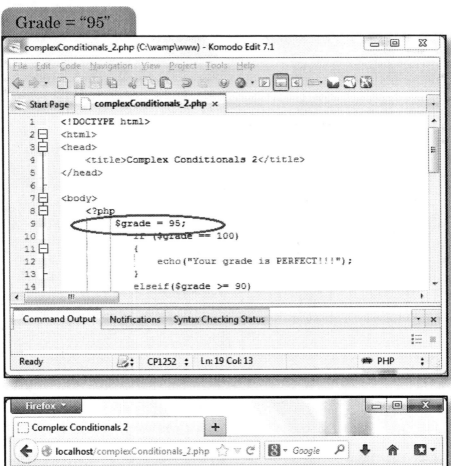

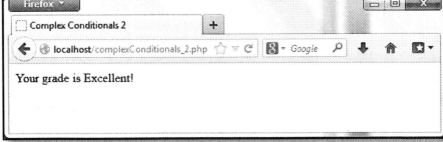

Figure 4.24: Changing the value of *$grade* to 95 and viewing the output.

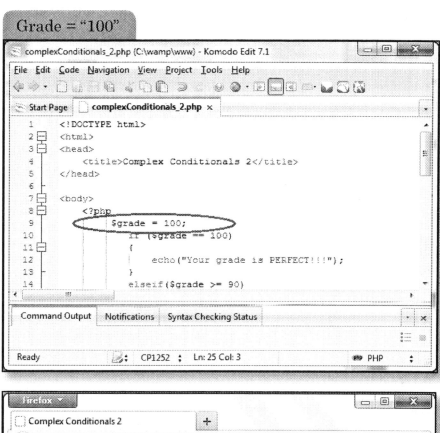

Grade = "100"

Figure 4.25: Changing the value of $grade to 100 and viewing the output.

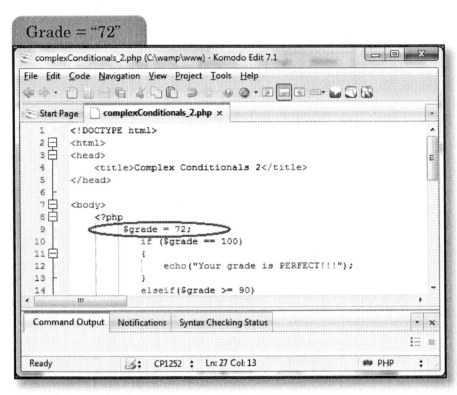

Figure 4.26: Changing the value of *$grade* to 72 and viewing the output.

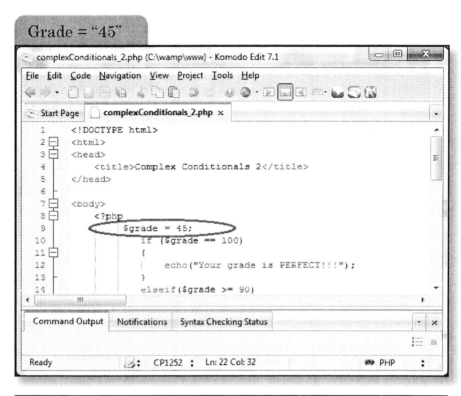

Grade = "45"

```
1    <!DOCTYPE html>
2    <html>
3    <head>
4        <title>Complex Conditionals 2</title>
5    </head>
6
7    <body>
8        <?php
9            $grade = 45;
10               if ($grade == 100)
11           {
12                   echo("Your grade is PERFECT!!!");
13           }
14               elseif($grade >= 90)
```

Your grade is Below Average

Figure 4.27: Changing the value of *$grade* to 45 and viewing the output.

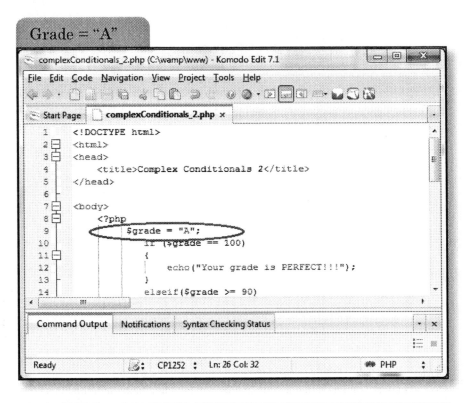

Grade = "A"

```
1    <!DOCTYPE html>
2    <html>
3    <head>
4        <title>Complex Conditionals 2</title>
5    </head>
6
7    <body>
8        <?php
9            $grade = "A";
10           if ($grade == 100)
11           {
12               echo("Your grade is PERFECT!!!");
13           }
14           elseif($grade >= 90)
```

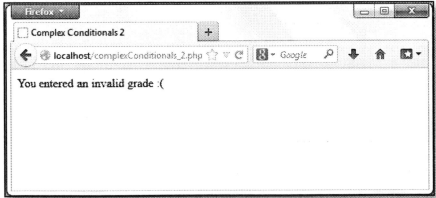

You entered an invalid grade :(

Figure 4.28: Changing the value of *$grade* to "A" and viewing the output.

# 4.4 Switch Statement

The *switch-statement* is ideal for those situations where a variable or expression has to be tested against a range of different values. This is the structure and syntax of the *switch-statement:*

**Switch-Statement**

```
switch ($variable) {
    case value1:
        statements for value1. . .
        break;
    case value2:
        statements for value2. . .
        break;
    default:
        statements for default. . .
}
statements after switch
```

The first line begins with the *switch* keyword followed by the name of the test variable in parentheses, *$variable,* whose values are to be tested.

The *case* keyword defines the program statements to be executed if the value following the *case* keyword matches the current value of $*variable,* the test variable.

The *break* keyword terminates the *switch-statement.* Why is the *break* statement needed? When a case value matches the test variable's current value, the statements for that case value are executed. After this, the program continues down the *switch-statement,* executing the statements of all the other case values, as well as the *default* case, whether those values match the test variable or not! Clearly, we don't want this to happen which is why we include the *break* statement as the last statement for a case value's associated statements.

The *default* keyword defines statements to be executed if none of the case values match the test variable.

Let's work on an example.

**PROBLEM:** Create a *switch-statement* routine that will determine the numerical grade bracket a letter grade corresponds to, and display the grade bracket's description accordingly. Use the following table of grades:

| Letter Grade | Output Message |
|---|---|
| A | A means your grade is from 91 to 100. |
| B | B means your grade is from 81 to 90. |
| C | C means your grade is from 71 to 80. |
| D | D means your grade is from 61 to 70. |
| F | F means your grade is from 51 to 60. |
| default | The grade you entered is invalid. |

**SOLUTION:**

### CODE LISTING: SOLUTION FOR SWITCHCASEBREAKCONDITIONAL.PHP

```php
<!DOCTYPE html>

<html>
<head>
    <title>Switch-Case-Break
Conditionals</title>
</head>
<body>
    <?php
        $grade = 'A';
            switch($grade)
            {
                case 'A':
                    echo("A means your
grade is from 91-100.");
                break;
```

```php
                case 'B':
                        echo("B means your
grade is from 81-90.");
                break;
                case 'C':
                        echo("C means your
grade is from 71-80.");
                break;
                case 'D':
                        echo("D means your
grade is from 61-70.");
                break;
                case 'F':
                        echo("F means your
grade is from 51-60.");
                break;
                default:
                        echo("The grade you
entered is invalid");
                }
        ?>
</body>
</html>
```

**1**    **Step 1:** Create a blank HTML5 document and save it under the filename *switchCaseBreakConditional.php*.

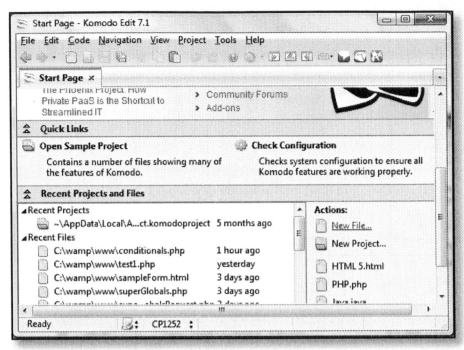

Figure 4.29: Komodo Edit start page.

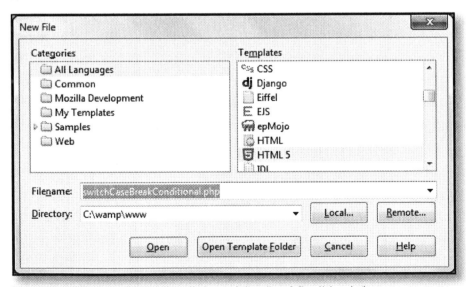

Figure 4.30: Creating a new file called switchCaseBreakConditional.php.

Type in the <title> tag "Switch-Case-Break Conditional". Include the opening and closing PHP script tags in the document <body>.

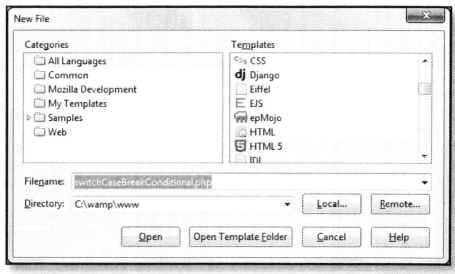

Figure 4.31: Opening a new HTML5 document in Komodo Edit.

**Step 2:** Assign the initial value 'A' to the variable *$grade*. Encode the entire code solution and save your file again.

```
<!DOCTYPE html>

<html>
<head>
    <title>Switch-Case-Break
Conditionals</title>
</head>
<body>
    <?php
        $grade = 'A';
            switch($grade)
            {
                case 'A':
                    echo("A means your
grade is from 91-100.");
                break;
                case 'B':
```

```
                    echo("B means your
grade is from 81-90.");
                break;
                case 'C':
                    echo("C means your
grade is from 71-80.");
                break;
                case 'D':
                    echo("D means your
grade is from 61-70.");
                break;
                case 'F':
                    echo("F means your
grade is from 51-60.");
                break;
                default:
                    echo("The grade you
entered is invalid");
            }
    ?>
</body>
</html>
```

**Step 3:** Launch your browser, type the filename in the address bar and click *Go* or press the *enter* key. Wait a second or two.

Figure 4.32: Accessing switchCaseBreakConditional.php in the browser.

## OUTPUT:

**4** **Step 4:** View your output.

If *$grade* = 'A'

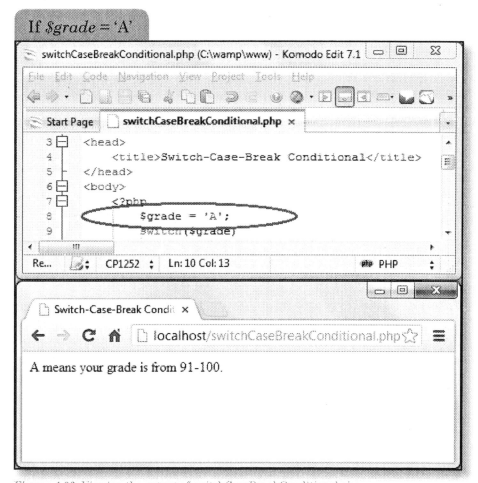

Figure 4.33: Viewing the output of switchCaseBreakConditional.php.

## MODIFY THE ASSIGNED VALUE:

**5** **Step 5:** Replace the values of *$grade* with B, C, D and F and see the results.

| Grade | Expected Output Message |
|-------|-------------------------|
| $grade = 'A' | A means your grade is from 91-100. |
| $grade = 'B' | B means your grade is from 81-90. |
| $grade = 'C' | C means your grade is from 71-80. |
| $grade = 'D' | D means your grade is from 61-70. |
| $grade = 'F' | F means your grade is from 51-60. |
| $grade = 'a' | The grade you entered is invalid. |
| $grade = 'E' | The grade you entered is invalid. |

**6** **Step 6:** View the output.

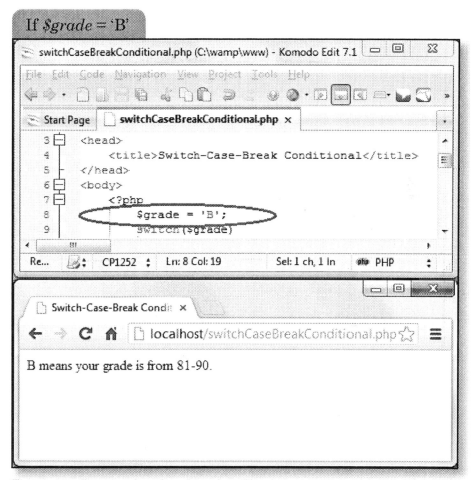

Figure 4.34: Changing the value of *$grade* to 'B' and viewing the output.

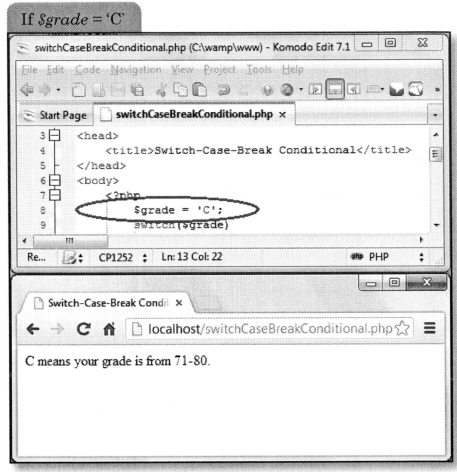

Figure 4.35: Changing the value of *$grade* to 'C' and viewing the output.

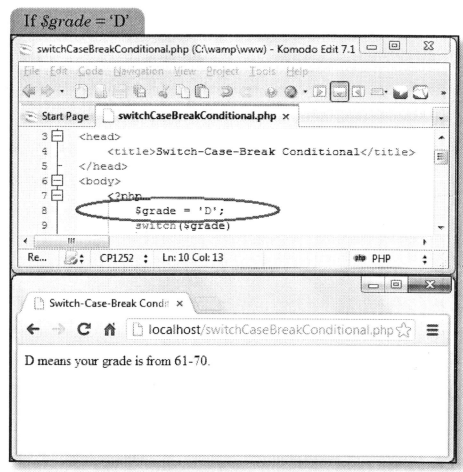

Figure 4.36: Changing the value of *$grade* to 'D' and viewing the output.

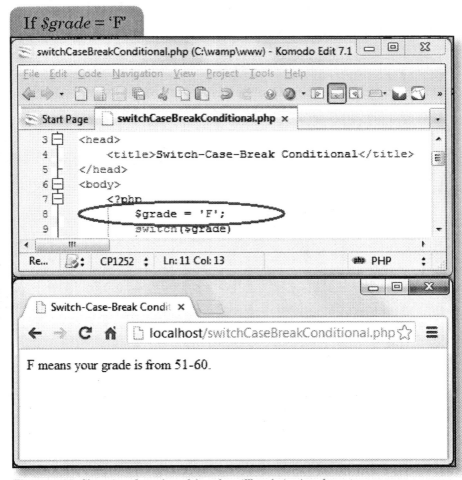

**Figure 4.37:** Changing the value of *$grade* to 'F' and viewing the output.

Replace *$grade* with a value outside of the typical range, say 'a' and 'E'. Take note of the result.

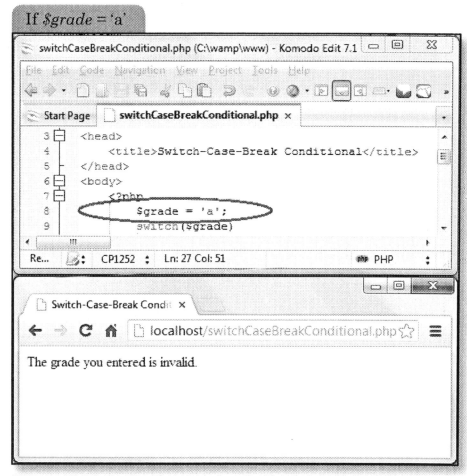

Figure 4.38: Changing the value of *$grade* to 'a' and viewing the output.

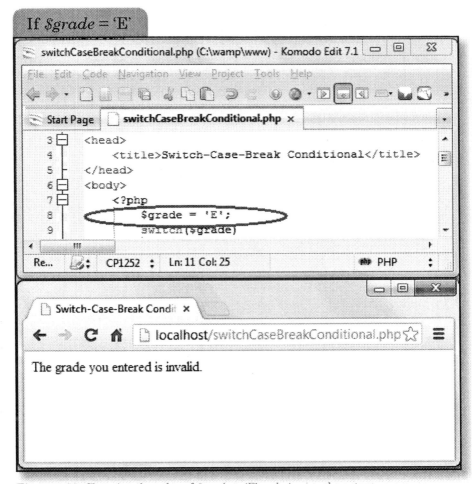

Figure 4.39: Changing the value of *$grade* to 'E' and viewing the output.

We mentioned that the *switch-statement* is case sensitive and this is proven true if you tried assigning either "a", "b", "c", "d" or "f" to the variable *$grade*. Assigning any of these lowercase grades will cause the program to report the grade as invalid.

The *switch-statement* can overcome this limitation by adding another *case* after the first *case* listed. This is how it is done. If we want both characters 'A' and 'a' to be treated as the same grades, then we must declare two successive *cases*:

```
case 'A':
case 'a':
    action
break;
```

This goes inside the basic switch-case-break structure, like this:

```php
<?php
    $variable = value;
        switch($variable)
        {
                case A:
                case a:
                        action;
                break;

                default:
                        default action;
                }
?>
```

In this structure, the program will look at the variable's value. It will test if the value is equal to 'A', if not, it will look for a break statement. Since there is none, it will continue to test and this time see if the value is equal to 'a'—all because of the next *case* 'a' statement that followed. If the value is equal to 'a', then the following *action* is performed. This resolves the case sensitivity issue of switch-case-break conditional.

However, this *case* series is ideal only for a maximum of three cases. If there are already more than three cases to put in series, then the more practical tool to use is an *if-else* statement having multiple conditions and including an OR logical operator.

To reinforce this discussion, we'll apply the *case* series in the previous example, *switchCaseBreakConditional.php,* to make sure the program routine will catch both uppercase and lowercase grades assigned to *$grade*.

Let's see what happens to the output of *switchCaseBreakConditionals_2.php* when the *$grade* is set to 'a' in the code.

```
<body>
    <?php
        $grade = 'a';
```

Running the program will give the result:

Figure 4.40: Changing the value of *$grade* to 'a' and viewing the output.

This is because the existing code does not provide the *case* for lowercase 'a'.

**PROBLEM:** Tweak the code for *switchCaseBreakConditional.php* so that it will now include a *case* for the lowercase grades 'a', 'b', 'c', 'd' and 'f'. Keep the assigned value for *$grade* to 'a'.

**SOLUTION:**

## CODE LISTING: SOLUTION FOR
## SWITCHCASEBREAKCONDITIONAL_2.PHP

```
<!DOCTYPE html>

<html>
<head>
    <title>Switch-Case-Break Conditional
2</title>
</head>
<body>
    <?php
        $grade = 'a';
            switch($grade)
            {
                case 'A':
                case 'a':
                    echo("A means your
grade is from 91-100.");
                break;
                case 'B':
                case 'b':
                    echo("B means your
grade is from 81-90.");
                break;
                case 'C':
                case 'c':
                    echo("C means your
grade is from 71-80.");
                break;
                case 'D':
                case 'd':
                    echo("D means your
grade is from 61-70.");
                break;
```

```
                case 'F':
                case 'f':
                    echo("E means your
grade is from 51-60.");
                break;
                default:
                    echo("The grade you
entered is invalid.");
                }
    ?>
</body>
</html>
```

**1** **Step 1:** Create a blank HTML5 document and save it under the filename *switchCaseBreakConditional_2.php*.

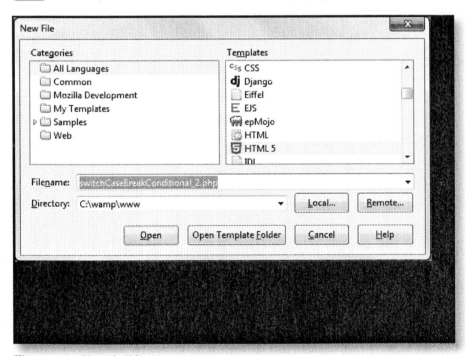

Figure 4.41: Komodo Edit start page.

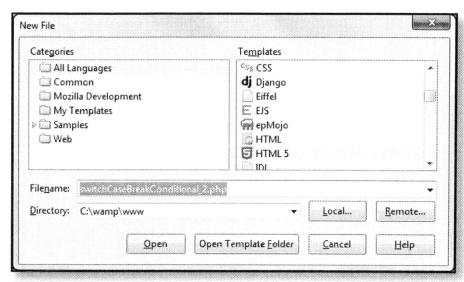

Figure 4.42: Creating a new file called switchCaseBreakConditional_2.php.

**2** **Step 2:** Type in the <title> tag "Switch-Case-Break Conditional 2". Include the opening and closing PHP script tags in the document <body>.

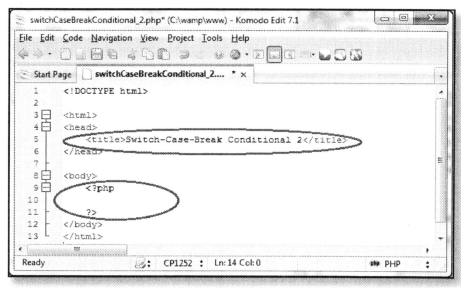

Figure 4.43: Adding a title and PHP tags to the document.

**Step 3:** Assign the initial value, 'a', to the variable *$grade*. Encode the entire code solution given and save your file again.

```
<!DOCTYPE html>

<html>
<head>
    <title>Switch-Case-Break Conditional
2</title>
</head>
<body>
    <?php
        $grade = 'a';
            switch($grade)
            {
                case 'A':
                case 'a':
                    echo("A means your
grade is from 91-100.");
                    break;
                case 'B':
                case 'b':
                    echo("B means your
grade is from 81-90.");
                    break;
                case 'C':
                case 'c':
                    echo("C means your
grade is from 71-80.");
                    break;
                case 'D':
                case 'd':
                    echo("D means your
grade is from 61-70.");
                    break;
                case 'F':
                case 'f':
                    echo("E means your
```

```
grade is from 51-60.");
                break;
                default:
                    echo("The grade you
entered is invalid.");
            }
    ?>
</body>
</html>
```

**4**  **Step 4:** Launch your browser, type the filename in the address bar and click *Go to* or press the *enter* key. Wait a second or two.

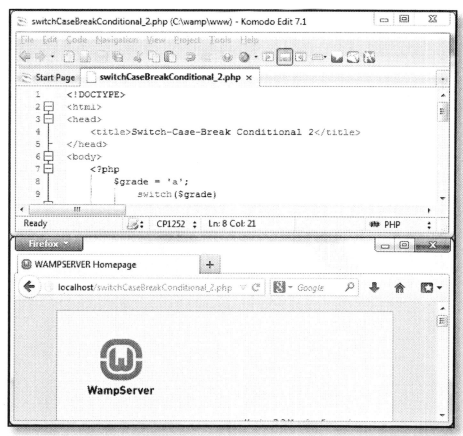

Figure 4.44: Accessing switchCaseBreakConditional_2.php in the browser.

## OUTPUT:

**5** **Step 5:** View your output.

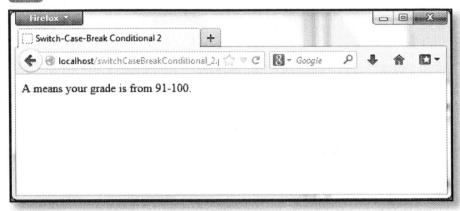

Figure 4.45: Viewing the output of switchCaseBreakConditional_2.php.

## MODIFY THE ASSIGNED VALUE:

**6** **Step 6:** Replace the values of *$grade* with the following values and see the results. The first one has been shown previously. Start with the second row's value, *$grade* = 'B' or *$grade* = 'c'.

| Grade | Expected Output Message |
|---|---|
| $grade = 'A' or 'a' | A means your grade is from 91-100. |
| $grade = 'B' or 'b' | B means your grade is from 81-90. |
| $grade = 'C' or 'c' | C means your grade is from 71-80. |
| $grade = 'D' or 'd' | D means your grade is from 61-70. |
| $grade = 'F' or 'f' | F means your grade is from 51-60. |
| $grade = 'X' or 'x' | The grade you entered is invalid. |
| $grade = '85' or 'Xx' | The grade you entered is invalid. |

**7** **Step 7:** View the output.

## If $grade = 'B' or 'b'

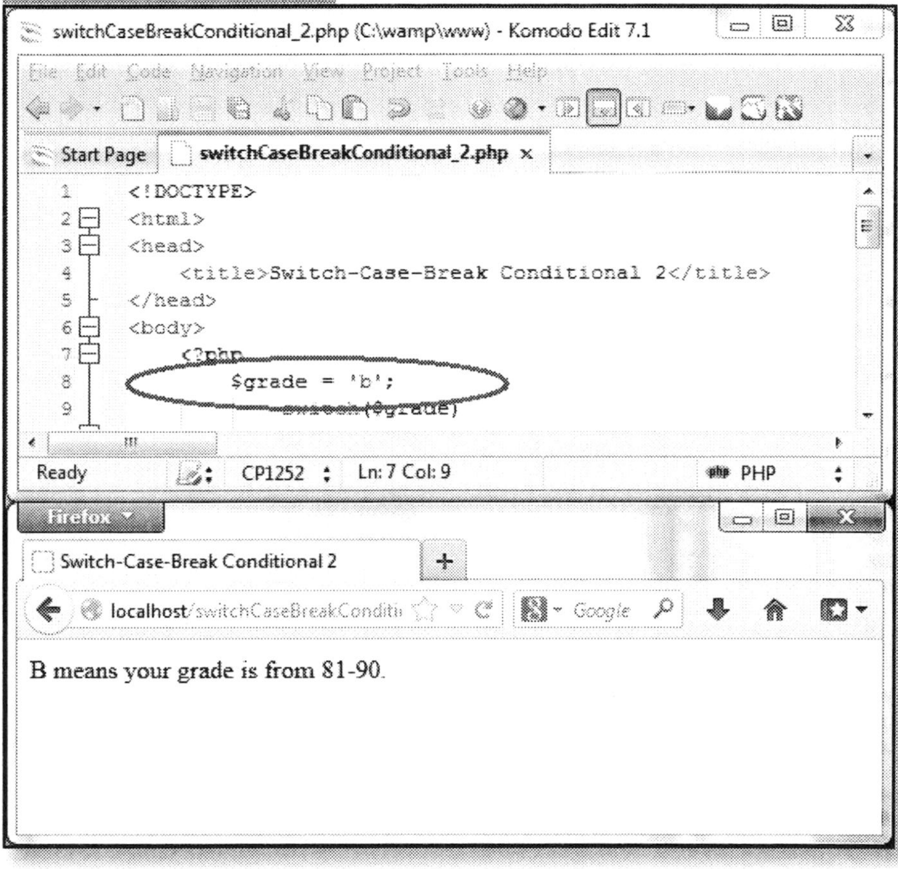

Figure 4.46: Changing the value of *$grade* to 'b' and viewing the output.

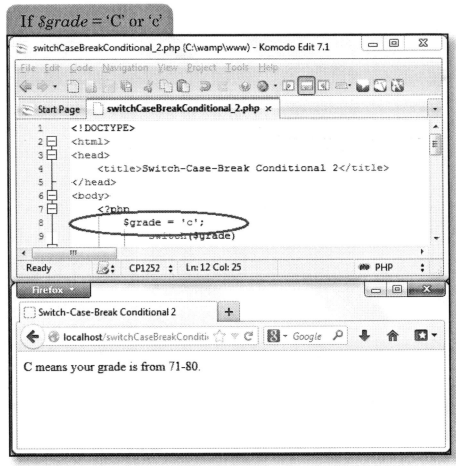

Figure 4.47: Changing the value of *$grade* to 'c' and viewing the output.

Figure 4.48: Changing the value of *$grade* to 'd' and viewing the output.

Figure 4.49: Changing the value of *$grade* to 'f' and viewing the output.

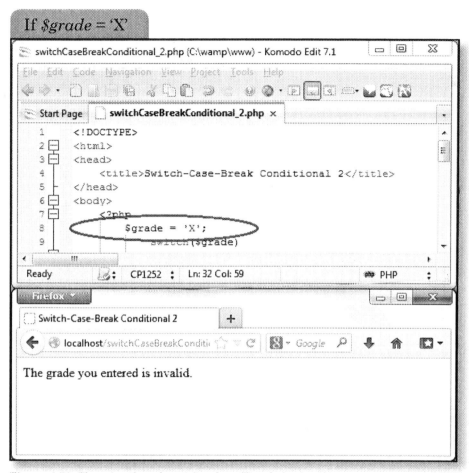

Figure 4.50: Changing the value of *$grade* to 'X' and viewing the output.

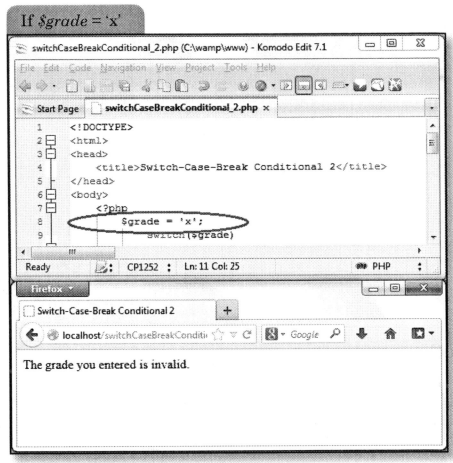

Figure 4.51: Changing the value of *$grade* to 'x' and viewing the output.

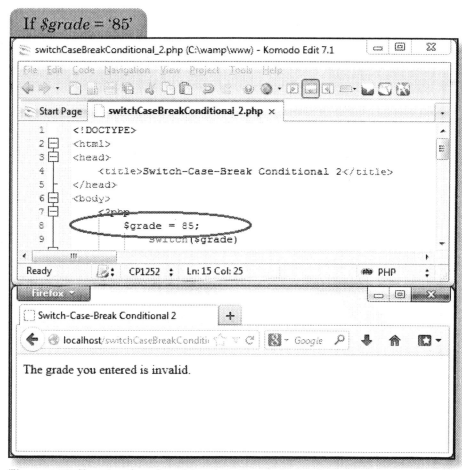

Figure 4.52: Changing the value of *$grade* to 85 and viewing the output.

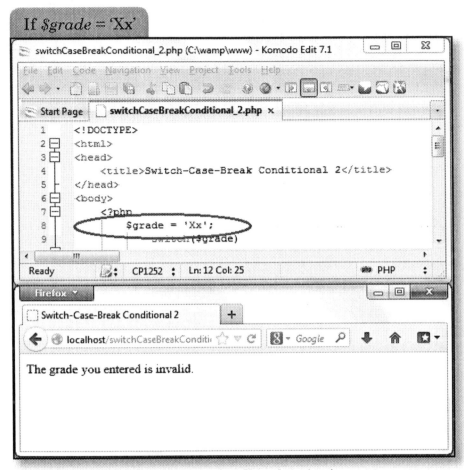

Figure 4.53: Changing the value of *$grade* to 'Xx' and viewing the output.

In summary, the *switch-statement* offers a simpler and more compact structure than an *if-elseif-statement,* especially when there are a large number of values, string or numeric, to test against.

Just don't forget the *break* statement at the end of each *case* code block.

# 4.5 TERNARY OPERATOR—*COMPACT IF-ELSE*

Earlier in this chapter, we discussed **operators**, in particular **comparative** and **logical operators** which are mainly used in **conditional expressions**. All those **operators** we presented work on either a single operand (for example: !$isTrue) or on two operands (for example: $a == $b).

The **ternary** operator works on three **operands** or more specifically, three **expressions**. This is its syntax:

**Ternary**

```
(conditional-cxpression1 ) ? expression2 :
expression3
```

The preceding **ternary expression** will return the value of *expression2* if *conditional-expression1* evaluates to **true**; otherwise it will return the value of *expression3*. Most of the time, to make use of the returned value, the **ternary expression** would be used in an assignment statement in the following manner:

```
$variable = (cond-expr1)? expr2 : expr3
```

At first, it may be difficult to read code that uses the **ternary** operator as it is easy to miss the question mark (?) and the colon (:). But, using the **ternary expression** is a great way to replace an *if-else* statement that takes up at least four lines with only one line thus resulting in compact code.

Let's work on an example.

**PROBLEM:** Create a program that will determine if a user's age is greater than or equal to 18. If it is, then the message "You can vote." should be displayed. Otherwise, the output must display "You cannot vote." Use the ternary operator in implementing the program's logic.

**SOLUTION:**

```
<!DOCTYPE html>
<html>
<head>
    <title>Ternary Operator</title>
</head>
<body>
    <?php
        $age = 19;
        $voteStatus = ($age >= 18) ? "You
can vote!" : "You cannot vote!";
        print ($voteStatus);
    ?>
</body>
</html>
```

1 **Step 1:** Create a blank HTML5 document and save it under the filename *ternaryOperations.php*.

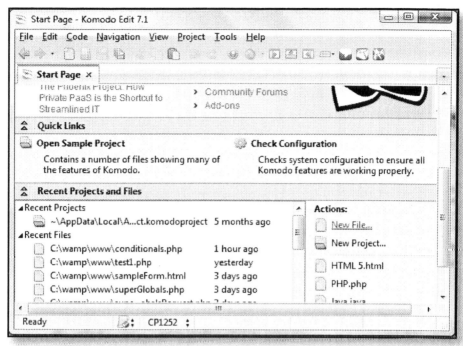

Figure 4.54: Komodo Edit start page.

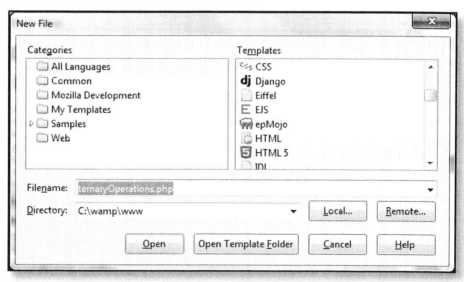

Figure 4.55: Creating a new file called ternaryOperations.php.

Type in the <title> tag "ternaryOperations.php". Include the opening and closing PHP script tags in the document <body>.

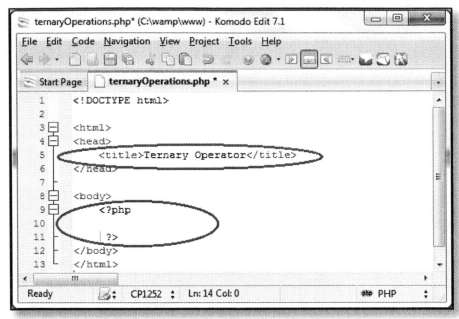

Figure 4.56: Adding a title and PHP tags to the document.

**2** **Step 2:** Assign the initial value 19 to the variable *$age*. Encode the entire code solution given and save your file.

```php
<!DOCTYPE html>
<html>
<head>
   <title>Ternary Operator</title>
</head>
<body>
   <?php
        $age = 19;
        $voteStatus = $age >= 18) ? "You
can vote!" : "You cannot vote!"
        print ($voteStatus . "<br/>You are
" . $age . " years old.");
   ?>
</body>
</html>
```

**3** **Step 3:** Launch your browser, type the filename in the address bar and click *Go to* or press the *enter* key. Wait a second or two.

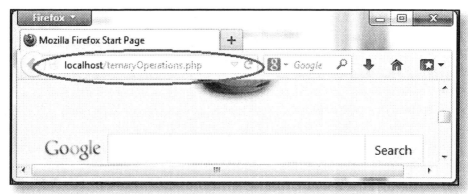

Figure 4.57: Accessing ternaryOperations.php in the browser.

## OUTPUT:

**4** **Step 4:** View your output.

Figure 4.58: Viewing the output of ternaryOperations.php.

**MODIFY THE ASSIGNED VALUE:**

**5** **Step 5:** Replace the values of *$age* with the following values and see the results. The first one has been shown previously. Start with the second row's value, *$age* = 60.

| Grade | Expected Output Message |
|-------|-------------------------|
| $age = 19 | You can vote! |
| $age = 60 | You can vote! |
| $age = 16 | You cannot vote! |

**6** **Step 6:** View the output.

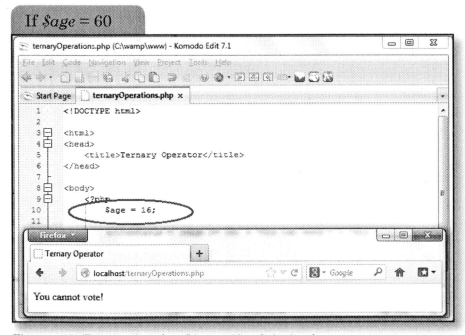

Figure 4.59: Changing the value of *$age* to 60 and viewing the output.

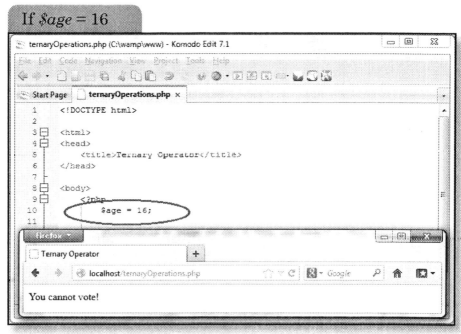

Figure 4.60: Changing the value of *$age* to 16 and viewing the output.

1. What are conditionals?
   a. Statements that define a condition.
   b. Requirements that will be evaluated for nullity of value.
   c. Logical statements that can hold any value and be evaluated based on that value.
   d. Statements that evaluate an expression condition to be true or false and perform the corresponding action associated with either true or false value.

2. What conditional operator does the condition "<=" depict?
   a. Greater than or equal to.
   b. Is equal to.
   c. Less than.
   d. Less than or equal to.

3. What is an example of a complex conditional?
   e. If statement.
   f. Switch statement.
   g. If-else statement.
   h. A series of if-else-if statements.

4. What are switch-case-break conditionals best defined as?
   i. A shorthand notation of an if statement.
   j. A switch based on a case that breaks apart randomly.
   k. A conditional that has many cases.
   l. A longer version of an if statement.

5. Is switch-case-break case sensitive?
   a. Yes.
   b. No.
   c. Maybe.
   d. By default, yes, but it can be customized by adding multiple cases that would remove the case sensitivity.

6. What are ternary operators?
   a. A one line if-else statement associated with a variable.
   b. Conditionals that have complex conditions structure.
   c. Operators that assign a value to a variable.
   d. Operators that evaluate a condition and perform a certain action.

7. What do the symbols (?) and (:) in ternary statements mean, respectively?
   a.  If and else.
   b.  OR and AND.
   c.  Greater than and less than.
   d.  Plus and minus.

## CHAPTER 4 LAB EXERCISE

1. Create a PHP program that will display a form asking an individual to input their first name, last name, age, and citizenship.

The form must have text input fields for the first name, last name and age; radio buttons for the yes and no reply for citizenship, and a "Register" and a "Reset" or "Clear Fields" button.

2. Create an HTML5 document and save it as *voter_registration.html* inside the www or htdocs folder.

3. Adopt the following form layout and form fields: *voterFirstName*, *voterLastname*, *votersAge* and *isCitizen*. Place these elements in table form for a clean look.

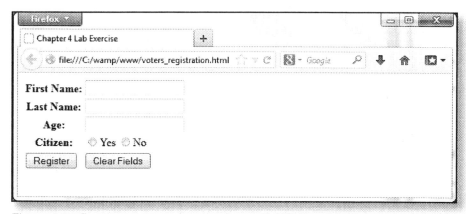

Figure 4.61: Creating a voter registration form with HTML and PHP.

Use *maxlength* attribute to limit the number of characters of *voterFirstName* and *voterLastName* to 15 and *votersAge* to three.

```
<table>
        <tr>
            <th>
```

```html
                First Name:
            </th>
            <td>
                <input name="voterFirstName"
maxlength="15">
            </td>
        </tr>
        <tr>
            <th>
                Last Name:
            </th>
            <td>
                <input name="voterLastName"
maxlength="15">
            </td>
        </tr>
        <tr>
            <th>
                Age:
            </th>
            <td>
                <input name="votersAge"
maxlength="3">
            </td>
        </tr>
        <tr>
            <th>
                Citizen:
            </th>
            <td><input type="radio"
name="isCitizen" value="true">Yes
            <input type="radio"
name="isCitizen" value="false">No</td>
        </tr>
        <tr>
            <td><input type="submit"
value="Register"></td>
            <td><input type="reset"
value="Clear Fields"></td>
        </tr>
    </table>
```

4. Create a new text file and save it as *voters_registration.php* in your www or htdocs folder.

5. Determine if the age is greater than or equal to 18. Type the code in your *voters_registration.php* file. Use $_POST superglobals.

```php
<?php
    $voterFirstName = $_
POST['voterFirstName'];
    $voterLastName = $_
POST['voterLastName'];
    $isCitizen = $_POST['isCitizen'];
    $votersAge = $_POST['votersAge'];

    if($votersAge >= 18 && $isCitizen ==
true)
    {
        print($voterFirstName . " " .
$voterLastName . "</br>");
        print($votersAge . " years old.</
br>");
        print("Is a citizen.</br>");
        print("You are allowed to vote.");
    }
    else
    {
        print($voterFirstName . " " .
$voterLastName . "</br>");
        print($votersAge . " years old.</
br>");
        print("Is a citizen.</br>");
    print("You are not allowed to vote.");
    }

?>
```

6. This is how the output should appear:

Figure 4.62: Viewing the output of voters_registration.html.

## Chapter 4 Lab Solution:

### Code Listing: HTML Form

```
<!DOCTYPE html>

<html>
<head>
    <title>Chapter 4 Lab Exercise</title>
</head>
<body>
    <form action="voter_registration.php"
method="post">
    <table>
        <tr>
            <th>
                First Name:
            </th>
            <td>
                <input
name="voterFirstName" maxlength="15">
            </td>
```

```
        </tr>
        <tr>
            <th>
                Last Name:
            </th>
            <td>
                <input
name="voterLastName" maxlength="15">
            </td>
        </tr>
        <tr>
            <th>
                Age:
            </th>
            <td>
                <input name="votersAge"
maxlength="3">
            </td>
        </tr>
        <tr>
            <th>
                Citizen:
            </th>
            <td><input type="radio"
name="isCitizen" value="true">Yes
            <input type="radio"
name="isCitizen" value="false">No</td>
        </tr>
        <tr>
            <td><input type="submit"
value="Register"></td>
            <td><input type="reset"
value="Clear Fields"></td>
        </tr>
    </table>
    </form>
</body>
</html>
```

```php
<?php
    $voterFirstName = $_
POST['voterFirstName'];
    $voterLastName = $_
POST['voterLastName'];
    $isCitizen = $_POST['isCitizen'];
    $votersAge = $_POST['votersAge'];

    if($votersAge >= 18 && $isCitizen ==
"true")
    {
        print("You are " . $voterFirstName
. " " . $voterLastName . ", " . $votersAge
. " years old.</br>");
        print("You are a citizen.</br>");
        print("You are allowed to vote.");
    }
    elseif($votersAge >= 18 && $isCitizen
== "false")
    {
        print("You are " . $voterFirstName
. " " . $voterLastName . ", " . $votersAge
. " years old.</br>");
        print("You are not a citizen.</
br>");
        print("You are not allowed to
vote.");
    }
    elseif($votersAge < 18 && $isCitizen
== "true")
    {
        print("You are " . $voterFirstName
. " " . $voterLastName . ", " . $votersAge
. " years old.</br>");
        print("You are a citizen.</br>");
```

```
        print("You are not allowed to
vote.");
    }
    else
    {
        print("You are " . $voterFirstName
. " " . $voterLastName . ", " . $votersAge
. " years old.</br>");
        print("You are not a citizen.</
br>");
        print("You are not allowed to
vote.");
    }

?>
```

Figure 4.63: Viewing the output of voters_registration.html.

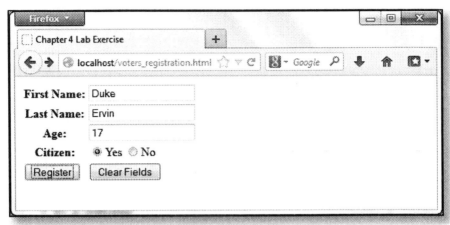

Figure 4.64: Clicking the register button to submit the form.

After clicking the *Register* button, this is how the output will look:

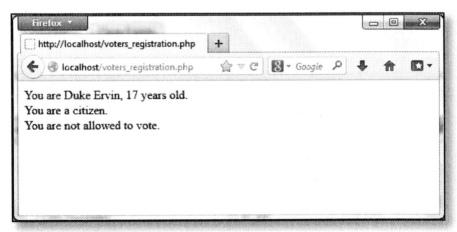

Figure 4.65: Viewing the output of voters_registration.php.

## CODE LISTING: VOTERS_REGISTRATION.HTML

```
<!DOCTYPE html>

<html>
<head>
    <title>Chapter 4 Lab Exercise</title>
</head>
<body>
    <form action="voters_registration.php"
method="post">
    <table>
        <tr>
            <th>
                First Name:
            </th>
            <td>
                <input
name="voterFirstName" maxlength="15">
            </td>
        </tr>
        <tr>
            <th>
                Last Name:
            </th>
            <td>
                <input
name="voterLastName" maxlength="15">
            </td>
        </tr>
        <tr>
            <th>
                Age:
            </th>
            <td>
                <input name="votersAge"
```

```
maxlength="3">
            </td>
        </tr>
        <tr>
            <th>
                Citizen:
            </th>
            <td><input type="radio"
name="isCitizen" value="true">Yes
            <input type="radio"
name="isCitizen" value="false">No</td>
        </tr>
        <tr>
            <td><input type="submit"
value="Register"></td>
            <td><input type="reset"
value="Clear Fields"></td>
        </tr>
    </table>
    </form>
</body>
</html>
```

## CODE LISTING: VOTERS_REGISTRATION.PHP

```php
<?php
    $voterFirstName = $_
POST['voterFirstName'];
    $voterLastName = $_
POST['voterLastName'];
    $isCitizen = $_POST['isCitizen'];
    $votersAge = $_POST['votersAge'];

    if($votersAge >= 18 && $isCitizen ==
"true")
    {
        print("You are " . $voterFirstName
```

```
. " " . $voterLastName . ", " . $votersAge
. " years old.</br>");
        print("You are a citizen.</br>");
        print("You are allowed to vote.");
    }
    elseif($votersAge >= 18 && $isCitizen
== "false")
    {
        print("You are " . $voterFirstName
. " " . $voterLastName . ", " . $votersAge
. " years old.</br>");
        print("You are not a citizen.</
br>");
        print("You are not allowed to
vote.");
    }
    elseif($votersAge < 18 && $isCitizen
== "true")
    {
        print("You are " . $voterFirstName
. " " . $voterLastName . ", " . $votersAge
. " years old.</br>");
        print("You are a citizen.</br>");
        print("You are not allowed to
vote.");
    }
    else
    {
        print("You are " . $voterFirstName
. " " . $voterLastName . ", " . $votersAge
. " years old.</br>");
        print("You are not a citizen.</
br>");
        print("You are not allowed to
vote.");
    }

?>
```

# CHAPTER SUMMARY:

In this chapter you first learned about **expressions** and **conditional expressions** and how they are formed from **operands, operators, comparison operators**, and **logical operators**.

You saw that **conditional expressions** are the essential components of PHP's branching control structures and how this structure is implemented by four conditional statements in PHP, namely:

-the *if-statement*,
-the *if-else-* and *if-elseif-statements*,
-the *switch-statement*,
-and the *ternary operator*.

We also covered multiple examples to fully understand the syntax, structure and implementation of all these conditionals.

In the next chapter, we will discuss looping control structures.

# CHAPTER 5
## CONTROL STRUCTURES - LOOPS

### CHAPTER OBJECTIVES:

• You will be able to understand and analyze the different looping or iteration control structures in PHP.
• You will master the syntax and structure of the *while-loop, do-while-loop, for-loop,* and *foreach-loop* statements in PHP.
• You will learn how to use these different loops in actual code.

In the last chapter, we studied **branching control structures** where specific code blocks are executed or not executed based on the results of evaluating **conditional expressions**.

In this chapter, we study **looping control structures**, also known as **iteration control structures**, where we repeatedly execute or iterate through a specific block of code. The results of evaluating **conditional expressions** will determine the number of times we **loop** or **iterate** through a block of code.

> ### Looping Control Structure

A **looping control structure** consists of:
        a. a **conditional expression,** and
        b. a clearly defined block of code.

This block of code will be repeatedly executed as long as the **conditional expression** evaluates to TRUE.

---

**TIP:** You should fully understand the concepts of **expressions** and **conditional expressions** and how they are formed from **operands, operators, comparison operators** and **logical operators**. These concepts were explained in detail with numerous examples in Chapter 4.

---

PHP implements the following **looping statements** to implement **iteration control structures.**
      a. *while-loop*        c. *for-loop*
      b. *do-while-loop*     d. *foreach-loop*

# 5.1 WHILE-LOOP

This is the syntax and structure of the *while-loop*.

```
while (conditional expression) {
    code block of statements
}
first statement after while-loop
```

Program execution of the *while-loop* begins by evaluating the **conditional expression** declared at the beginning of the loop. If the evaluated result is TRUE, the code block of statements is executed. Then the **conditional expression** is evaluated again and as long as the result is TRUE, the code block of statements is executed. Once the **conditional expression** evaluates to FALSE, the code block is ignored and program execution jumps to the first statement after the *while-loop*.

> While-Loop

Note that in the code block of statements of the while statement, there must exist some statement(s) that will cause the **conditional expression** to evaluate to FALSE. For example, if your **conditional expression** is *count < 10*, then there must be a statement (for example: *count++*) in the code block to eventually cause the variable *count* to take on the value 10 or some other value greater than 10. Otherwise, the loop will never terminate!

Let's work on an example:

**PROBLEM:** Create a *while-loop* that will count from one to 10. Each number should be displayed on separate lines. Make sure the initial value for the conditional statement is TRUE. Use the variable name *$number*.

## SOLUTION:

**1** **Step 1:** Create a new HTML5 document. Name it *whileLoops_1. php*. Save it in your www or htdocs folder.

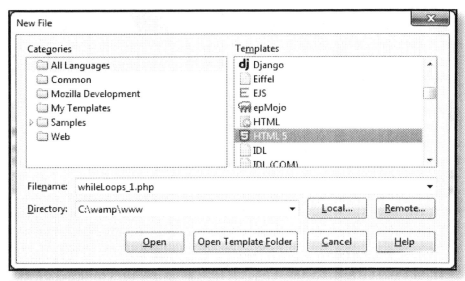

Figure 5.1: Opening a new HTML5 document in Komodo Edit.

**2** **Step 2:** Type the following program statements in your PHP document.

## CODE LISTING: WHILELOOPS_1.PHP

```
<!DOCTYPE html>

<html>
<head>
    <title>While Loop Example 1</title>
</head>

<body>
    <?php
        $number = 0;
        while($number < 11) //do while
$number is less than 11
        {
            print($number); // display the
value of $number
            print("</br>");   // insert a
line break
```

```
        $number++;          // increase
the value of $number by 1
        }
    ?>
</body>
</html>
```

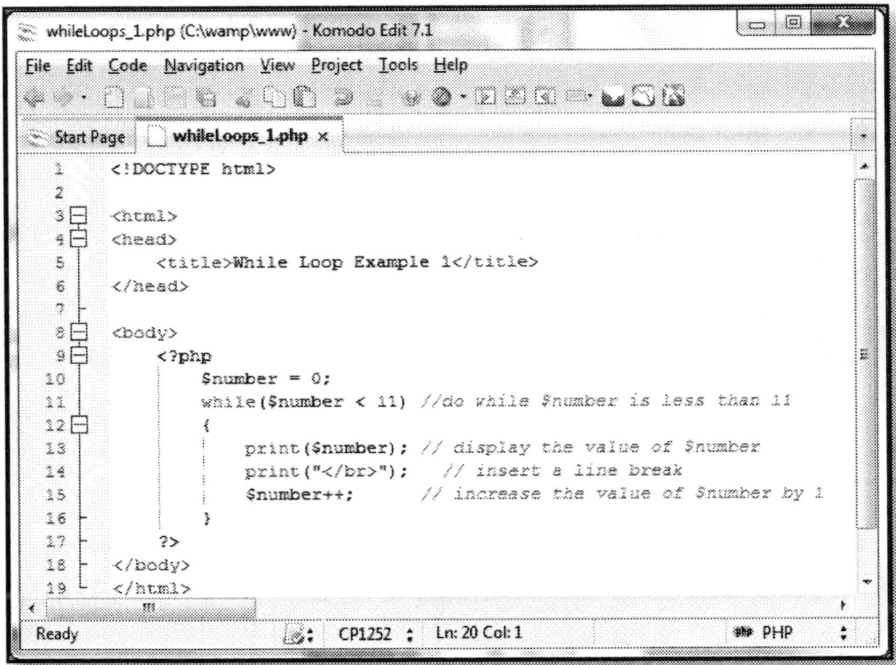

Figure 5.2: Inputting the statements of *whileLoops1.php*.

**3** **Step 3:** Save your file again.

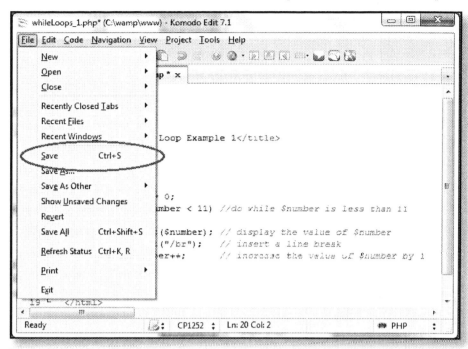

Figure 5.3: Saving a file in Komodo Edit.

**4** **Step 4:** Run your output.

Figure 5.4: Output of *whileLoops_1.php*.

What would happen in the example given if the **conditional expression** evaluates to FALSE? Try it out and see what happens.

**5** **Step 5:** Tweak the variable assignment portion by assigning the value *11* to *$number*

```php
<?php
    $number = 11;
```

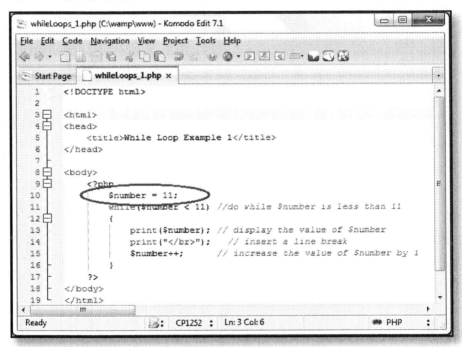

Figure 5.5: Change the initial value of the counter variable *$number* to 11.

**6** **Step 6:** Save your document.

**7** **Step 7:** Run your output.

Figure 5.6: Blank output after changing initial value of *$number* to 11.

Nothing was displayed. This is because the **conditional expression** evaluates to FALSE. This will cause the loop's code block to be ignored, resulting in a blank page.

Let's try another example. This time, we'll instruct the loop to count by fives.

**PROBLEM:** Create a *while-loop* that will count by fives from zero to 50. Each number should be displayed on separate lines. Make sure the conditional statement's initial value is TRUE. Use the variable name *$number*.

**SOLUTION:**

**1** **Step 1:** Create a new HTML5 document. Name it *whileLoops_2.php*. Save it under your www or htdocs folder.

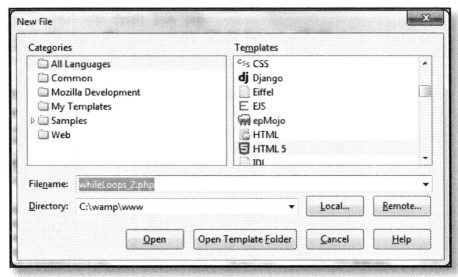

Figure 5.7: Opening a new HTML5 document in Komodo Edit.

**2** **Step 2:** Type the following program statements in your PHP document:

## CODE LISTING: WHILELOOPS_2.PHP

```
<!DOCTYPE html>

<html>
<head>
    <title>While Loop Example 2</title>
</head>
```

```
<body>
    <?php
        $number = 0;
        while($number < 51) //do while
$number is less than 51
        {
            print($number); // display the
value of $number
            print("</br>"); // insert a
line break
            $number += 5;    // increase
the value of $number by 5
        }
    ?>
</body>
</html>
```

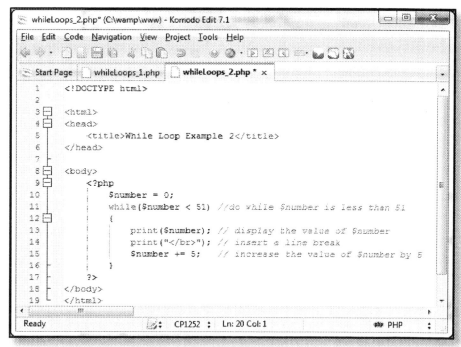

Figure 5.8: Inputting the statements of *whileLoops_2.php*.

**3** **Step 3:** Run your output.

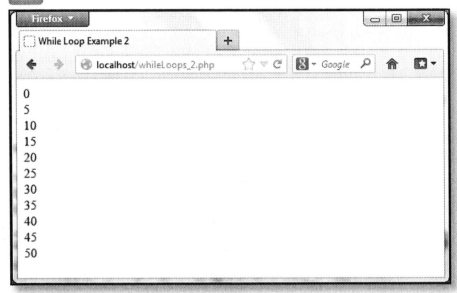

Figure 5.9: Output of *whileLoops_2.php*.

What would happen if the initial condition is set to FALSE? To find out, try doing the following:

**Step 4:** Tweak the variable assignment portion by assigning the value *52* to *$number*.

```php
<?php
    $number = 52;
```

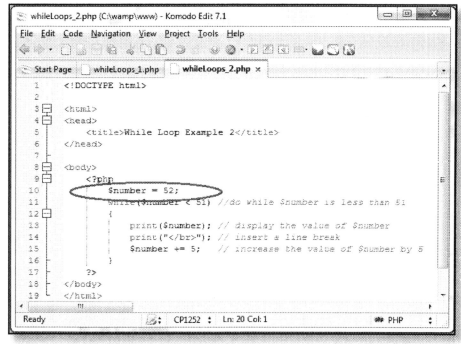

Figure 5.10: Change the initial value of the counter variable *$number* to 52 in *whileLoops_2.php*.

**5** **Step 5:** Save your document.

**6** **Step 6:** Run your output.

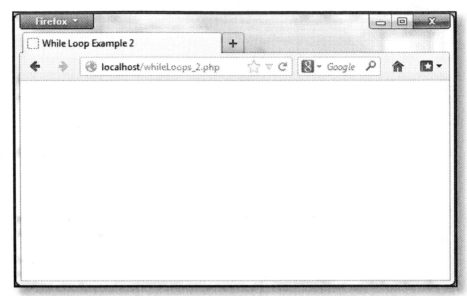

Figure 5.11: Blank output after changing initial value of $number to 52 in whileLoops_2. php.

As expected, the screen is blank because the **conditional expression** evaluated to FALSE upon entering the *do-while-loop*.

For our third example of a *while-loop,* let's retrieve a simple array that has seven elements or members. (Later on in this chapter, we will tackle the *foreach-loop* which is the best way to retrieve the elements of any array.)

**PROBLEM:** Create a *while-loop* that will read an array consisting of seven members: Kingdom, Phylum, Class, Order, Family, Genus and Species. Each array member must be displayed separately on a line. Use the variable names *$taxonomy* for the array and *$x* for the array counter.

**SOLUTION:**

**1** **Step 1:** Create a new HTML5 document. Name it *whileLoops_3. php.* Save it under your www or htdocs folder.

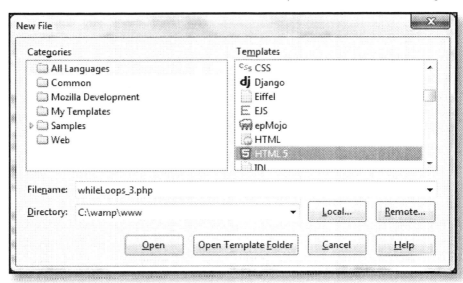

Figure 5.12: Opening a new HTML5 document in Komodo Edit.

**2** **Step 2:** Type the following program statements in your PHP document.

## CODE LISTING: WHILELOOPS_3.PHP

```
<!DOCTYPE html>

<html>
<head>
    <title>While Loops Example 3</title>
</head>

<body>
    <?php
        //This is the array declaration
        $taxonomy = array("Kingdom",
"Phylum", "Class", "Order", "Family",
"Genus", "Species");

        $x = 0;      //Set the array
counter to zero
        while($x < count($taxonomy))
```

```
/*compare if $x is less than the number of
counted array elements*/
        {
            print($taxonomy[$x]); //
display the array member($x)
            print("</br>");         //
insert a line break
            $x++;                    //
access the next array member
        }
    ?>
</body>
</html>
```

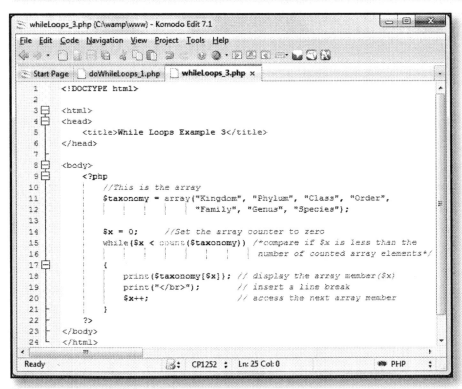

Figure 5.13: Inputting the statements of *whileLoops_3.php*.

**3** **Step 3:** Save your file again.

**4** **Step 4:** Run your output.

Figure 5.14: Output of *whileLoops_3.php*.

# 5.2 DO-WHILE-LOOP

The *do-while-loop* is just like the *while-loop* except that the
**conditional expression** is placed at the end of the *do-while-loop*
statement, just after the code block. This is
the syntax and structure of the *do-while-loop*.

**Do-While-Loop**

```
do {
    code block of statements
} while (conditional expression)
first statement after do-while-statement
```

In the *while-loop* statement, program execution begins by first
evaluating the **conditional expression.** But in the *do-while-loop*,
program execution begins by first executing the loop's code block and
then evaluating the **conditional expression** which is at the end of the
statement. If the **conditional expression** evaluates to TRUE then the
code block will be executed again. If not, the *do-while-loop* terminates.

Let's modify our first example, *whileLoop_1.php,* and create a *do-while-*

*loop* version of that example.

**PROBLEM:** Create a program using a *do-while-loop* that will count from one to ten. Each number should be displayed on separate lines. Use the variable name *$number*.

**SOLUTION:**

**1** **Step 1:** Create a new HTML5 document. Name it *doWhileLoops_1.php*. Save it under your www or htdocs folder.

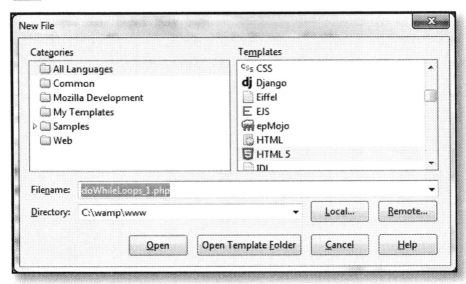

Figure 5.15: Opening a new HTML5 document in Komodo Edit.

**2** **Step 2:** Type the following program statements in your PHP document.

## CODE LISTING: DOWHILELOOPS_1.PHP

```
<!DOCTYPE html>

<html>
<head>
    <title>Do-While Loops Example 1</
title>
</head>
```

```
<body>
    <?php
        $number = 1;
        do                       // Do
statement
        {
            print($number); // display the
value of $number
            print("</br>"); // insert a
line break
            $number++;          // increase
the value of $number by 1
        }
        while($number < 11) //do while
$number is less than 11
    ?>
</body>
</html>
```

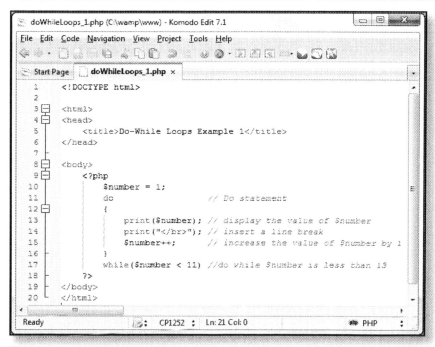

Figure 5.16: Inputting the statements of *doWhileLoops_1.php*.

**3** **Step 3:** Save your file again.

**4** **Step 4:** Run your output.

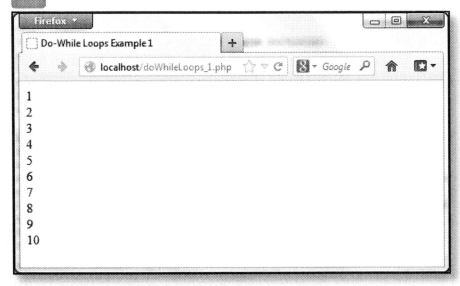

Figure 5.17: Output of *doWhileLoops_1.php*.

The *do-while-loop* version generated an identical output as the *while-loop* version.

What would happen if the **conditional expression** is initially FALSE?

**5** **Step 5:** Modify the assigned value in the conditional statement.

**6** **Step 6:** Tweak the variable assignment portion by assigning the value *11* to *$number*

```php
<?php
    $number = 11;
```

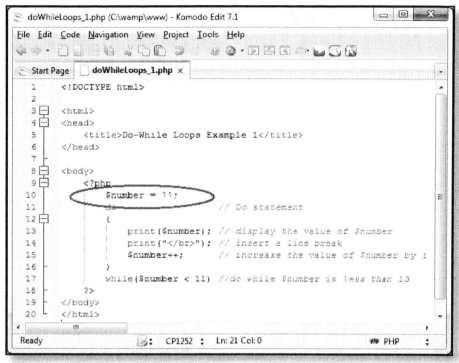

Figure 5.18: Change the initial value of the counter variable *$number* to 11 in
*doWhileLoops_1.php*.

**7** Step 7: Save your file.

**8** Step 8: Run your output.

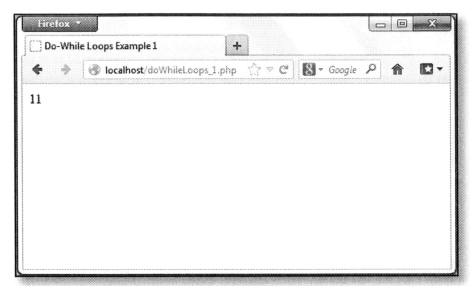

Figure 5.19: Output of *doWhileLoops_1.php* after changing initial value of *$number* to 11.

The assigned value—*11*—to the variable *$number* caused the **conditional expression** *($number <11)* to evaluate to FALSE. Thus, the loop is terminated. But this evaluation is done at the end of the loop, after the code block had already been unconditionally executed. Thus, we get that single output of 11.

So when do you use the *while-loop* or the *do-while-loop?* That will, of course, depend on the program logic you have to implement. Just remember that in the *do-while-loop*, its code block will be executed at least once whether or not the statement's conditional expression evaluates to TRUE or FALSE. In situations where you need this behavior, the *do-while-loop* is handy.

# 5.3 FOR-LOOP

So far, we have studied the *while-* and *do-while-* statements, the two simplest PHP **iteration structures**. A not-so-simple PHP loop and yet compact and powerful **iteration structure** and a preferred favorite among programmers is the *for-loop* statement whose structure and syntax is:

```
for (set-start; continue-condition;
increment){
    // block of code to loop through
}
first statement after for-loop
```

**For-Loop**

All the logic and parameters required to control the *for-loop* logic are declared in its first line within the parentheses after the *for* keyword. There are three statements that have to be declared within the parentheses. They have been appropriately labelled *set-start, test-condition* and *increment* to denote the essential function of each statement. Note that only the first two statements end with a semi-colon.

The *set-start* statement sets the starting value of the loop's counter variable. The counter variable keeps track of the number of times the loop is executed. How this variable is incremented (or decremented) is set in the *increment* statement.

The *continue-condition* statement declares the **conditional expression** for the loop's continued execution. This condition is evaluated at the beginning of each loop. If the evaluated result is TRUE, the loop is executed. Otherwise, the loop terminates.

The *increment* statement sets the value by which the counter variable will be incremented (or decremented) for every execution of the loop. Most of the time, this variable is incremented by 1 but any value is allowed, including negative values. The counter variable's current value lets us know at any time how many iterations the loop has already undergone.

The *for-loop* statement is used much more often than the *while-* and *do-while-* statements, especially when you know how many times you have to iterate through a code block. The feature that makes the *for-loop* the preferred iteration structure among programmers is that all the logic required to start, continue and terminate the loop can be directly read from the *for-loop*'s first line. This is unlike the *while-* and *do-while-* loops, where only the **conditional expression** for those loops' continued execution is explicitly declared. Thus, in *while-* and *do-while* loops, you have to read and search through the code to find what variable (and its initial value) will be used as the loop's counter and by what value it will be incremented.

Let's analyze a simple *for-loop* that counts from 1 to 10.

```
for ($i = 1; $i <= 10; $i++;)
{
    echo ($i . </br>)
}
```

The *set-start* statement, $i =1, sets the counter variable $i to its starting value 1. $i will be incremented by 1 (as defined in the *increment* statement, $i++) at the end of every execution of the *for-loop's* code block.

At the very start of the *for-loop*'s execution, the *test-condition* $i <=10 is evaluated. This **conditional expression** will evaluate to TRUE, since the value of $i is 1 at the start of execution. It will evaluate to TRUE for the first 10 iterations of the code block but at the start of the 11th iteration, $i will be 11 thus causing the *for-loop* to terminate.

Now let's study examples of *for-loops* that display integers by twos, threes and backwards. This will require incrementing and decrementing by values other than 1.

**PROBLEM:** Create a *for-loop* that will count by twos and threes, and then will count backwards by fours from 40 down to four.

**SOLUTION:**

**1** **Step 1:** Create a new HTML5 file and save it as *forLoops_1.php* inside your www or htdocs folder.

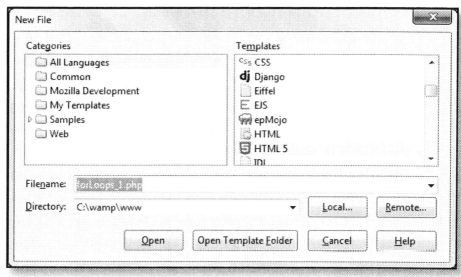

**2** **Step 2:** Input the following program statements.

## CODE LISTING: FORLOOPS_1.PHP

```php
<!DOCTYPE html>

<html>
<head>
    <title>For-loop Example 1</title>
</head>
<body>
    <?php
        echo("Count by twos from 0 to
10:</br>");
        for($i = 0; $i <=10; $i+=2)  //
count by two's from 0-10
            {
                echo($i . "</br>");
            }

        echo("Count by threes from 0 to
15:</br>");
```

```
        for($i = 0; $i <=15; $i+=3)   //
count by threes from 0-15
            {
                echo($i . "</br>");
            }

        echo("Count backwards by fours
from 40 down to 4:</br>");
        for($i = 40; $i >=4; $i-=4)   //
count backwards by fours from 40 down to 4
            {
                echo($i . "</br>");
            }
    ?>
</body>
</html>
```

This is how your code will look in Komodo Edit:

Figure 5.21: Inputting the statements of *forLoops_1.php*.

**3** **Step 3:** Save your file again.

**4** **Step 4:** Run your output.

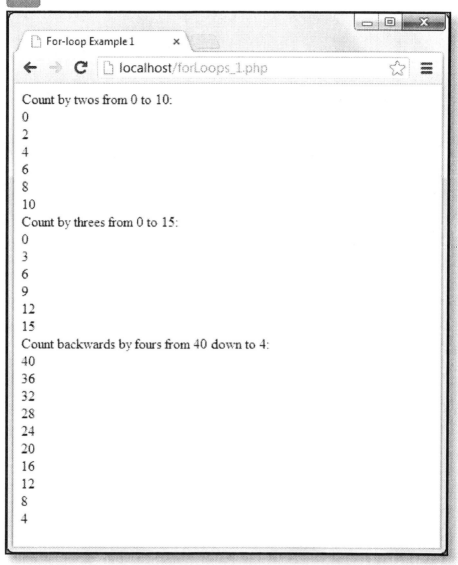

Figure 5.22: Output of *forLoops_1.php*

## 5.4 FOREACH-LOOPS

The *foreach-loop* statement is a modified *for-loop* statement that works only on arrays and objects. It won't work with any other data type. (Objects will be studied in Chapter 10.) The purpose of the *foreach-loop* is to make it easy to consecutively retrieve the elements of any type of array.

> **ForEach-Loop**

> TIP: Arrays were presented in Chapter 3 and it is vital that you clearly understand the differences between indexed (or simple) arrays, associative arrays and multi-dimensional arrays. You should know how to create any of those arrays, how to populate them, and how to reference and retrieve their members.

When used to iterate over the members of an **indexed** or **simple** array, the structure and syntax of the *foreach-loop* statement is:

```
foreach ($arrayName as $elementValue) {
    block of code
}
```

When used to iterate over the members of an **associative** array, the structure and syntax of the *foreach-loop* statement is:

```
foreach ($arrayName as $keyValue =>
$elementValue) {
    block of code
}
```

*$arrayName* is the name of the array whose elements you want to access.

*$keyValue* stores the value of the key of the current array element.

*$elementValue* stores the value of the current array element.

Notice that there is no need to define a counter variable and set its initial and incrementing value, nor is there a need to define a conditional expression. The *foreach-loop* will automatically and consecutively step through all memory locations or indices of an array (whether they store elements or not).

Now, before we go into some examples, let's preview two concerns regarding accessing an array's elements through the *foreach-loop*. These two concerns will be discussed in detail in the next chapters but for now you should at least be aware of them.

First, the *foreach-loop* will return copies (variables *$keyValue* and *$elementValue*) of the array's elements. You can use these variables just as you would use any other variable. You could also assign new values to them. But assigning new values to *$keyValue* or to *$elementValue* will not affect the array elements since these two variables are just copies of the values of the array elements. In another chapter, we will discuss how to modify the elements of an array through the *foreach-loop*.

The second concern deals with arrays with empty memory locations. We have kept things simple by dealing with fully populated arrays but in real life using the *foreach-loop* to access an array's elements always includes code that assumes that the array will have empty memory locations. This will be discussed in detail in later chapters.

Now, let's study an example of using the *foreach-loop* on an array.

PROBLEM: Create an associative array that contains the first names of seven people and their corresponding GPAs as shown in the following table.

| First Names | GPA |
|---|---|
| Adam | 4.00 |
| Ervin | 3.75 |
| Erin | 3.9 |
| Jim | 3.59 |
| Eric | 3.0 |
| Duane | 2.11 |
| Sally | Not given |

## SOLUTION:

**1** **Step 1:** Create a new HTML5 document and save it in the www folder with the filename *foreachLoops_1.php*. Use the array variable name *$gpas*.

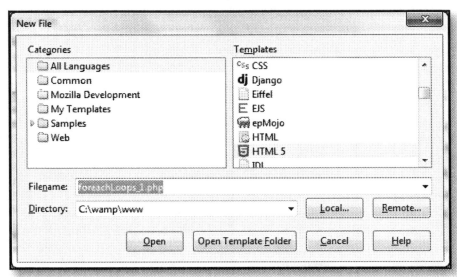

Figure 5.23: Opening a new HTML5 document in Komodo Edit.

**2** **Step 2:** Input the following program statements.

Declare the array as follows:

```php
<?php
        $gpas;
        $gpas["Adam"] = 4.0;
        $gpas["Ervin"] = 3.75;
        $gpas["Erin"] = 3.9;
        $gpas["Jim"] = 3.59;
        $gpas["Eric"] = 3.0;
        $gpas["Duane"] = 2.11;
        $gpas["Sally"] = "Not given";
?>
```

The *foreach-loop* routine should look like:

```php
foreach ($gpas as $key => $value)
        {
                print("Name: " . $key);
                print("<br/>GPA: " . $value);
                print("<br/>");
        }
```

This is the complete code listing:

## CODE LISTING: FOREACHLOOPS_1.PHP

```php
<!DOCTYPE html>
<html>
<head>
    <title>Foreach Loop Example 1</title>
</head>
<body>
    <?php
        $gpas;
        $gpas["Adam"] = 4.0;
        $gpas["Ervin"] = 3.75;
        $gpas["Erin"] = 3.9;
        $gpas["Jim"] = 3.59;
        $gpas["Eric"] = 3.0;
        $gpas["Duane"] = 2.11;
        $gpas["Sally"] = "Not given";

        foreach ($gpas as $key => $value)
        {
                print("Name: " . $key);
                print("<br/>GPA: " . $value);
                print("<br/>");
        }
    ?>
</body>
</html>
```

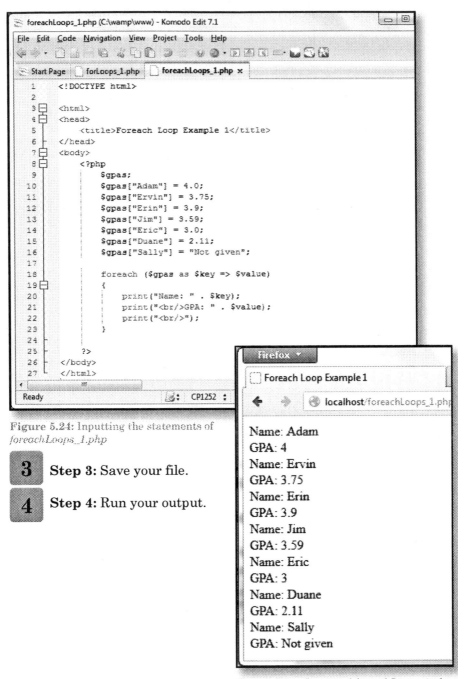

```
  1    <!DOCTYPE html>
  2
  3    <html>
  4    <head>
  5        <title>Foreach Loop Example 1</title>
  6    </head>
  7    <body>
  8        <?php
  9            $gpas;
 10            $gpas["Adam"] = 4.0;
 11            $gpas["Ervin"] = 3.75;
 12            $gpas["Erin"] = 3.9;
 13            $gpas["Jim"] = 3.59;
 14            $gpas["Eric"] = 3.0;
 15            $gpas["Duane"] = 2.11;
 16            $gpas["Sally"] = "Not given";
 17
 18            foreach ($gpas as $key => $value)
 19            {
 20                print("Name: " . $key);
 21                print("<br/>GPA: " . $value);
 22                print("<br/>");
 23            }
 24
 25        ?>
 26    </body>
 27    </html>
```

Figure 5.24: Inputting the statements of *foreachLoops_1.php*

**3** Step 3: Save your file.

**4** Step 4: Run your output.

Foreach Loop Example 1

localhost/foreachLoops_1.php

Name: Adam
GPA: 4
Name: Ervin
GPA: 3.75
Name: Erin
GPA: 3.9
Name: Jim
GPA: 3.59
Name: Eric
GPA: 3
Name: Duane
GPA: 2.11
Name: Sally
GPA: Not given

Figure 5.25: Output of *foreachLoops_1.php*.

**PROBLEM:** Create a variation in the output layout so that the names fall in the first column and the respective GPAs are displayed across from each name.

**SOLUTION:**

**1** **Step 1:** Modify the code and place the table elements code right below the array declaration.

```
echo("<table border='0'>");
echo("<tr>");
echo("<th>Name</th>");
echo("<th>GPA</th>");
echo("</tr>");
```

**2** **Step 2:** Tweak the *foreach-loop* and insert the appropriate table data cell alignment codes.

```
foreach ($gpas as $key => $value)
{
      echo("<tr>");
      echo("<td align='left'>" .
$key . "</td>");
      echo("<td align='center'>" .
$value . "</td>");
      echo("</tr>");
}
```

The complete code listing should now look like this:

```
<!DOCTYPE html>
<html>
<head>
    <title>Foreach Loop Example 1</title>
</head>
<body>
    <?php
        $gpas;
        $gpas["Adam"] = 4.00;
        $gpas["Ervin"] = 3.75;
        $gpas["Erin"] = 3.90;
        $gpas["Jim"] = 3.59;
        $gpas["Eric"] = 3.00;
        $gpas["Duane"] = 2.11;
        $gpas["Sally"] = "Not given";

        echo("<table border='0'>");
        echo("<tr>");
        echo("<th>Name</th>");
        echo("<th>GPA</th>");
        echo("</tr>");

        foreach ($gpas as $key => $value)
        {
            echo("<tr>");
            echo("<td align='left'>" .
$key . "</td>");
            echo("<td align='center'>" .
$value . "</td>");
            echo("</tr>");
        }
        echo("</table>");
    ?>
</body>
</html>
```

```
foreachLoops_2.php* (C:\wamp\www) - Komodo Edit 7.1                    [_][□][ x ]

File  Edit  Code  Navigation  View  Project  Tools  Help

◄ ► ·  ☐ ☐ ☐ ☐  ◢ ☐ ☐ ☞       ☞ ☺ · ☐ ☑ ☐ ☞ ☜ ☉ ☒

← ☜ Start Page  ☐ forLoops_1.php  ☐ foreachLoops_1.php  ☐ foreachLoops_2.php * ×  → ·

 1        <!DOCTYPE html>
 2        <html>
 3        <head>
 4            <title>Foreach Loop Example 1</title>
 5        </head>
 6        <body>
 7            <?php
 8                $gpas;
 9                $gpas["Adam"] = 4.00;
10                $gpas["Ervin"] = 3.75;
11                $gpas["Erin"] = 3.90;
12                $gpas["Jim"] = 3.59;
13                $gpas["Eric"] = 3.00;
14                $gpas["Duane"] = 2.11;
15                $gpas["Sally"] = "Not given";
16
17                echo("<table border='0'>");
18                echo("<tr>");
19                echo("<th>Name</th>");
20                echo("<th>GPA</th>");
21                echo("</tr>");
22
23                foreach ($gpas as $key => $value)
24                {
25                    echo("<tr>");
26                    echo("<td align='left'>" . $key . "</td>");
27                    echo("<td align='center'>" . $value . "</td>");
28                    echo("</tr>");
29                }
30            ?>
31        </body>
32        </html>
◄        III                                                              ►

Ready              ☑:  CP1252  :  Ln: 33 Col: 0                    php PHP    :
```

Figure 5.26: Inputting the statements of *foreachLoops_2.php*

**3**  **Step 3:** Save your file as *foreachLoops_2.php*.

**4**  **Step 4:** Run your output.

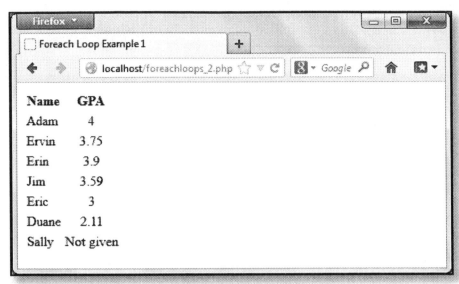

Figure 5.27: Output of *foreachLoops_2.php*

Using *foreach-loop,* let's do some mathematical manipulations in another associative array. The second example will involve computing for the GPA of a student given the subject grades.

**PROBLEM:** Write a program where seven academic subjects along with the final grades are listed. At the end of the list the average GPA is computed. See the following table for the values.

| Subjects | Grades |
| --- | --- |
| Algebra | 3.50 |
| Biology | 3.75 |
| Arts | 3.00 |
| Writing | 2.50 |
| Communications | 2.50 |
| Languages | 4.00 |
| History | 3.75 |

## SOLUTION:

**1** **Step 1:** Open an HTML5 document template. In the <title> tag, type your title as *foreachLoops_3.php*. Save your file in the www or htdocs folder. I will no longer include an image here since you are already familiar with this step.

**2** **Step 2:** With the Komodo Edit *foreachLoops_3.php* file still open, type the following program statements.

Declare the associative array as follows:

```php
$subject;
$subject['Algebra'] = 3.50;
$subject['Bioloqy'] = 3.75;
$subject['Arts'] = 3.00;
$subject['Writing'] = 2.50;
$subject['Communications'] = 2.50;
$subject['Languages'] = 4.00;
$subject['History'] = 3.75;
```

To compute for the average, all the grades must be totaled then divided by the number of subjects. Therefore, you must include in the declaration two variables that will hold the sum, *$gpt,* and the average, *$gpa,* of the grades:

```php
$gpa=0;
$gpt=0;
```

In the *foreach-loop*, include the instruction that will list the different subjects and the corresponding grade. This is also the portion where you will include the process to add all the grades.

```php
foreach($subject as $name => $value)
        {
            echo("<tr>");
            echo("<td align='left'>" .
$name . "</td>");
            echo("<td align='center'>" .
```

```php
$value . "</td>");
            echo("</tr>");
            $gpt += $value;
        }
```

This is the complete code listing:

## CODE LISTING: FOREACHLOOPS_3.PHP

```php
<!DOCTYPE html>
<html>
<head>
    <title>Foreach Loop Example 3</title>
</head>
<body>
    <?php
        $subject;
        $subject['Algebra'] = 3.50;
        $subject['Biology'] = 3.75;
        $subject['Arts'] = 3.00;
        $subject['Writing'] = 2.50;
        $subject['Communications'] = 2.50;
        $subject['Languages'] = 4.00;
        $subject['History'] = 3.75;
        $gpa=0;
        $gpt=0;

        echo("<table border='1'>");
        echo("<tr>");
        echo("<th>Subject</th>");
        echo("<th>Grade</th>");
        foreach($subject as $name =>
$value)
        {
            echo("<tr>");
            echo("<td align='left'>" .
$name . "</td>");
```

```
                echo("<td align='center'>" .
$value . "</td>");
            echo("</tr>");
            $gpt += $value;
        }

        $gpa = ($gpt/count($subject));
        echo("<tr>");
        echo("<th align='left'>Average
GPA</th>");
        printf("<th align='center'>%0.2f</
th>", $gpa);
        echo("</tr></table>");
    ?>
</body>
</html>
```

**3** **Step 3:** Save your file.

**4** **Step 4:** Run your output.

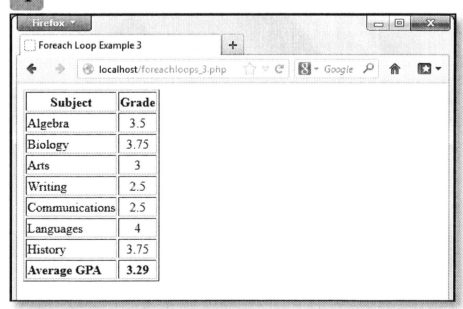

| Subject | Grade |
|---|---|
| Algebra | 3.5 |
| Biology | 3.75 |
| Arts | 3 |
| Writing | 2.5 |
| Communications | 2.5 |
| Languages | 4 |
| History | 3.75 |
| **Average GPA** | **3.29** |

Figure 5.28: Output of *foreachLoops_3.php*

1. What are loops?
   a. An endless iteration of a code segment.
   b. Commands that execute a block of a code a fixed number of times.
   c. Commands that repeat the process of a code segment depending on the condition set in the program.
   d. Control structures that ignore the repetition of a process.

2. What is the main difference between *while-loops* and *do-while-loops*?
   a. *While-loops* are shorter than *do-while-loops*.
   b. *Do-while-loops* have more complex coding than *while-loops*.
   c. *Do-while-loops* iterate at least once even if the condition is initially set to FALSE; *while-loops* ignore the loop if the initial value is FALSE.
   d. There is no difference at all.

3. What is a *for-loop*?
   a. *For-loops* are loops that iterate a code segment four times.
   b. *For-loops* are loops that have longer coding than *while* and *do-while* loops.
   c. *For-loops* are a compact type of loop that contain the logic and parameters of the loop all in one line.
   d. *For-loops* are control structure designed to handle loops involving arrays.

4. Which loop would be wise to use when dealing with complex arrays?
   a. *while-loop*
   b. *do-while-loop*
   c. *for-loop*
   d. *foreach-loop*

# CHAPTER 5 LAB EXERCISE

**PROBLEM 1:** Create a loop routine that will display the following output. Don't cheat! You may only print() or echo() one asterisk symbol at a time and not a string of asterisks.

```
*
**
***
****
*****
******
*******
********
*********
**********
***********
************
```

**PROBLEM 2:** Write a program that will compute for the total score of a basketball team at the end of the game. Sum up the total points gained by each of the players from the first half and second half of the game. The following table represents the associative array and the points the team gained during the game.

| Player's Name | Points- First Half | Points- Second Half |
|---|---|---|
| Brandon Bass | 5 | 3 |
| Avery Bradley | 0 | 2 |
| Jordan Crawford | 6 | 2 |
| Kevin Garnett | 7 | 5 |
| Jeff Green | 3 | 3 |
| Courtney Lee | 1 | 4 |
| Fab Melo | 0 | 2 |
| Paul Pierce | 15 | 10 |

| Shavlik Randolph | 0 | 0 |
|---|---|---|
| Rajon Rondo | 20 | 8 |
| Jared Sullinger | 0 | 3 |
| Jason Terry | 9 | 10 |
| D.J. White | 3 | 2 |
| Chris Wilcox | 1 | 2 |
| Terrence Williams | 0 | 0 |

**PROBLEM 3:** Create a program that will compute for an investment's monthly earnings. The program must be able to generate a report with the following information:

1) Principal amount invested
2) Interest rate (annual)
3) Term or duration of the investment in years (6 months is entered as 0.5, 3 months = 0.25, and so on.)
4) Monthly current balances
5) Aggregate balance at the end of the investment term

The term or duration and interest rate will vary depending on the numbers input in the form. However, the following conditions must prevail to accurately compute for the earnings.

1) Monthly interest rate is computed as:
Monthly Interest Rate = $interestRate/12

2) Monthly interest must be reported and should be computed as:
Monthly Interest = $principal *$monthlyInterestRate

3) Monthly current balances must also be reported and should be computed as:
Monthly Balance = $principal + $monthlyInterest

4) Future investment value at end of the term is computed as :
Total Investment = the last monthly balance

Principal amount, annual interest rate and term must all be treated as $superglobal variables.

Prepare two document files for the solution. The superglobals will be handled by a form page. The computation is taken care of by a separate document containing a pure PHP script which will handle all the computations and processing of output.

This is how the form page should look:

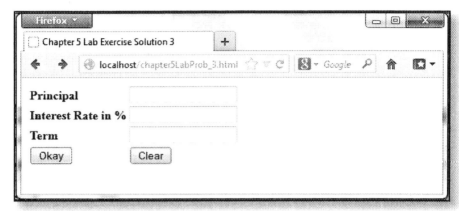

Figure 5.29: Form page or input screen display for Lab Exercise 3.

Format the output as follows:

| Principal Amount | | |
|---|---|---|
| Annual Interest Rate | | |
| Term | | |
| Earnings History | | |
| Month | Monthly Interest Earned | Current Balance |
| Month 1 | | |
| Month 2 | | |
| Month 3 | | |
| ... | | |
| Month n | | |
| | Investment's future value at end of term | |

# CHAPTER 5 LAB EXERCISE SOLUTIONS:

## SOLUTION 1:

### CODE LISTING: CHAPTER LAB PROBLEM 1 SOLUTION
*CHAPTERLABPROB_1.PHP*

```php
<?php
    for($i=0;$i<=10;$i++)
    {
        for($j=0;$j<=$i;$j++)
        {
            print("*\t");
        }
        print("</br>");
    }
?>
```

## SOLUTION 1 OUTPUT:

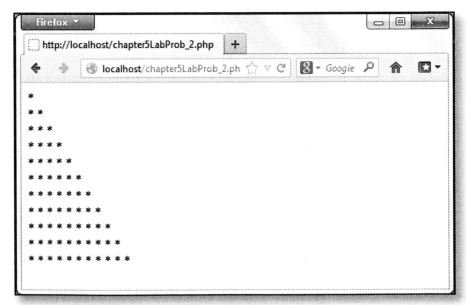

Figure 5.30: Output of Lab Exercise 1 (*chapter5LabProb_1.php*)

## SOLUTION 2:

## CODE LISTING: CHAPTER LAB
## PROBLEM 2 SOLUTION
### *CHAPTERLABPROB_2.PHP*

```php
<!DOCTYPE html>
<html>
    <head>
        <title>Chapter 5 Lab Exercise Solution 2</title>
    </head>
    <body>
<?php
    $boston = array
                (
                    "Brandon Bass" => array (5, 3),
                    "Avery Bradley" => array (0, 2),
                    "Jordan Crawford" => array (6, 2),
                    "Kevin Garnett" -> array (7, 5),
                    "Jeff Green" => array (3, 3),
                    "Courtney Lee" => array (1, 4),
                    "Fab Melo" => array (0, 2),
                    "Paul Pierce" => array (15, 10),
                    "Shavlik Randolph" => array (0, 0),
                    "Rajon Rondo" => array (20, 8),
                    "Jared Sullinger" => array (0, 3),
                    "Jason Terry" => array (9, 10),
                    "D.J. White" => array (3, 2),
                    "Chris Wilcox" => array (1, 2),
                    "Terrence Williams" => array (0, 0)
                );
                $totalScore = 0;

//add all points to get the total score
                foreach($boston as $key)
                {
                    foreach($key as $value)
                    {

                    $totalScore += $value;
                    }
                }

                //set up the table heading
                echo("<table border='1'>");
```

```php
                        echo("<tr>");
                        echo("<th>Player Name</th>");
                        echo("<th>Points-First Half</th>");
                        echo("<th>Points-Second Half</th>");
                        echo("</tr>");

                        echo("<tr>");
                        echo("<td>Brandon Bass</td>");
                        echo("<td align='center'>" .
$boston['Brandon Bass'][0] . "</td>");
                        echo("<td align='center'>" .
$boston['Brandon Bass'][1] . "</td>");
                        echo("</tr>");

                        echo("<tr>");
                        echo("<td>Avery Bradley</td>");
                        echo("<td align='center'>" .
$boston['Avery Bradley'][0] . "</td>");
                        echo("<td align='center'>" .
$boston['Avery Bradley'][1] . "</td>");
                        echo("</tr>");

                        echo("<tr>");
                        echo("<td>Jordan Crawford</td>");
                        echo("<td align='center'>" .
$boston['Jordan Crawford'][0] . "</td>");
                        echo("<td align='center'>" .
$boston['Jordan Crawford'][1] . "</td>");
                        echo("</tr>");

                        echo("<tr>");
                        echo("<td>Kevin Garnett</td>");
                        echo("<td align='center'>" .
$boston['Kevin Garnett'][0] . "</td>");
                        echo("<td align='center'>" .
$boston['Kevin Garnett'][1] . "</td>");
                        echo("</tr>");

                        echo("<tr>");
                        echo("<td>Jeff Green</td>");
                        echo("<td align='center'>" .
$boston['Jeff Green'][0] . "</td>");
                        echo("<td align='center'>" .
$boston['Jeff Green'][1] . "</td>");
                        echo("</tr>");

                        echo("<tr>");
                        echo("<td>Courtney Lee</td>");
                        echo("<td align='center'>" .
$boston['Courtney Lee'][0] . "</td>");
```

```
                    echo("<td align='center'>" .
$boston['Courtney Lee'][1] . "</td>");
                    echo("</tr>");

                    echo("<tr>");
                    echo("<td>Fab Melo</td>");
                    echo("<td align='center'>" .
$boston['Fab Melo'][0] . "</td>");
                    echo("<td align='center'>" .
$boston['Fab Melo'][1] . "</td>");
                    echo("</tr>");

                    echo("<tr>");
                    echo("<td>Paul Pierce</td>");
                    echo("<td align='center'>" .
$boston['Paul Pierce'][0] . "</td>");
                    echo("<td align='center'>" .
$boston['Paul Pierce'][1] . "</td>");
                    echo("</tr>");

                    echo("<tr>");
                    echo("<td>Shavlik Randolph</td>");
                    echo("<td align='center'>" .
$boston['Shavlik Randolph'][0] . "</td>");
                    echo("<td align='center'>" .
$boston['Shavlik Randolph'][1] . "</td>");
                    echo("</tr>");

                    echo("<tr>");
                    echo("<td>Rajon Rondo</td>");
                    echo("<td align='center'>" .
$boston['Rajon Rondo'][0] . "</td>");
                    echo("<td align='center'>" .
$boston['Rajon Rondo'][1] . "</td>");
                    echo("</tr>");

                    echo("<tr>");
                    echo("<td>Jared Sullinger</td>");
                    echo("<td align='center'>" .
$boston['Jared Sullinger'][0] . "</td>");
                    echo("<td align='center'>" .
$boston['Jared Sullinger'][1] . "</td>");
                    echo("</tr>");

                    echo("<tr>");
                    echo("<td>Jason Terry</td>");
                    echo("<td align='center'>" .
$boston['Jason Terry'][0] . "</td>");
                    echo("<td align='center'>" .
$boston['Jason Terry'][1] . "</td>");
```

```php
                echo("</tr>");

                echo("<tr>");
                echo("<td>D.J. White</td>");
                echo("<td align='center'>" .
$boston['D.J. White'][0] . "</td>");
                echo("<td align='center'>" .
$boston['D.J. White'][1] . "</td>");
                echo("</tr>");

                echo("<tr>");
                echo("<td>Chris Wilcox</td>");
                echo("<td align='center'>" .
$boston['Chris Wilcox'][0] . "</td>");
                echo("<td align='center'>" .
$boston['Chris Wilcox'][1] . "</td>");
                echo("</tr>");

                echo("<tr>");
                echo("<td>Terrence Williams</td>");
                echo("<td align='center'>" .
$boston['Terrence Williams'][0] . "</td>");
                echo("<td align='center'>" .
$boston['Terrence Williams'][1] . "</td>");
                echo("</tr>");

                echo("<tr>");
                echo("<th>End Game Score</th>");
                echo("<td align='center'
colspan='2'>" . $totalScore . "</td>");
                echo("</tr>");

?>
</body>
</html>
```

## SOLUTION 2 OUTPUT:

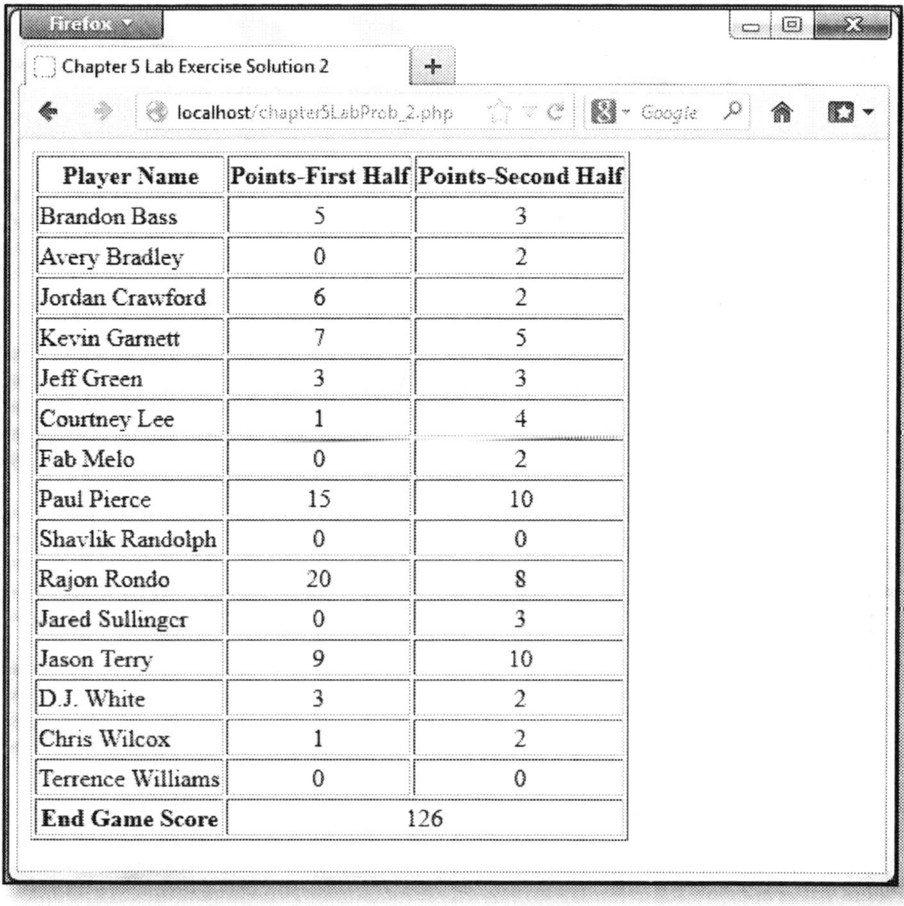

| Player Name | Points-First Half | Points-Second Half |
|---|---|---|
| Brandon Bass | 5 | 3 |
| Avery Bradley | 0 | 2 |
| Jordan Crawford | 6 | 2 |
| Kevin Garnett | 7 | 5 |
| Jeff Green | 3 | 3 |
| Courtney Lee | 1 | 4 |
| Fab Melo | 0 | 2 |
| Paul Pierce | 15 | 10 |
| Shavlik Randolph | 0 | 0 |
| Rajon Rondo | 20 | 8 |
| Jared Sullinger | 0 | 3 |
| Jason Terry | 9 | 10 |
| D.J. White | 3 | 2 |
| Chris Wilcox | 1 | 2 |
| Terrence Williams | 0 | 0 |
| **End Game Score** | 126 | |

Figure 5.31: Output of Lab Exercise 2 (*chapter5LabProb_2.php*)

## SOLUTION 3:

### CODE LISTING: CHAPTER LAB PROBLEM 3 SOLUTION
### *CHAPTERLABPROB_3.HTML*

```
<!DOCTYPE html>
<html>
<head>
    <title> Chapter 5 Lab Exercise
```

```
Solution 3</title>
</head>

<body>
    <form action="chapter5LabProb_3.php"
method="post">
        <table>
            <tr>
                <th align=left>Principal</
th>
                <td><input
name="principal" /></td>
            </tr>
            <tr>
                <th align=left>Interest
Rate in %</th>
                <td><input
name="interestRate" /></td>
            </tr>
            <tr>
                <th align=left>Term</th>
                <td><input name="term"
/></td>
            </tr>
            <tr>
                <td><input type="submit"
value="Okay" /></td>
                <td><input type="reset"
value="Clear" /></td>
            </tr>
        </table>
    </form>
</body>
</html>
```

## Solution 3: Form Output

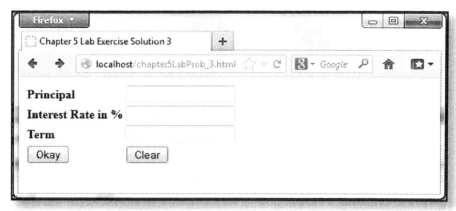

Figure 5.32: Input Screen for Lab Exercise 3 *(chapter5LabProb_3.php)*

### Code Listing: Chapter Lab Problem 3 Solution
### *CHAPTERLABPROB_3.PHP*

```php
<?php

    $principal = $_REQUEST['principal'];
    $interestRate = ($_
REQUEST['interestRate'] / 100);
    $term = $_REQUEST['term'];

    $mi = 0;
    $mir = 0;
    $mb = $principal;

    $months = ($term * 12);
    $mir = ($interestRate / 12);

  $final=0;
    echo("<table border='1'>");
    echo("<tr>");
    echo("<td>Principal Amount</td>");
    echo("<td colspan='2' align='center'>" .
$principal . "</td>");
    echo("</tr>");
```

```php
    echo("<td>Annual Interest Rate (In
Decimal)</td>");
    echo("<td colspan='2' align='center'>" .
$interestRate . "</td>");
    echo("</tr>");
    echo("<td>Term (In months)</td>");
    echo("<td colspan='2' align='center'>" .
$months . "</td>");
    echo("</tr>");
    echo("<tr>");
    echo("<td colspan='3'
align='center'>Earnings History</td>");
    echo("</tr>");
    echo("<tr>");
    echo("<td>Month</td>");
    echo("<td>Monthly Interest Earned</td>");
    echo("<td>Current Balance</td>");
    echo("</tr>");

    for($i = 1; $i<=$months; $i++)  {
        $mi = ($mb*$mir);

        $mb = ($mb+$mi);
        echo("<tr>");
        echo("<td align='center'>Month " . $i
. "</td>");

        printf("<td>%0.2f</td>", $mi);

        printf("<td>%0.2f</td>", $mb);

        $final=$mb;
    }

    echo("<tr>");
    echo("<td colspan='2'>Investment's future
value at end of term</td>");
    printf("<td>%0.2f</td>", $final);
    echo("</tr></table");
?>
```

## SOLUTION 3 OUTPUT:

Principal: 600, Interest: 10%, Term: (5 months) 0.41667

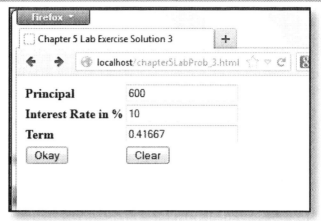

Figure 5.33: First set of input values for Lab Exercise 3

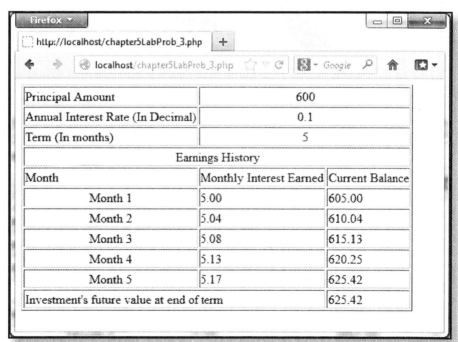

Figure 5.34: Output for first set of input values - Principal: 600, Int: 10%, Term: (5 months) 0.41667

Principal: 100, Interest: 10%, Term: (12 months) 1 year

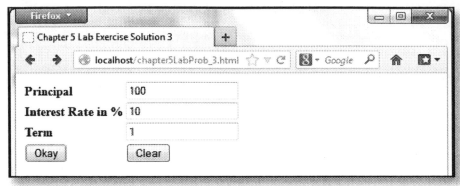

Figure 5.35: Second set of input values for Lab Exercise 3

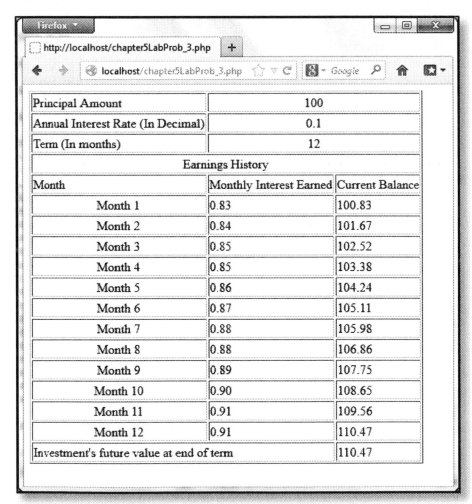

| Principal Amount | 100 | |
|---|---|---|
| Annual Interest Rate (In Decimal) | 0.1 | |
| Term (In months) | 12 | |
| Earnings History | | |
| Month | Monthly Interest Earned | Current Balance |
| Month 1 | 0.83 | 100.83 |
| Month 2 | 0.84 | 101.67 |
| Month 3 | 0.85 | 102.52 |
| Month 4 | 0.85 | 103.38 |
| Month 5 | 0.86 | 104.24 |
| Month 6 | 0.87 | 105.11 |
| Month 7 | 0.88 | 105.98 |
| Month 8 | 0.88 | 106.86 |
| Month 9 | 0.89 | 107.75 |
| Month 10 | 0.90 | 108.65 |
| Month 11 | 0.91 | 109.56 |
| Month 12 | 0.91 | 110.47 |
| Investment's future value at end of term | | 110.47 |

Figure 5.36: Output for second set of input values - Principal: 100, Int: 10%, Term: (12 Months) 1 Year

# CHAPTER SUMMARY:

In this chapter you studied the structure and syntax, as well as numerous examples, of the different looping or iteration structures in PHP: *while-loop, do-while-loop, for-loop* and *foreach-loop*.

Among those four looping structures, the *foreach-loop* is the only iteration structure that is specifically designed to handle all types of arrays, making it possible to manipulate them with ease.

In the next chapter, we will discuss custom PHP functions.

# CHAPTER 6
## CUSTOM PHP FUNCTIONS

**CHAPTER OBJECTIVES:**

- You will be able to define what PHP functions are.
- You will learn the format and syntax used in creating and calling functions.
- You will learn about function arguments which are used to pass values to functions and functions parameters which are used to receive the values passed to functions.
- You will learn how to return values from functions.
- You will learn how to organize your own functions into *PHP function container files* and how to retrieve them with the PHP built-in functions *include* and *require*.

# 6.1 INTRODUCTION AND OVERVIEW

Functions are an indispensable feature of programming languages because:

- in a well-designed computer system, 98% of that system's code will reside in functions, and
- a full understanding of functions is vital to mastering the widely-used paradigm of OOP (object-oriented programming) which lets programmers build modular, reusable code and makes it easy to build large applications that are simple to maintain.

Space limitations prevent us from tackling all the features and capabilities of PHP functions. We will only be discussing the fundamentals, as stated in the chapter objectives, that will get the beginner started with functions.

Now, you may have been unaware of it, but since Chapter 1 you have been using functions. Specifically, you have used or called, not only once but several times, three out of PHP's thousands of built-in functions, namely: *echo()*, *print()* and *printf()*.

Here are actual instances from Chapter 1 where you used those functions.

```php
echo("</br>This is my second PHP
statement");

print("Hello! ");

printf("I am %d years old", 21);
```

In Chapter 3, you used the *array()* function. The instance in which you called the *array()* function may look more complicated than the preceding instances, but it follows the same format and syntax of function calls.

```php
$salary = array("Doe" => 30000,
                "Smith" => 28000,
                "Rogers" => 50000,
                "Adam" => 120000,
                "Brown" => 60000);
```

TIP: Nov 27, 2012, a user at www.stackoverflow.com reported that there were 5,845 built-in or internal functions listed at the official PHP website, www.php.net. In addition, hundreds of developers provide fully tested and debugged functions in specialized code libraries which they produce and distribute, mostly for free. If you are looking for a feature or capability that you want to program into a website, chances are that feature or capability already exists as several functions in some developers' code library. Searching for that code library and learning how to use it will definitely take far less time than programming and debugging it yourself. One large and popular library is PEAR (PHP Extension and Application Repository). Check it out at pear.php.net.

# 6.2 CALLING FUNCTIONS

**Functions** (called *subroutines* in other, especially older, programming languages) are self-contained compilations of program statements that,especially older ones perform a specific task, a specific *function.*

For example, the primary job of the *echo(), print() and printf()* functions is to display in a browser the string value which is passed as an argument to them within the parentheses that must always follow the function name.

As for the *array()* function, it creates an array from the values which are passed as arguments to the function. These values become the array's *elements* or *members*. The *array()* function then returns a variable reference to the array.

**Functions**

(Take a moment here to review the examples of *echo(), print(), printf()* and *array()* in the previous chapters.)

> **TIP:** A well-designed function will perform only one task. If you find a function doing more than one task, then it should be re-coded into several functions where each function performs only one task.

A call to a function is equivalent to a program statement. When you call a function, program control jumps to the first line of the function. When the function finishes executing its code, program control transfers to the statement immediately after the function call.

```
$retValue = functionName(arg1, arg2,...);
// function call
Program statement executed after
functionName finishes executing.
```

You can optionally control a function's processing by passing any number of values, called *arguments*, to the function.

For example, the *echo()* and *print()* functions were each passed one argument which is a string. This string is what the *echo()* and *print()*

functions will display in the browser. Next, the *printf()* function was passed two arguments, the first a string, the second an integer. Both the string and the integer will be displayed in the browser as "I am 21 years old." Lastly, the *array()* function was passed five arguments which will become the *members* or *elements* of the *associative* array *$salary*.

Functions can also optionally pass a value, called a *return value,* back to you.

Calling or executing a function executes the program statements of that function. When you call or execute a function, you can use any of the following formats.

```
1. functionName();

2. functionName( arg1, arg2,..., argN );

3. $returnValue = functionName();

4. $returnValue = functionName( arg1,
   arg2, . . .);
```

➤ *functionName* – This is the unique name you give the function. No two functions can have the same name.

➤ *arg1, arg2, . . ., argN* – This is an optional list of comma-separated literals or variable names, called *arguments,* which are values passed to the function. There is no limit to the number of arguments that you can pass. These arguments allow you to control the function's execution and they are what give a function its power and flexibility.

➤ *$returnValue* – This is an optional variable which receives and stores an optional value returned by the function. By using a variable to hold a function's return value, we make that value available to the rest of the script.

Let's look at one more example of a function call which uses all the optional components of a function call – the argument list and the return value. We will be referring to this example several times later in this chapter.

```
$noDaysInMonth = days_in_month( $month,
$year );
```

The *days_in_month()* function was written and contributed by a user of
www.stackoverflow.com. It returns the number of days in a given month
(*$month*) of any past and future year (*$year*), taking into account leap
years.

Functions are an essential component of any programming language.
You simply have to have them for the following reasons:

a. You eliminate duplicating code.

Let's say you write a routine that forms three-character,
uppercase initials by taking the first letter of a person's first
name, middle name and last name. (For example, the initials
GWB would be formed from George Walker Bush.)

Without functions, you would have to copy and paste this routine
for every person's name you have to process. But with functions,
you can place this routine in a function, call that function and
pass the first name, middle name and last name as arguments.
Then, the function would return the three character initials as a
return value. For example:

```
$givname = "George";
$midname = "Walker";
$surname = "Bush";
$initials = formInitials( $givname,
$midname, $surname);
```

The previous four lines of code can be compacted into one line in
this way.

```
$initials = formInitials( "George",
"Walker", "Bush");
```

In either of the two previous forms, the variable *$initials* will
contain the characters, in uppercase, "GWB".

b. Functions can be reused in other scripts.

You now have an error-free *formInitials()* function which you (and other programmers) can use in future scripts. You don't even have to read or know what program statements make up the function. All you need to know is the function's name, what it does, what arguments to pass to it, and what (if any) its return value is.

c. Functions greatly reduce errors.

Again, let's say that without functions you have to resort to the copying and pasting in order to duplicate program statements. Let's say that you copy and pasted a routine twenty times. Now a situation arises where you have to make a slight adjustment to that routine—this means that now you have to go to those twenty locations and make those changes. Besides the time and effort of making twenty separate edits, more likely than not, some typing error will creep in that will completely wreck your code. And you won't know about it until the script actually bombs!
But if your routine had been created as a function, you would only have to make the change once.

d. Functions help you divide and conquer.

Programming, or the writing of actual code, should be preceded by lengthy, systematic analysis. Before the foundation of a house or building is laid out, days and weeks were definitely spent on surveying the land, analyzing the soil, selecting the appropriate materials, and then drafting and finalizing the construction blueprints. A similar process of analysis and design is performed even before the first line of computer code is written.

A careful, lengthy and systematic analysis of the system you are implementing in PHP code will reveal that the entire system can be broken down into a hierarchy of tasks or jobs. Each of those tasks can be programmed into a function which will fit nicely into a hierarchy of functions. Once all the functions have been developed and tested, including their interfaces with other functions, then the top-level controlling routines can be finalized.

In fact, a well-designed system will have as much as 98 percent of its code in functions, with the remaining 2 percent consisting of top-level control code to control the execution of those functions.

# 6.3 THE INCLUDE() AND REQUIRE() FUNCTIONS

In the previous section, we covered all the aspects of how to call or execute functions, including passing arguments to functions and retrieving and storing the function's return value. We'll get down to the nitty-gritty of creating functions in the next section. For now, we will cover how to organize the various functions you will be coding and how to easily access them. By "organizing" we mean where or in what files do you place or store the functions you will create so that they can be easily found and accessed?

In all the previous chapters, we have written our PHP code within PHP tags in an HTML structured document that has .php as its filename extension (not .html). However, this is not the practice in real life PHP coding. Ideally, the only PHP code in the HTML-structured document would be one function call to the top-level control function in a hierarchy of PHP functions, such as:

```
<php
    main();
?>
```

The main task of *main()* (or whichever appropriate name you choose) is to control the execution of the second-level control functions in the hierarchy of functions. The code for the *main()* function itself would reside in a separate .php file.

Functions should be stored in separate PHP *function container files* to facilitate orderliness, retrieval and maintenance. Let's say that in one project, the development team coded, tested and debugged 100 functions. Suppose that each function averaged 20 lines, with the shortest functions having only two lines and the longest function having a hundred lines. Experienced programmers would not place all those 100 functions in one PHP script file (which would be at least 2000 lines of code and require 40 sheets of hardcopy printouts). They would first classify and group the functions according to their main tasks and then place or store functions with similar tasks in separate PHP *function container files*. For example, functions handling graphics would be placed in graphics.php. Functions dealing with calculating discounts would go in discounts.php, and so on.

**Function Container Files**

Programmers can then read into the main script file, on an as-needed basis, whatever *function container file* is needed. To accomplish this, programmers would use any of the following four functions:

```
include("phpScriptName");

include_once("phpScriptName");

require("phpScriptName");

require_once("phpScriptName");
```

All four functions allow the functions in file *phpScriptName* to be integrated into the current script file just as if the code had been copied and pasted.

**include()**

The only difference between *include()* and *require()* is that *include()* merely raises a PHP warning (E_WARNING) if the file to be included can't be found, while *require()* raises a fatal error (E_COMPILE_ERROR) and stops running the script.

*Include_once()* and *require_once()* are used to prevent nested includes. To understand nested includes, let's consider the following four PHP scripts – *1stScript.php*, *2ndScript.php*, *myFuncsA.php* and *4thScript. php*.

**require()**

```
// 1stScript.php
<php
    include("myFuncsA.php")
    validateParameters();
?>

// 2ndScript.php
<php
    include("myFuncsA.php")
    function computeValues( param1, param2)
{
        program statements;
        return $computedValue;
```

```
    }
    validateParameters();

?>


// myFuncsA.php
<php
    function validateParameters() {
        program statements;
        return expression;
    }
?>


// 4thScript.php
<php
    include("1stScript.php");
    include("2ndScript.php");
?>
```

*1stScript.php* and *2ndScript.php* both include *myFuncsA.php* wherein the function *validateParameters()* is defined and coded. So far so good! But now here comes *4thScript.php* which includes both *1stScript.php* and *2ndScript.php*. This is our *nested includes* situation!

The problem will occur when *4thScript.php* includes *2ndScript.php* because when this happens *2ndScript.php* will include *myFuncA.php* which contains the definition of *validateParameters()*. But *1stScript. php* already included *myFuncA.php* and in this process defined *validateParameters()*. So when *2ndScript.php* included *myFuncA.php*, it defined *validateParameters()* again, thus causing a fatal error which displayed a long error message, a portion of which reads:

```
Cannot redeclare validateParameters()
(previously declared in myFuncA.php) . . .
```

A function can only be declared once, which occurred when *2ndScript. php* included *myFuncA.php,* causing the function *validateParameters()* to be redefined.

To get around this problem, we use *include_once()* in *4thScript.php*.

```
// 4thScript.php
<php
    include_once("1stScript.php");
    include_once("2ndScript.php");
?>
```

*Include_once()* and *require_once()* include the specified file or script only once during the current script execution. If you call *include_once()* or *require_once()* again to include the same file or script, nothing will happen.

The *include()* or *require()* function calls should be placed in the <head> section of the HTML document.

It should also be understood that when you include a script file of PHP functions, you do NOT automatically execute those functions. A function can only be executed with a correctly formatted function call with the correct number and sequence of required parameters.

Let's work on some examples.

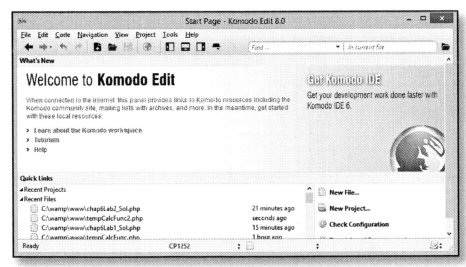

Figure 6.1: Start file creation in the Komodo Edit start page by clicking *New File*.

Choose *New file* and a window will pop up. Select PHP template and set www or htdocs as the directory in which to save a new file called *includeMe.php.*

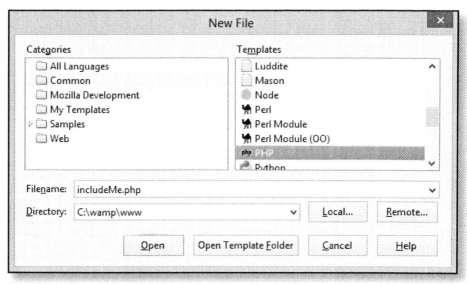

Figure 6.2: Komodo Edit's New File dialogue window. Type the file name *includeMe.php* and save the file in your www or htdocs folder.

With the new PHP file open, type the following code within the PHP *opening* and *closing tags*.

```php
<?php
    print("This statement is called from
the file includeMe.php using the include
command.");
?>
```

Figure 6.3: *includeMe.php* code in Komodo Edit.

Save and run this script.

This code will produce the following output:

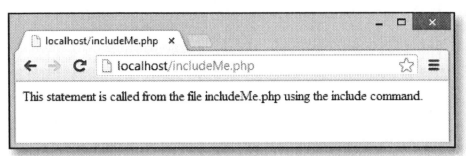

Figure 6.4: Output when *includeMe.php* script is run.

Create another PHP file using the template but this time, use *include. php* as the filename.

In the *include.php* file, type the following code that prints the same statement and then inserts a break tag. Then put in an *include* command and place it inside *includeMe.php*.

Your code should look like this:

```php
<?php

print("The following statement below is
printed out using the include function.
");
print("</br>");

include("includeMe.php");

?>
```

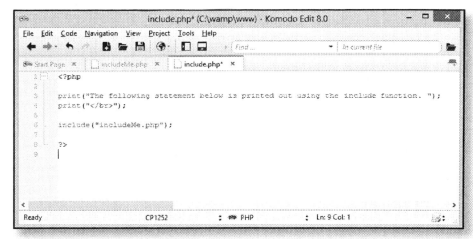

Figure 6.5: The complete code listing for *include.php* as viewed in Komodo Edit.

Your output from the new file should look like this:

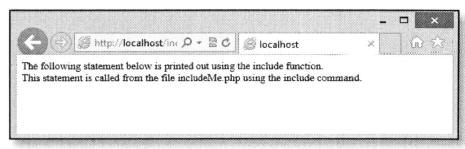

Figure 6.6: Output for *include.php* when ran.

*Include* can be repeated multiple times by just replicating the *include* function statement within the program.

Modify *include.php* by copying the code below, then run it.

```php
<?php
    print("The following statement
below is printed out using the include
function.");
    print("</br>");
    include("includeMe.php");
    print("</br>");
    include("includeMe.php");
    print("</br>");
```

```php
    include("includeMe.php");
    print("</br>");
    include("includeMe.php");
?>
```

Here is how the new output should look:

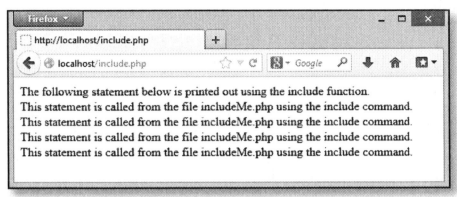

Figure 6.7: Output for modified *include.php* when run.

Now, replace *include* with *require* in our previous *include.php* code and add a few more *print statements*. Also, change the file inside the *require* statement as shown in the code below and then save the file as *include_2.php*.

## CODE LISTING: INCLUDE_2.PHP

```php
<?php
    print("The following statement below is
printed out using the include function.");
    print("</br>");

    require("includeMeXX.php");
    print("</br>");

    include("includeMe.php");
    print("</br>");
    include("includeMe.php");
    print("</br>");
    include("includeMe.php");
```

```
    print("The following statement below is
printed out using the include function.");
    print("</br>");
    print("The following statement below is
printed out using the include function.");
    print("</br>");
    print("The following statement below is
printed out using the include function.");
    print("</br>");
?>
```

Notice that when the error was found in the *require* statement, none of the code after the statement was processed and the program stopped.

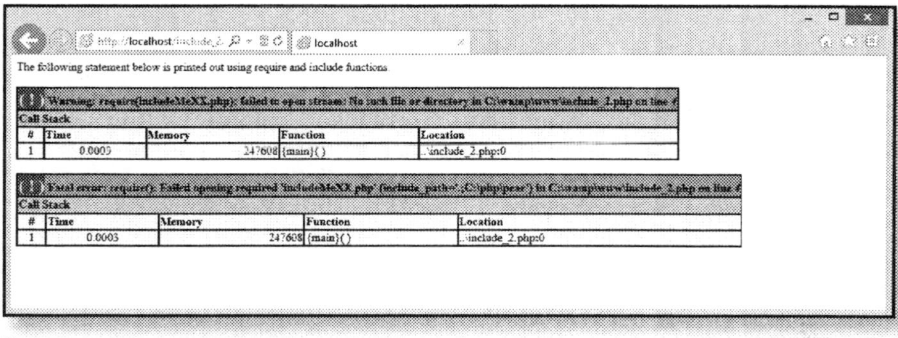

Figure 6.8: Output for *include_2.php* when ran.

As for the *include* function, instead of getting an error, the error is ignored. For example, type and save the following code under the file name *include_3.php* and run the output:

## CODE LISTING: INCLUDE_3.PHP

```php
<?php
    print("The following statement
below is printed out using the include
function.");
    print("</br>");
    include("includeMeXX.php");
    print("</br>");
```

```
    include("includeMe.php");
    print("The following statement
below is printed out using the include
function.");
    print("</br>");
    print("The following statement
below is printed out using the include
function.");
    print("</br>");

    print("The following statement
below is printed out using the include
function.");
    print("</br>");
?>
```

If all *print* and *include* statements were processed, the output will display six sentences. But because one of the *include* statements called a non-existent or "null" file—*includeMeXX.php*, the program will interpret that section of the code as an error and print out an error statement in the browser. When *require* is used instead of *include*, the program will halt as well.

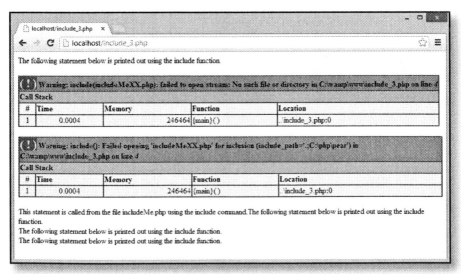

Figure 6.9: Output for *include_3.php* when ran.

# 6.4 CREATING A SIMPLE FUNCTION

Now let's study how to write our own functions. This is the format and syntax we have to follow.

```
function functionName( param1, param2, . . 
. paramN ) {
    program statements;
    return expression;
}
```

The first line must begin with the keyword *function*. Then, comes the name of your function. This name must follow certain rules.

A valid *functionName* starts with a letter or underscore, followed by any number of letters, numbers, or underscores. Function names are not case sensitive.

We earlier said that a function is a "self-contained collection of program statements that perform a specific task." When you name a function, that name should give you an idea of the "specific task" the function will perform. The function name should be followed by a set of parentheses, (). If the function will be programmed to receive arguments, then a comma separated list of parameters (param1, param2, ... paramN) that will receive the arguments should be placed within the parentheses. You can specify as many parameter variables as needed but for each parameter that you specify, a corresponding argument has to be passed to the function when it is called. Put another way, the order and number of arguments in the function call should match the order and number of parameters in the function definition.

Whether your function will receive arguments or not, the parentheses, (), must follow the function name.

> **NOTE:** What's the difference between arguments and parameters? An *argument* is a value you pass to a function and a *parameter* is the variable within the function that receives the argument. In real life, the terms are used interchangeably.

After the parentheses, comes the function's main code block, which are delimited by curly brackets {}. Within this code block you can write any PHP program statement including calls to other functions including the current function, a practice known as *recursion*.

The *return* statement returns *expression*.

> **TIP:** Just in case you have forgotten just what an *expression* is, you can review section 1 of chapter 4 "Simple Control Structure—*If* Statement".

A *return* statement can be placed anywhere in the function's code block but once the *return* statement is executed, the function immediately terminates and control is returned to the calling script, specifically the first program statement after the function call.

Let's create a simple function. Prepare two file templates: a PHP *function container file* and a HTML document that will call the functions from the container file.

**1** **Step 1**: Create a PHP template with the file name *functions.php*. This will be our *function container file*. Click *New File*.

```php
<?php
    function greeting()
    {
        print("Hello! This is a greeting!</br>");
    }
    function loop(){


        for($i=0; $i<=10; $i++)
        {
            for($j=0; $j<=$i; $j++)
            {
                print("*\t");
            }
            print("<br/>");
        }
    }
```

Figure 6.10: Komodo Edit start page. Click on New File.

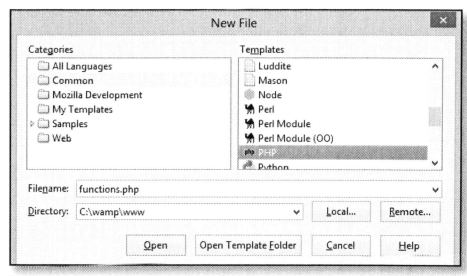

Figure 6.11: Komodo Edit's New File dialogue window. Type the file name *functions.php* and save the file in your www or htdocs folder.

Once the *functions.php* file is created, begin writing the first *function* —*greeting()*.

**2** **Step 2:** In your *functions.php* file, type the following code.

```php
<?php
    function greeting()
    {
    echo("Hello! This is a greeting!");
    }
?>
```

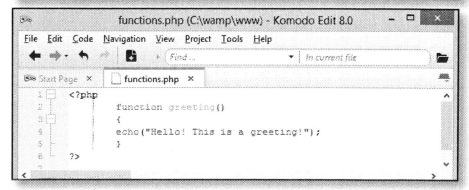

Figure 6.12: Output for *functions.php* when run.

The statement enclosed by the opening and closing curly brackets is the code that is actually called by the HTML document that requires the *function*. The PHP functions script container file must properly contain these functions and the HTML document must properly *include* or *require* the functions.

Now let's add a second function, *loop()*, to our container file. This loop routine will display asterisks (*) in a triangular structure.

```php
<?php
    function greeting()
    {
        print("Hello! This is a
greeting!</br>");
    }
    function loop()
    {
        for($i=0; $i<=10; $i++)
    {
        for($j=0; $j<=$i; $j++)
        {
            print("*\t");
        }
    print("<br/>");
    }
    }
?>
```

The complete code listing should now look like this:

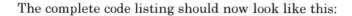

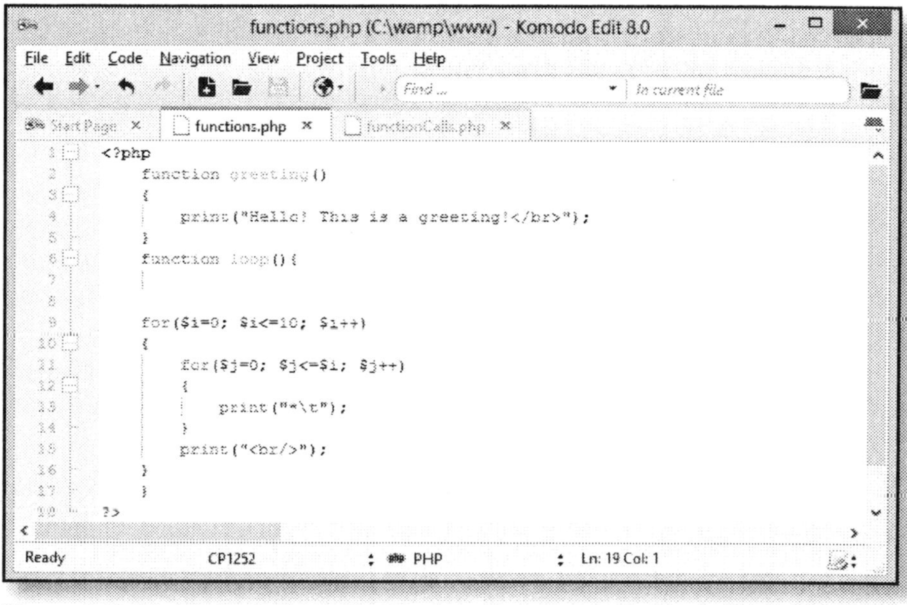

```php
<?php
    function greeting()
    {
        print("Hello! This is a greeting!</br>");
    }
    function loop(){

        for($i=0; $i<=10; $i++)
        {
            for($j=0; $j<=$i; $j++)
            {
                print("*\t");
            }
            print("<br/>");
        }
    }
?>
```

Figure 6.13: Modified code listing for *functions.php*.

After adding your second function, create your HTML master document that will call the *functions* from the *functions.php* container file.

**3** **Step 3:** Click your *functionCalls.php* file in Komodo Edit to make it the active document.

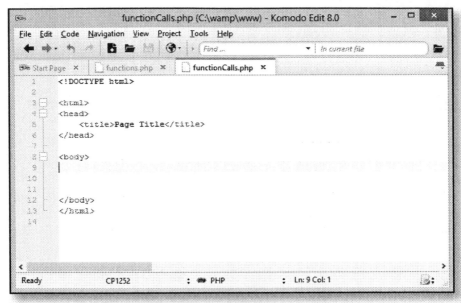

Figure 6.14: New HTML5 document template for *functionCalls.php*

**Step 4**: Type in the following codes. Make sure the functions container file *functions.php* is *required* in the head section of the *functionCalls.php* document. Save the document when you are done.

## CODE LISTING: FUNCTIONCALLS.PHP

```
<!DOCTYPE html>
<html>
<head>
<title>Function Calls</title>
    <?php
        require("functions.php");
    ?>
</head>
<body>
    <?php

    ?>
</body>
</html>
```

If you attempt to run *functionCalls.php* this early, no output will be displayed except for a parse error. This is because none of the *functions* were called yet.

When *function containers* are *included* or *required* in a document, it does not necessarily mean that the *functions* are automatically called, too. The *functions* will have to be explicitly called within the HTML document. This modularity for writing out *functions* makes extensive coding much simpler and easier to deal with.

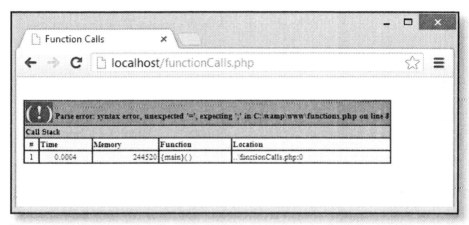

Figure 6.15: Output for *functionCalls.php* when run.

To properly call the function, the *functions* must be specifically called from within the HTML document by including their *function name*.

```
<body>
    <?php
        greeting();

        loop();
    ?>
</body>
```

To call out the two *functions*—*greeting* and *loop*, the *functionCalls.php* document has to be updated.

**5** **Step 5**: Tweak your code as follows:

### CODE LISTING: UPDATED FUNCTIONCALL.PHP

```
<!DOCTYPE html>
<html>
<head>
<title>Function Calls</title>
    <?php
        require("functions.php");
    ?>
</head>
<body>
    <?php
        greeting();
        loop();
    ?>
</body>
</html>
```

**6** **Step 6**: Save the updated document and view your output.

Figure 6.16: Output for *functionCalls.php* after properly calling the functions *greeting()* and *loop()* in the program.

# 6.5 FUNCTION ARGUMENTS

Passing arguments to a function is not just a way for programmers to communicate with the function. Arguments give functions their immense power and flexibility because arguments control the processing logic of functions. Let's look again at a previous example, the *days_in_month()* function. The complete definition of the function is listed here.

**Arguments**

```
function days_in_month($month, $year)
{
return $month == 2 ? ($year % 4 ? 28 :
($year % 100 ? 29 : ($year % 400 ? 28 :
29))) : (($month - 1) % 7 % 2 ? 30 : 31);
}
```

Although it looks complicated, the function's code block is just one line consisting of nested ternary operators. The function is called with two parameters:

 a. *$month* – the numeric representation of each of the twelve months
 b. *$year* - a four-digit integer representing the year.

The function's return value is the number of days it has calculated for the specific *$month* and specific *$year* passed to it. An actual call to the function for the number of days in February, 2014 would be:

```
$noDaysInMonth = days_in_month( 2, 2014 )
```

The function would return 28 which will be stored in the variable *$noDaysInMonth*.

Now, let's imagine that we couldn't pass arguments to functions. In the case of the *days_in_month()* function, we would have to write code for a version of that function for every month of every year we want to calculate!

Functions without arguments would be useless! But with parameters, we have one function to handle all the months of all the past and future years, on to eternity!

Here are some rules governing passing arguments to functions.

a. If more than one argument is to be passed to a function, the arguments have to be separated by commas.

b. The number and order of the arguments passed to the function must match the number and order of the parameters as declared in the function definition. If the function declaration requires three parameters, then three corresponding arguments must be passed.

Let's take a previous example, a function that declared three parameters. This is the function's partial declaration:

```
Function formInitials( $givname, $midname,
$surname) { program statements
}
```

A correct call to this function would be:

```
$initials = formInitials( "George",
"Walker", "Bush")
```

There are three arguments for three parameters and the order of the arguments corresponds to the order of the parameters. The argument "George" corresponds to the parameter $givname, the argument "Walker" to $midname, the argument "Bush" to $surname. Change the order of the arguments and you get erroneous results!

c. Arguments can be any of the eight PHP data types, namely: integers, floating-point numbers, strings, booleans, arrays, objects, resources (or handles) and even null. (Although passing a null value to a function is a rarity.)

d. There is no limit to the number of arguments you can pass to a function. However, it is impractical to use more than five or six. Imagine the difficulty and high probability of errors if you define and use a function that required more than six arguments!

**TIP:** By using arrays, you can pass any number of arguments to functions but still keep the interface simple because you are only passing one variable, the array, to the function.

Let's work on some examples.

**1** **Step 1**: Create a new PHP *function script container file* in a PHP template and use the file name *functionArgs.php*.

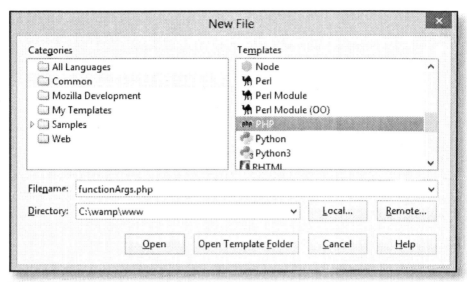

Figure 6.17: Komodo Edit's New File dialogue window for the file *functionArgs.php*.

**2** **Step 2**: Save it in your www or htdocs folder.

**3** **Step 3**: In the *functionArgs.php* file, create the function named *dogAgeCalc()* and pass the parameter *$dogAge* to the function.

```php
<?php
function dogAgeCalc($dogAge)
    {
```

**4** **Step 4**: Write the code that will multiply the dog's age by seven.

```php
    $humanAge = $dogAge*7;
print("The dog's age in human years is " .
$humanAge .".");
```

**5** **Step 5:** Close the script.

This script will calculate a dog's given age in human years. For

example, if the dog is 7 years old he would be equivalent to a 49-year-old human. Here is the complete code listing for the dog age calculator.

## CODE LISTING: FUNCTIONARGS.PHP

```php
<?php
    function dogAgeCalc($dogAge)
    {
        $humanAge = $dogAge*7;
        print("The dog's age in human
years is " . $humanAge .".");
    }
?>
```

If you attempt to run the code, it will display a blank output because no value is assigned yet to the variable *$age*. This is how the script's output will look:

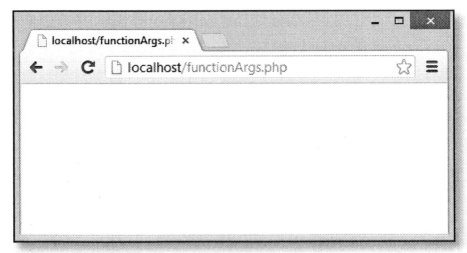

Figure 6.18: Output for *functionArgs.php* when ran.

Now to make this *php function* container file useful, we have to create another PHP document written in an HTML template.

**6** **Step 6:** Open a new HTML document template and name the file *computeDogAge.php*.

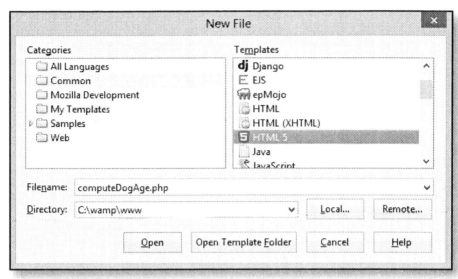

**7** **Step 7:** Include the opening and closing PHP script tags. In the <head> section of the document, *include()* the PHP function container file *functionArgs.php*. The calls to the *include()* and *require()* function must reside in the <head> section.

```
<!DOCTYPE html
<html>
<head>
<title>Dog Age Calculator</title>
    <?php include("functionArgs.php"); ?>
</head>
```

**8** **Step 8:** Call the function *dogAgeCalc* in the <body> section and assign the value five to *$age*, which is then passed to the *function*.

```
<body>
    <?php
        dogAgeCalc(5);
```

**Step 9**: Close the script and the document.

```
    ?>
</body>
</html>
```

The complete code listing and output are shown as follows:

## CODE LISTING: COMPUTEDOGAGE.PHP

```php
<!DOCTYPE html>
<html>
<head>
<title>Dog Age Calculator</title>
    <?php include("functionArgs.php"); ?>
</head>
<body>
    <?php
        dogAgeCalc(5);
    ?>
</body>
</html>
```

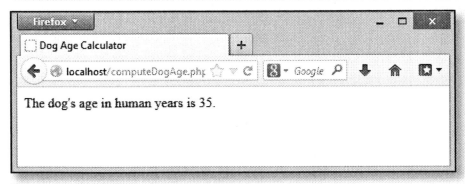

Figure 6.20: Output for *computeDogAge.php* when ran.

# 6.6 THE RETURN STATEMENT

PHP functions can return only a single value with the *return* statement. The *return* statement is optional but if no return value is provided by the function, the function (on its own) will return null. The syntax for the *return* statement is:

**Return**

```
return expression;
```

> **TIP:** Just in case you have forgotten just what an *expression* is, you can review section 1 of chapter 4 "Simple Control Structure—*If* Statement".

What if you want to return more than one value from a function? Use an array!

Note, however, that if a function returns more than one value, this might be an indication of bad design. Keep in mind that a function should accomplish only one task!

Let's take a look at the following example.

The *square(int)* function accepts an integer as a parameter and returns the square of that integer.

## CODE LISTING: RETURNEXAMPLE1_INTERNAL.PHP

```php
<!DOCTYPE html>
<html>
<head>
    <?php
        function square($value)
        {
            $value = $value*$value;
            return($value);
        }
    ?>
<title>Return Function Example 1</title>
</head>
```

```
<body>
    <?php
        print("The value of 2 squared is "
. square(2). ".");
    ?>
</body>
</html>
```

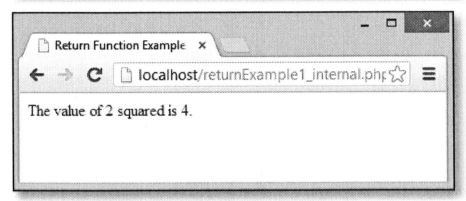

Figure 6.21: Output for *returnExample1_internal.php*.

Now, let's modify the script so that the return value of the function *square()* is stored in the variable *$x*.

```
<body>
    <?php
print("The value of 2 squared is " .
square(2));

        $x = square(25);
```

Now, add a *print()* statement to print the value of *$x*.

```
print("</br> The value of the returned
number is " . $x);
```

Your updated code listing and output should now be:

## CODE LISTING: RETURNEXAMPLE2_INTERNAL.PHP

```
<!DOCTYPE html>
<html>
<head>
<title>Return Function Example 2</title>
    <?php
        function square($value)
        {
            $value = $value*$value;
            return($value);
        }
    ?>
</head>
<body>
    <?php
        print("The value of 2 squared is "
. square(2));
        $x = square(25);
        print("</br> The value of the
returned number is " . $x);
    ?>
</body>
</html>
```

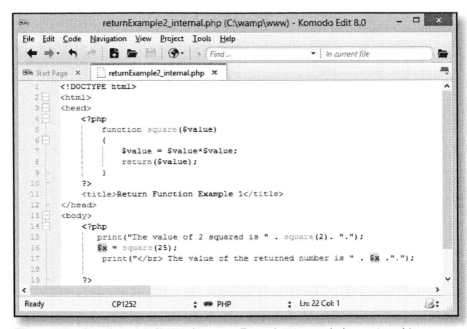

Figure 6.22: Complete code listing for *returnExample2_internal.php* as viewed in Komodo Edit.

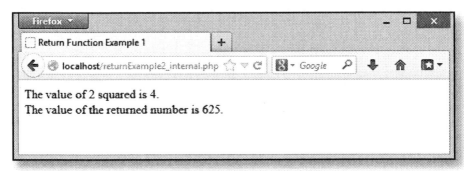

Figure 6.23: Output for *returnExample2_internal.php* when ran.

## QUESTIONS FOR REVIEW

1. What are functions?
   a. Blocks of related code that are stored under a specific keyword that may be called and repeatedly used.
   b. Equations that produce a curve.
   c. A complete code listing that performs a preset process in PHP.
   d. Keywords consisting of code, functions and commands.

2. What are arguments?
   a. Values or strings that are passed into a function.
   b. A collision of two or more different opinions.
   c. Variables that contain a specific value.
   d. Comma separated values that complete a function.

3. How does the return statement work?
   a. Return ends the execution of a function and returns a value to the caller of the function.
   b. Return will make the code start from a no-value argument and repeat itself.
   c. Return prints out the value that was passed onto a function.
   d. Return processes the list of operations and then returns the result.

4. Which function will produce an error and terminate the script if the filename passed to that function as an argument cannot be found?
   a. include
   b. include_once
   c. require
   d. None of the above.

# CHAPTER 6 LAB EXERCISE

1. Write a function that will convert Celsius temperatures to Fahrenheit. Write another function that will convert Fahrenheit temperatures to Celsius. Here are the formulas.

Formulas:
Fahrenheit to Celsius: Tc = (5/9)*(Tf-32)
Celsius to Fahrenheit: Tf = (9/5)*Tc+32

Use the following parameters for this first exercise:

    a. Value to convert: 50
    b. Function name for:
        Fahrenheit to Celsius conversion – Celsius ( )
        Celsius to Fahrenheit conversion –Fahrenheit ( )
    c. Function parameter variable: $temp

Use the two-document method to accomplish this. The first document should be the *function container file* named *tempCalcFunc.php*. The second document is the *chap6Lab1_Sol.php* saved using an HTML document template.
Use the function *include* to reference the container file. Display the result as a two decimal floating point number.

2. Modify your program so that the user can enter a temperature value using a form. Radio buttons will be used to indicate whether the temperature is in Celsius or Fahrenheit. When the user clicks the submit button the corresponding result must be displayed.

Use the same function container file used in Lab Exercise 1, *tempCalcFunc.php*. Create another PHP script file in an HTML document template for the form. Use the filename *chap6Lab2_Sol.php*.

# CHAPTER 6 LAB SOLUTION:

## CODE LISTING: TEMPCALCFUNC.PHP

```php
<?php
    function Celsius($temp)
    {
        $temp = ((($temp*9)/5)+32);
        print("The value in Fahrenheit is
");
        return($temp);
    }
    function Fahrenheit($temp)
    {
        $temp = (($temp-32)*5/9);
        print("The value in Celsius is ");
        return($temp);
    }
?>
```

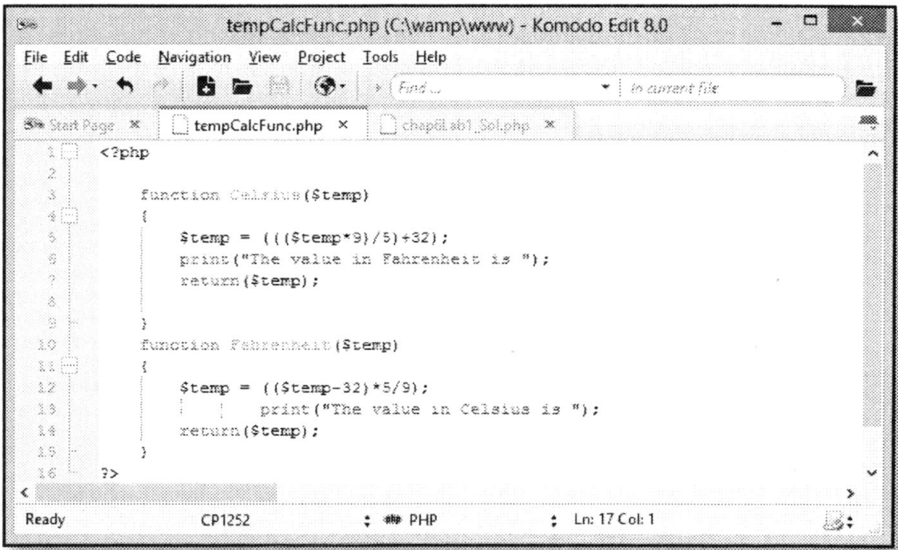

Figure 6.24: Complete code listing for *tempCalcFunc.php* as viewed in Komodo Edit.

## CODE LISTING: CHAP6LAB1_SOL.PHP

```php
<!DOCTYPE html>
<html>
<head>
<title>Chapter 6 Lab Exercise 1</title>
    <?php
        include("tempCalcFunc.php");
    ?>
</head>
<body>
    <?php
        printf("%0.2f", Celsius(50));
        print (".");
        print ("<br/>");
        printf("%0.2f", Fahrenheit(50));
        print (".");
    ?>
</body>
</html>
```

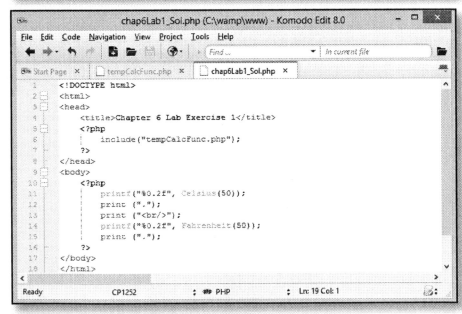

Figure 6.25: Complete code listing for *chap6Lab1_Sol.php* as viewed in Komodo Edit.

## CODE LISTING: TEMPCALCFUNC2.PHP

```php
<?php
    $tempInput = $_POST['temp'];
    $cond = $_POST['type'];
    $newTemp = 0;

function Celsius($temp)
    {
        $temp = ((($temp*9)/5)+32);
        return($temp);
    }
function Fahrenheit($temp)
    {
        $temp = ((($temp-32)*5)/9);
        return($temp);
    }

if($cond == "1")
    {
        $newTemp = celsius($tempInput);
        echo("The temperature in
Fahrenheit is " . $newTemp.".");
    }
        else if($cond == "2")
    {
        $newTemp = fahrenheit($tempInput);
        echo("The temperature in Celsius
is " . $newTemp.".");
    }
?>
<form action="chap6Lab2_Sol.php">
<input type="submit" value="Return" />
</form>
```

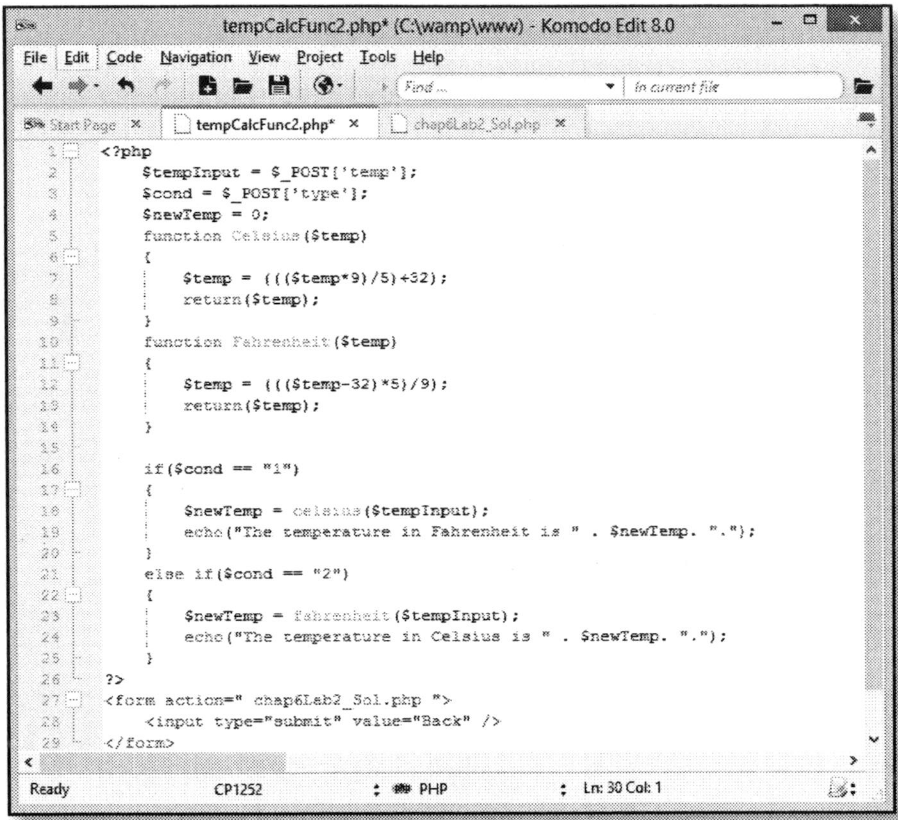
tempCalcFunc2.php* (C:\wamp\www) - Komodo Edit 8.0
File Edit Code Navigation View Project Tools Help
Find ...
In current file
Start Page
tempCalcFunc2.php*
chap6Lab2_Sol.php
<?php
$tempInput = $_POST['temp'];
$cond = $_POST['type'];
$newTemp = 0;
function Celsius($temp)
{
$temp = ((($temp*9)/5)+32);
return($temp);
}
function Fahrenheit($temp)
{
$temp = ((($temp-32)*5)/9);
return($temp);
}
if($cond == "1")
{
$newTemp = celsius($tempInput);
echo("The temperature in Fahrenheit is " . $newTemp. ".");
}
else if($cond == "2")
{
$newTemp = fahrenheit($tempInput);
echo("The temperature in Celsius is " . $newTemp. ".");
}
?>
<form action=" chap6Lab2_Sol.php ">
<input type="submit" value="Back" />
</form>
Ready
CP1252
PHP
Ln: 30 Col: 1

**Figure 6.26**: Complete code listing for *tempCalcFunc2.php* as viewed in Komodo Edit.

## CODE LISTING: CHAP6LAB2_SOL.PHP

```html
<!DOCTYPE html>
<html>
<head>
<title>Chapter 6 Lab Exercise 2</title>
</head>
<body>
    <form action="tempCalcFunc2.php"
method="post">
    <table>
        <tr>
            <td colspan=2><strong>Enter the
temperature value and choose<br/>if it's in
Celsius or Fahrenheit:</strong></th>
        </tr>
        <tr>
            <td>Temperature</th>
            <td align="left"><input
type="text" name="temp"/></td>
        </tr>
        <tr>
            <td>Celsius
            <input type="radio" name="type"
value="1"/></th>
            <td>Fahrenheit
            <input type="radio" name="type"
value="2"/></th>
        </tr>
        <tr>
            <td align="left"><input
type="submit" value="Submit"/></td>
            <td align="left"><input
type="reset" value="Clear"/></td>
        </tr>
    </table>
    </form>
</body>
</html>
```

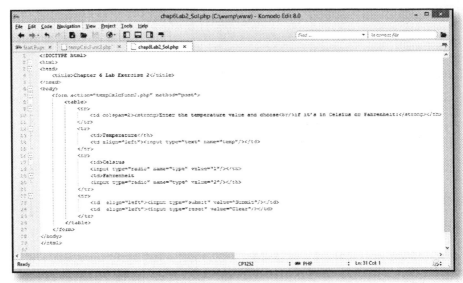

Figure 6.27: Complete code listing for *chap6Lab2_Sol.php* as viewed in Komodo Edit.

## Output: Conversion from Celsius to Fahrenheit.

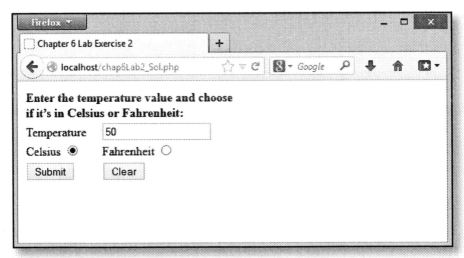

Figure 6.28: Output for Chapter 6 Lab Solution default page. The text box accepts the temperature value of 50 degrees Celsius.

Figure 6.28: Output after clicking the submit button: 50 degrees Celsius is converted to 122 degrees Fahrenheit.

## Output: Conversion from Fahrenheit to Celsius.

Figure 6.29: Chapter 6 Lab Solution default page. The text box accepts the temperature value of 50 degrees Fahrenheit.

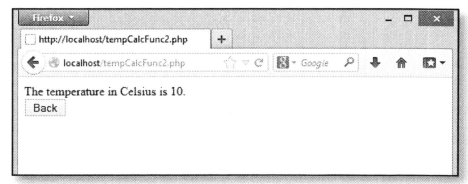

Figure 6.30: After clicking the submit button, 50 degrees Fahrenheit is converted to 10 degrees Celsius.

# Chapter Summary:

In this chapter, we covered only the fundamentals of functions, namely:

a. how to call or execute functions
b. how to create your own functions
c. how to organize your functions among several *function container files*
d. how to include the functions in *function container files* into your PHP scripts
e. how to pass arguments into a function's parameters
f. how to return a value from a function

In the next chapter we will discuss Server-File Input-Output. You will learn how files in the server are manipulated and be introduced to the different commands and functions used to perform these file processes.

# CHAPTER 7
## SERVER FILE I/O

**CHAPTER OBJECTIVES:**

- You will be able to define what server files are.
- You will be able to describe the rudiments of server files.
- You will learn how to access files on the server: read, write, open, close, append and delete.
- You will be able to describe what CSV files are and how to manipulate and organize these files into a usable form.

## 7.1 SERVING FILES ON THE SERVER

When we talk about files, we think of database files which are a compilation of tables consisting of identically formatted records. In web development, the word **file** is not limited to database files, as almost anything that appears more than once in a webpage automatically comprises a file.

When you visit Gmail or Yahoo Mail for instance, the aggregate user signups will constitute the user files. The emails that are stored in each of these accounts comprise the messages file. Collections of pictures, videos, and music on a webpage are all files, too.

The same goes for social networking sites such as Facebook, Twitter, LinkedIn, and Instagram. Most information found on their websites—including the comments, chats, and private messages—are all files. So are "likes" and all other postings. These files reside inside the server hosting these websites and get manipulated—read, written, opened, closed, appended and deleted—as the needs arise.

Commercial and business sites such as Oracle, Adobe, Linux, and Microsoft, including banking establishments and e-commerce portals, keep and treat almost all webpages, URL elements, and information as files.

Therefore, almost all website information is stored as files, which are then classified according to use, privilege, and security. Altogether they comprise an information database.

Now that we have a broad understanding of what server
files are and what comprises a server file, what does the term **file I/O**
or file input/ output mean in the context of PHP?

In PHP, *file input/output* concerns accessing files only on the server—
not on the local machine of the web browser. Primarily for security
reasons, we cannot let PHP scripts access any of the files on a local
machine.

Here is a list of functions that are introduced in this chapter and are
used in PHP server file input/output operations:

## PHP SERVER FILE INPUT/OUTPUT OPERATIONS

| Function | Description | Arguments |
|----------|-------------|-----------|
| fopen() | Opens a file. | File pointer, access mode |
| fclose() | Closes a file. | File pointer, access mode |
| fwrite() | Writes into a file that was opened in the server. | File pointer, resource file |
| fgets() | Reads a single line from a file. | Resource file, character size |
| fgetc() | Reads a single character from a file. | Resource file |
| file_get_contents() | Reads entire file into a string. | Resource file, character size |
| fread() | Reads from an open file. | File pointer, character size |
| fgetcsv() | Reads saved CSV files. | File pointer, character size |
| foef() | Checks if the "end of file" has been reached. *Limitations:* files opened in w, a, x modes cannot be read. | File pointer |

| unlink() | Deletes files. | Resource file |
| Or die() | Terminates a program if an error is encountered during the input or output process. Usually connected to the function *fopen*. | String parameter |
| filesize() | Gets the file size in bytes. | Null or integer value |

Table 7.1 List of commands and functions introduced.

Some file functions require specific *modes* as one of their arguments. These modes specify the type of access. Here is a list of *modes* used in PHP when calling the **fopen()** function.

| Mode | Description |
| --- | --- |
| r | Opens the file for reading only. The *file pointer* is positioned at the beginning of the file. |
| r+ | Opens the file for reading and writing. The *file pointer* is positioned at the beginning of the file. |
| w | Opens the file for writing only. Opens and clears the contents of files or creates a new file if it does not exist. In either case, you have a new empty file for writing data and the *file pointer* is positioned at the beginning of the file. |
| w+ | Opens the file for reading and writing. Opens and clears the contents of files or creates a new file if it does not exist. The *file pointer* is positioned at the beginning of the file. |
| a | Opens the file for appending (writing). Writes data to the end of an existing file. Creates a new file if it doesn't exist. The *file pointer* is positioned at the end of the file. |
| a+ | Opens the file for appending (writing) and reading. Writes data to the end of an existing file. Creates a new file if it doesn't exist. The *file pointer* is positioned at the end of the file. |
| x | Opens the file for writing only. Creates a new file. Returns FALSE and an error if the file already exists. |
| x+ | Opens the file for reading and writing. Creates a new file. Returns FALSE and an error if file already exists. |

Table 7.2 PHP file access modes.

We will begin our examples with a script that writes data to a text file and then a script which will retrieve the contents of that same text file.

**PROBLEM:** Code a PHP script that writes data, consisting of names, to a text file.

**SOLUTION:**

**1** **Step 1**: Begin by using Komodo Edit to create a new PHP document using the HTML document template.

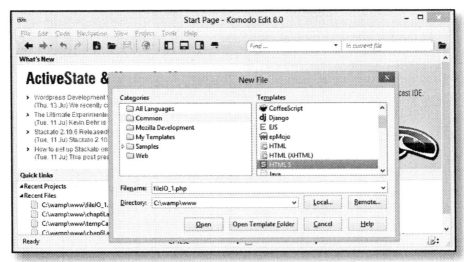

Figure 7.1: Creating a new HTML template to be named *fileIO_1.php* in Komodo Edit.

**2** **Step 2**: Save the file in your www or htdocs folder under the name *fileIO_1.php*

**3** **Step 3**: The name of the file we will write to is *"names.txt"* and we will store this filename in the variable *$fileName*.

```
<!DOCTYPE html>
<html>
<head>
    <title>Saving Files into the Server</
title>
</head>
<body>
    <?php
    $fileName = "names.txt";
```

**4** **Step 4**: Next we will access "names.txt" by using the **fopen()** function which takes two arguments, the *filename*, and the *mode*. This is the correct format for the **fopen()** function.

```
fopen($fileName, 'w')
```

The mode that we use is '**w**' which means to open the file for writing only.

**fopen()**

Now, the **fopen()** function returns a *file handle* which, among other uses, is a pointer associated with the file we opened and which we use to access the file's contents. We will store the *file handle* in the variable *$fp*. Our updated format for the **fopen()** function is now:

```
$fp = fopen($fileName, 'w')
```

**Tip:** *File handles* are *resource data types* which is one of the eight PHP data types. The file handle and not the filename is the primary means by which we perform input and output operations on the file. Every file that our program accesses must be assigned a unique *file handle*.

The **fopen()** function is usually connected with the command **or die,** which terminates the program and displays the error message "Can't open the file" if an error is encountered during the execution of the **fopen()** function. Our final program statement for the **fopen()** function is:

```
$fp = fopen($fileName, 'w') or die
("Can't open the file.");
```

Now that the **fopen()** function has successfully accessed *names.txt* by returning a *file handle* to it, we can start writing data to it. When we have completed writing data to it, we use the **fclose()** function.

**fclose()**

Every **fopen()** function must have a matching **fclose()** function. Failing to close a file properly with the **fclose()** function after accessing the file with the **fopen()** function could lead to some data corruption problems.

When you call the **fclose()** function, the server's file input-output system performs critical housekeeping tasks on the file. It could perform these housekeeping tasks during the various read, write, and update tasks on the file, but that would be grossly inefficient.

**5** **Step 5:** Now, we call the **fclose()** function, providing the file handle as the function's required argument.

```
fclose($fp);
```

**6** **Step 6:** Close the script and the HTML document.

```
    ?>
</body>
</html>

This is how the complete code listing will
look:

Code Listing: fileIO_1.php

<!DOCTYPE html>
<html>
<head>
    <title>Saving Files into the Server</
title>
</head>
<body>
    <?php
    $fileName = "names.txt";
    $fp = fopen($fileName, 'w') or die
("Can't open the file.");
    fclose($fp);
    ?>
</body>
</html>
```

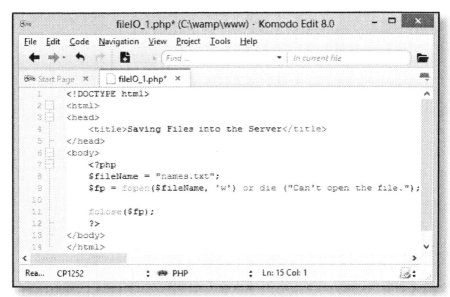

Figure 7.2: Initial code listing for *fileIO_1.php* as seen in Komodo Edit.

We now have the skeleton of most PHP input/output programs. In this skeleton, we specify the filename, call the **fopen()** function and then call the **fclose()** function.

Now, let's write the PHP code that actually writes data to the file *name. txt*. We declare a list of names and save it as an array, then create a loop that will iterate through the array.

**7** Step 7: Using the *array* function, create an array (referenced by the variable *$name*) whose members are the names *John, Guile, Lily, Ervin, Adam, Mary,* and *Irene*.

```
    $name = array("John", "Guile", "Lily",
 "Ervin", "Adam", "Mary", "Irene");
```

**8** Step 8: Now, we will store the names in array variable *$name* in the file *name.txt* We do this by looping through each member of the array and using the **fwrite()** function to write each name. At the end of each name, we append the *line-feed* character "\n". The *line-feed* character indicates where one name ends and another begins. It also indicates where we want a new line to begin.

**fwrite()**

```
for($i = 0; $i<=count($name);  $i++) {
        fwrite($fp, $name[$i] . "\n");
    }
```

The **fwrite()** function requires two arguments. First is the *file handle*, *$fp*, of the file **fwrite()** will write to. Second is the data to be written – the array member, *$name[$i]*.

This is how the complete code listing should look:

### CODE LISTING: APPENDED FILEIO_1.PHP

```
<!DOCTYPE html>
<html>
<head>
    <title>Saving Files into the Server</
title>
</head>
<body>
    <?php
    $fileName = "names.txt";
    $fp = fopen($fileName, 'w') or die
("Can't open the file");
    $name = array("John", "Guile", "Lily",
"Ervin", "Adam", "Mary", "Irene");
    for($i = 0; $i<=count($name);  $i++) {
        fwrite($fp, $name[$i] . "\n");
    }

    fclose($fp);
    ?>
</body>
</html>
```

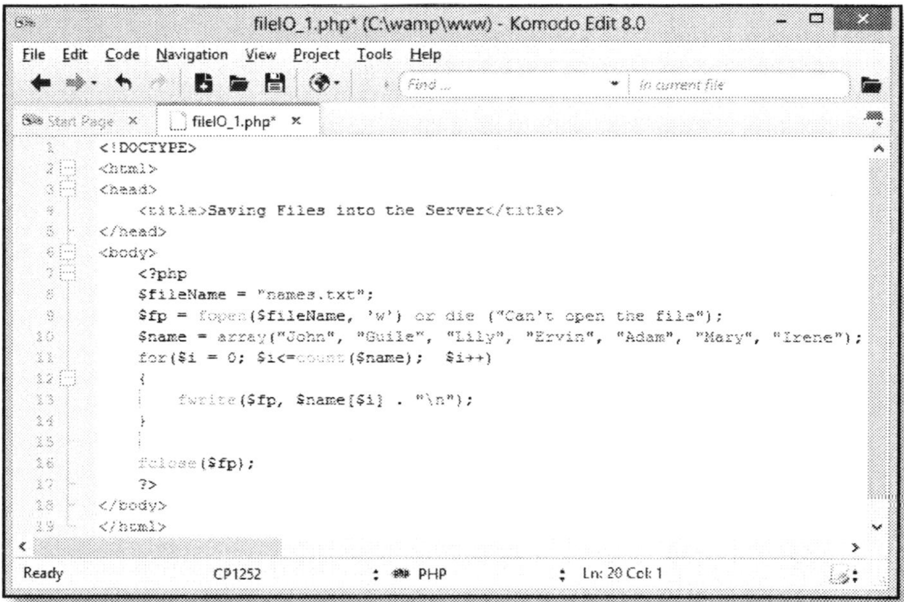

Figure 7.3: Complete code listing for *fileIO_1.php* as seen in Komodo Edit.

We'll run the program now only to check if the *names.txt* file was actually saved or written in your local server. Make sure you have saved your *fileIO_1.php* file.

Run *fileIO_1.php* from your local browser. For now, disregard any error message that displays.

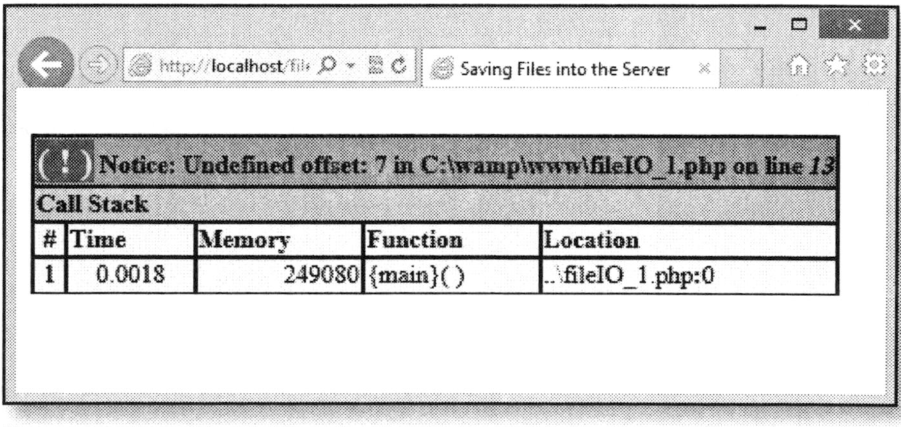

Figure 7.4: Output for *fileIO_1.php* when first ran.

Now that the page is running, we can check our special htdocs or www folder to look for the file *names.txt*.

Open your wamp/www or mamp/htdocs folder:

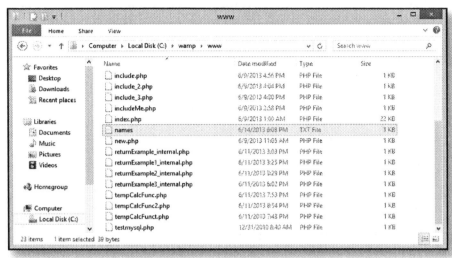

Figure 7.5: *Names.txt* opened through document browser.

Click on the filename and select "view using Notepad". Take note that when you open the text file it will display the names as a continuous single word text, as Notepad ignores the *line feed* character.

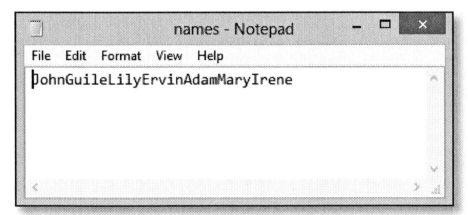

Figure 7.6: *Names.txt* viewed using Notepad.

Try viewing the *names.txt* file using another application such as WordPad and you will notice it displays the array members as a list:

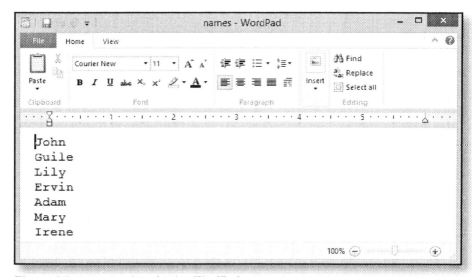

Figure 7.7: *names.txt* viewed using WordPad.

Here we can see the effect of the *line feed* character we appended to each name before writing that name to the text file using the **fwrite()** function:

```
fwrite($fp, $name[$i] . "\n");
```

WordPad interpreted the *line feed* character as an indicator to begin a new line. On the other hand, Notepad ignores the *line feed* character.

# 7.2 READING FILES ON THE SERVER

Now that the file *names.txt* has been written, or saved in the server, we are going to retrieve its contents. We will use three of PHP's frequently used file data retrieval functions, **fread()**, **file_get_contents()**, and **fgets()**.

The **fread()** function reads a string of characters from a file. It requires two arguments: a file handle (of *resource* data type) and the number of characters to read (of *integer* data type). An example is:

**fread()**

```
$string = fread($fp, 20);
```

In that example, 20 characters are read from the file pointed to by the *file handler $fp* and then stored in the variable *$string*. After this, the file pointer will be positioned at the $21^{st}$ character in the file.

**PROBLEM:** Read the entire contents of the file *names.txt* using the **fread()** function.

## SOLUTION:

**1** **Step 1:** Open *fileIO_1.php* in Komodo Edit and delete all program statements between the calls to the **fopen()** and **fclose()** functions.

**2** **Step 2:** Change the text between the <title> tags from "Saving Files into the Server" to "Reading Files from the Server."

**3** **Step 3:** In the call to the function **fopen()**, change the second argument, the mode, from 'w' to 'r'. The 'r' parameter means that we will access the file just to read its data.

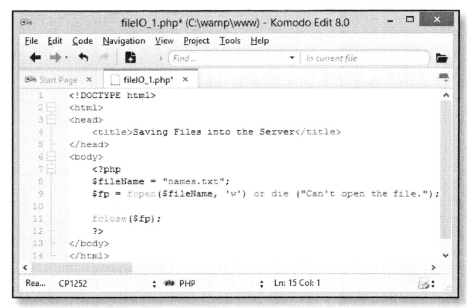

Figure 7.8: The program *fileIO_1.php* as reproduced from Figure 7.2 which we will save as *readFile_1.php*. All code between the calls to *fopen()* and *fclose()* has been removed.

 **Step 4:** Save your document as *readfile_1.php*. This is how your code listing should look after this step:

## CODE LISTING: READFILE_1.PHP

```php
<!DOCTYPE html>
<html>
<head>
    <title>Reading Files From The Server</title>
</head>
<body>
    <?php
        $fileName = "names.txt";
        $fp = fopen($fileName, 'r');
        fclose($fp);
    ?>
</body>
</html>
```

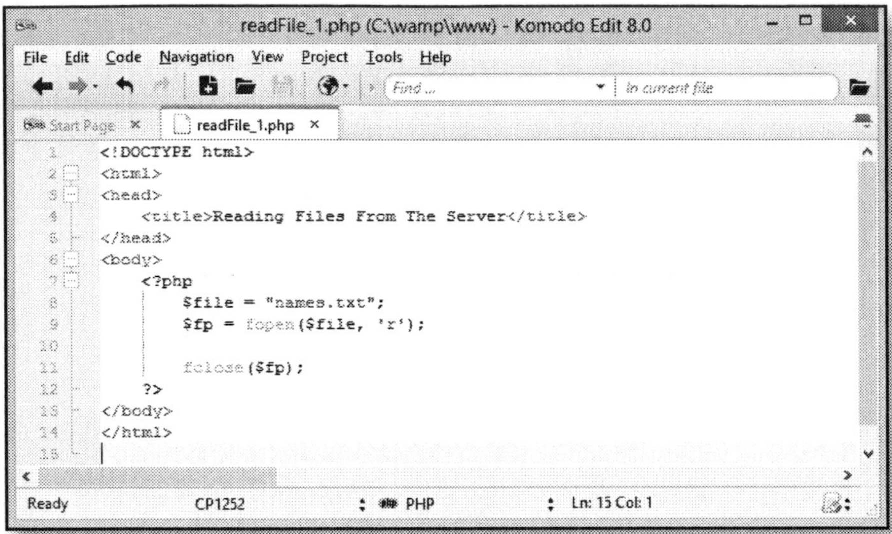

Figure 7.9: Complete code listing for *readFile_1.php* as seen in Komodo Edit.

**5** **Step 5:** Just after the call to **fopen()**, type the call to **fread()**.

```
$string = fread($fp, 20);
```

This is how the complete code listing should look:

## CODE LISTING: READFILE_2.PHP

```
<!DOCTYPE>
<html>
<head>
    <title>Reading Files From The Server</title>
</head>
<body>
    <?php
        $fileName = "names.txt";
        $fp = fopen($fileName, 'r');
        $string = fread($fp, 20);
        fclose($fp);
        echo($string);
```

```
      ?>
   </body>
   </html>
```

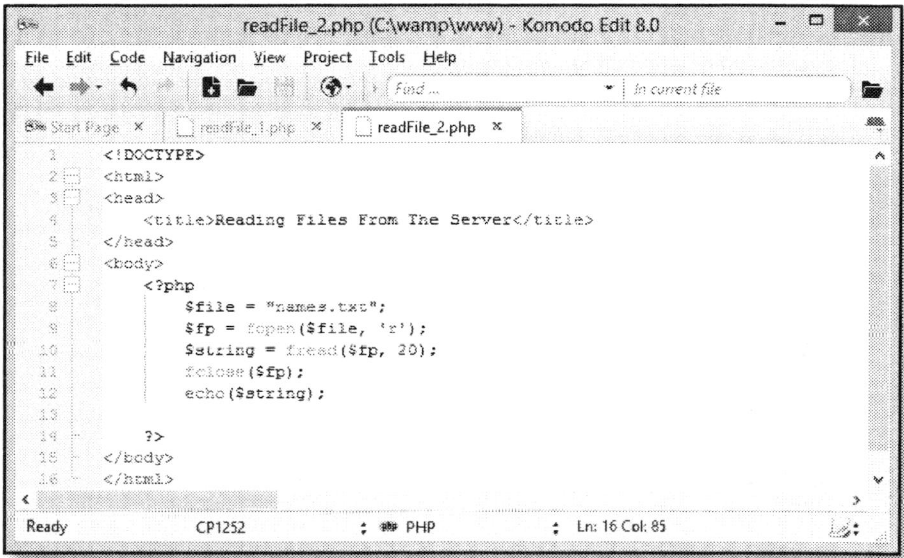

Figure 7.10: Complete code listing for *readFile_2.php*.

If we run the script, this is what the output will be:

John Guile Lily Ervi

Figure 7.11: Output of *readFile_2.php* when ran.

As you can see, not all the names were displayed in the browser because **fread()** retrieved only 20 characters, as we commanded it to do. To know exactly how many bytes to read from a file, we need the **filesize()** function, which will tell us exactly how many bytes are in a particular file.

**filesize()**

**1** **Step 1**: Create a new file and name it as *readFile_3.php*. Copy the code written in *readFile_2.php* exactly.

**2** **Step 2**: Locate the line which contains the call to **fread()**. Modify it from:

```
$string = fread($fp, 20);
```

to:

```
$string = fread($fp, filesize($file));
```

Note that the **filesize()** function accepts one argument, the *file handle* of the file it will access.

**3** **Step 3**: Check your whole code listing. Your updated code listing must now be:

```
<!DOCTYPE html>

<html>
<head>
    <title>Reading Files From The Server</title>
</head>
<body>
    <?php
        $fileName = "names.txt";
        $fp = fopen($fileName, 'r');
        $string = fread($fp,
filesize($file));
        fclose($fp);
        echo($string);
    ?>
</body>
</html
```

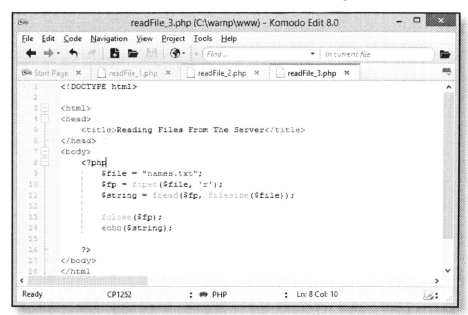

Figure 7.12: Complete code listing for readFile_3.php.

**4** **Step 4:** Run the script and view your output.

Figure 7.13: Output of readFile_3.php when run.

As you can see, the entire content of *names.txt* now gets displayed in the browser.

Let's read another text file still using the **fread()** and **filesize()** functions.

**5** **Step 5:** Create a new text file consisting of ten animal names and their corresponding scientific names as listed in the following table values. Save the new text file as *names_2.txt*. Make sure you save your new text file inside your www or htdocs folder.

| Common Name | Scientific Name |
| --- | --- |
| Ant | Hymenopterous formicidae |
| Bat | Chiroptera |
| Bear | Ursidae Carnivora |
| Camel | Camelus Camelidae |
| Cat | Felis Catus |
| Dog | Canis Familiaris |
| Frog | Anura Ranidae |
| Lion | Panthera Leo |
| Sheep | Bovidae Ovis |
| Tiger | Panthera Tigris |

Table 7.3: List of names for *names_2.txt*

You may use Komodo Edit to create and save your *names_2.txt* file.

Figure 7.14: *names_2.txt* file created using Komodo Edit.

**6**  **Step 6**: Change the line which assigns the string "names.txt" to the variable *$fileName* from:

```
$fileName = "names.txt";
```

to:

```
$fileName = "names_2.txt";
```

This is how your complete code listing should now look.

```
<!DOCTYPE html>

<html>
<head>
    <title>Reading Files From The Server</title>
</head>
<body>
    <?php
        $fileName = "names_2.txt";
        $fp = fopen($fileName, 'r');
        $string = fread($fp,
filesize($file));
        fclose($fp);
        echo($string);
    ?>
</body>
</html
```

**7**  **Step 7:** Save your file.

**8**  **Step 8:** Run your code and display the output.

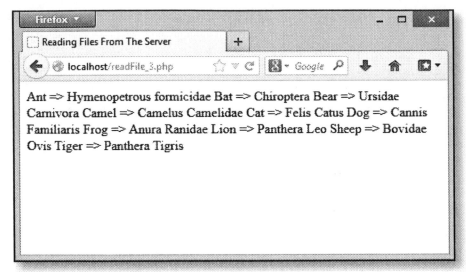

Figure 7.15: Output of *readFile_3.php* when run.

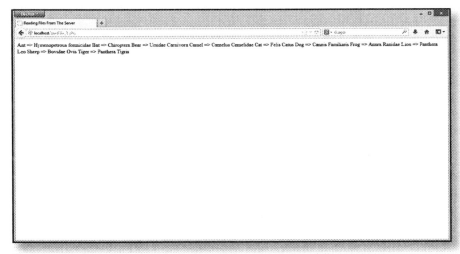

Figure 7.16: Output of *readFile_3.php* when run, viewed on full screen.

Figure 7.16 is a full screen version of Figure 7.15. Notice that whether your browser is shrunk, stretched, resized or maximized, you will see the common and scientific animal names displayed as one continuous line of text.

**file_get_contents()**

Now, let's use the **file_get_contents()** function to read *names_2.txt*. This function reads the contents of an entire file into a string without using a *file handle*. Therefore, we don't need to call the **fopen()** or **fclose()** functions.

**1** Step 1: Create a new HTML5 document template and name the file *readFile_4.php*. Save it in your www or htdocs folder.

**2** Step 2: Type the following code exactly as you see here.

## CODE LISTING: READFILE_4.PHP

```
<!DOCTYPE html>

<html>
<head>
    <title>Reading Files From The Server</
title>
</head>
<body>
    <?php
        $file = "names.txt";
        $string = file_get_contents($file);
        echo($string);
    ?>
</body>
</html>
```

You can see that our code is much simpler. We do not have to call the **fopen()** and **fclose()** functions. We just call the **file_get_contents()** function with two arguments: the name of the file we want to read and a Boolean value of either *true* or *false*.

The Boolean parameter TRUE in the *$string* assignment statement simply means to include the path in accessing the file. Since both our script and text files are in the www or htdocs folder, this second parameter has no effect.

---

Tip: The **file_get_contents()** function can accept up to five parameters. The first, the *filename*, is required, while the remaining four are optional. You can check out http://www.php. net/file_get_contents for more details on this function.

---

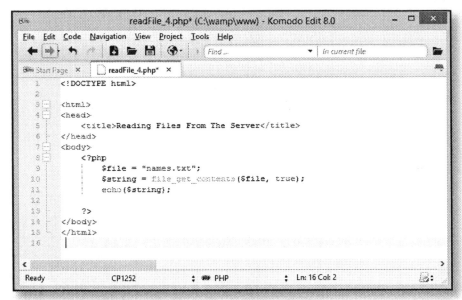

Figure 7.17: Code listing for *readFile_4.php*.

**3** **Step 3**: Save your file and run your output.

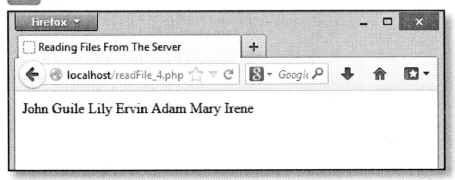

Figure 7.18: Output of *readFile_4.php* when ran.

The **file_get_contents()** function extracted the entire file content all at once and only in a matter of a few command lines.

Now, we will use the **fgets()** function to read our files. This function requires a *file handler* and so we will have to open the file with **fopen()** and then eventually close it with **fclose()**. Now, **fgets()** reads bytes from a file until it encounters a *line-feed* character or the end-of-file marker. It then stops reading bytes and leaves the file pointer at the character right after the *line-feed* character it encountered.

**fgets()**

**1** Step 1: Open an HTML5 document template and save this program as *readFile_5.php* in your www or htdocs folder.

**2** Step 2: Start off your code by including the PHP script tags.

```
<!DOCTYPE html>
<html>
<head>
    <title>Reading Files From The Server</title>
</head>
<body>
    <?php
```

**3** Step 3: Store the string "names.txt" in the variable *$fileName*.

```
$fileName = "names.txt";
```

**4** Step 4: Call the **fopen()** function using *read* mode.

```
$fp = fopen($fileName, 'r');
```

**5** Step 5: Call the **fgets()** function using the file handler variable *$fp* as the function's argument. We store the bytes that **fget()** will read from the file in the variable *$string*.

```
$string = fgets($fp);
```

**6** Step 6: Call **fclose()** and display the contents of *$string* with the **echo()** function.

```
fclose($fp);
echo($string);
```

```
    ?>
</body>
</html>
```

**7** Step 7: Close the PHP script tag and the HTML document. Be sure to save your document.

**8** Step 8: Your complete code listing should look like this:

## CODE LISTING: READFILE_5.PHP

```
<!DOCTYPE html>
<html>
<head>
    <title>Reading Files From The Server</
title>
</head>
<body>
    <?php
        $fileName = "names.txt";
        $fp = fopen($fileName, 'r');
        $string = fgets($fp);
        fclose($fp);
        echo($string);
    ?>
</body>
</html>
```

**9** Step 9: Run your script. You should see 'John' displayed in your browser.

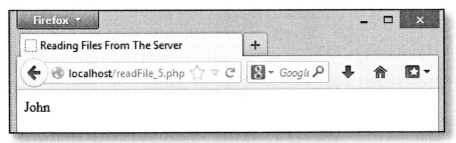

Figure 7.19: Output *readFile_5.php* when run.

Now let's use the same script to read the file *names_2.txt*.

**1** Step 1: With *readFile_5.php* still open in Komodo Edit, store the string "names_2.txt" in the variable *$fileName*.

```
        $fileName = "names_2.txt";
```

**Step 2:** Click on File >Save As... > and save the file as *readFile_6.php*.

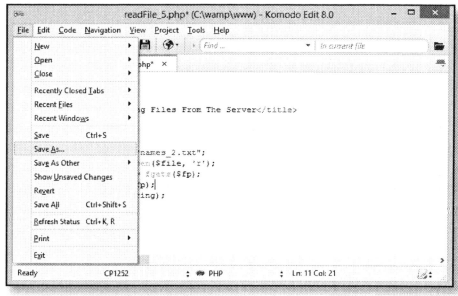

Figure 7.20: Save as dialogue box.

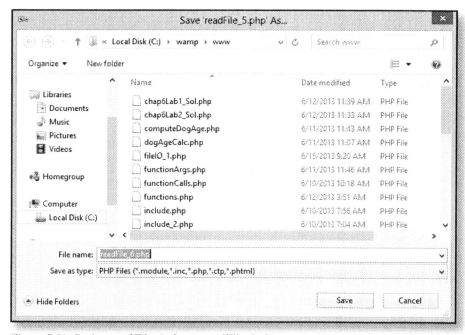

Figure 7.21: Saving *readFile_5.php* as *readFile_6.php*.

**3** **Step 3**: Run your script.

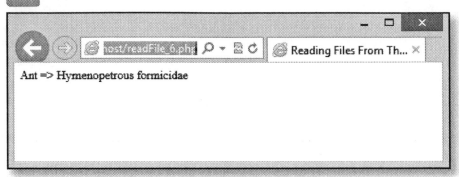

Figure 7.22: Output of *readFile_6.php* when ran.

You should see "Ant => Hymenopterous formicidae" in the browser.

Now, **fgets()** reads bytes from a file until it encounters a *line-feed* character or the end-of-file marker. It then stops reading bytes and leaves the file pointer at the character right after the *line-feed* character it encountered. So how can we read the entire file using the **fgets()** function?

We use a *while-loop* where we use the boolean **feof()** function as our conditional expression. This function returns TRUE if the *end-of-file* marker has been reached.

**feof()**

**1** **Step 1**: Create a new HTML5 document template. Include the PHP block script tags and name the file *readFile_7.php*.

```
<!DOCTYPE html>
<html>
<head>
    <title>Reading Files From The Server</title>
</head>
<body>
    <?php
```

**2** **Step 2:** Store the string "names.txt" in the variable *$fileName*.

```
$fileName = "names.txt";
```

**3** **Step 3:** Call the **fopen()** function using *read* mode.

```
$fp = fopen($fileName, 'r');
```

**4** **Step 4**: Initialize *$string* to the empty string "".

```
$string = "";
```

We need to do this because each time **fgets()** reads a line from the file we are accessing, we will append this line to *$string*. Initializing *$string* to an empty string makes sure that we are appending strings to strings.

**5** **Step 5**: Create the *while-loop*.

```
while(!feof($fp))
{
    $string .= fgets($fp, 256);
    $string .= "<br/>";
}
```

**6** **Step 6**: Close the file pointer.

```
fclose($fp);
```

**7** **Step 7**: Display the file.

```
echo($string);
```

**8** **Step 8:** Close the PHP script tag and the HTML document.

```
    ?>
</body>
</html>
```

**9** **Step 9**: This is how the complete code listing will look:

## CODE LISTING: READFILE_7.PHP

```php
<!DOCTYPE html>
<html>
<head>
    <title>Reading Files From The Server</title>
</head>
<body>
    <?php
        $file = "names.txt";
        $fp = fopen($file, 'r');
        $string = "";
        while(!feof($fp))
        {
            $string .= fgets($fp, 256);
            $string .= "<br/>";
        }
        fclose($fp);
        echo($string);
    ?>
</body>
</html>
```

**10** Step 10: Run the script.

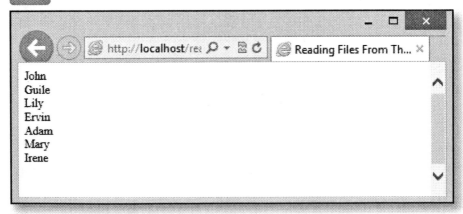

Figure 7.23: Output for *readFile_7.php*.

Each name is displayed on a different line.

Now, let's adjust the script to read *names_2.txt*. Store the string "names_2.txt" in the variable *$fileName* and then save the entire script as *readFile_8.php*. This is the complete code listing:

## CODE LISTING: READFILE_8.PHP

```
<!DOCTYPE html>
<html>
<head>
    <title>Reading Files From The Server</
title>
</head>
<body>
    <?php
        $file = "names 2.txt";
        $fp = fopen($file, 'r');
        $string = "";
        while(!feof($fp))
        {
            $string .= fgets($fp, 256);
            $string .= "<br/>";
        }
        fclose($fp);
        echo($string);
    ?>
</body>
</html>
```

Run *readFile_8.php* and view the output.

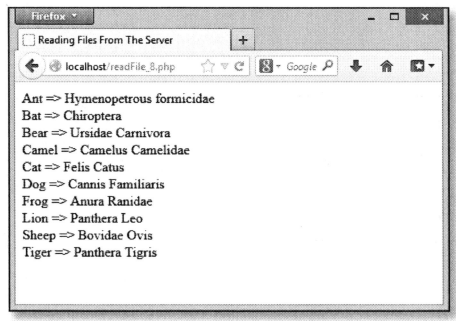

Figure 7.24: Output for *readFile_8.php*.

Here we have the complete list of animals and their scientific names as contained in the file *names_2.txt*.

# 7.3 APPEND AND DELETE

 **Appending** files in the server means the ability to add data to files. This new data is added to the end of the file, thus the term 'append'. Modifying or editing data that already exists in the file is more complicated and will not be discussed here.

To append or delete files, the file has to be opened first. The function used to open files is the familiar **fopen()** but with the *mode* set to 'a' which stands for 'append'.

**Fwrite()**, which we first used in our first example, *fileIO_1.php,* is the function we will use to append data to a server file. The function requires two arguments: the file pointer and the string of data to be written or appended to the file.

(Note also that in that first example, *fileIO_1.php,* we called **fopen()** with a 'w' mode. But here, we call **fopen()** with the 'a' mode. Why do you think that is?)

Now, let's diverge for a second and check to make sure that our WAMP server is still running and online. This is what we should see:

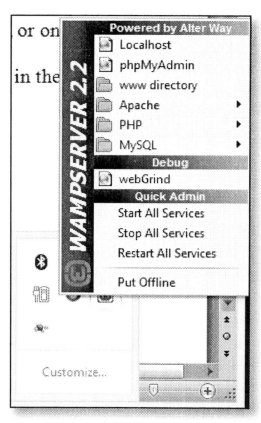

**1** **Step 1**: Create a new PHP file using the HTML5 template and save it in the www or htdocs folder. Save the file as *appendFile. php*.

Figure 7.25: WAMP server menu.

**2** **Step 2**: Embed the opening and closing PHP tags, declare the filename variable *$fileName* and call the **fopen()** function in mode 'a'. This should be your code:

```
<!DOCTYPE html>

<html>
<head>
    <title>Appending Files in the Server</title>
</head>

<body>

<?php
    $fileName = "names.txt";
    $fp = fopen($fileName, 'a');
```

**3** **Step 3**: We will be adding the names "John" and "Jane" to the file "names.txt" but first we store those names in the variables *$name1* and *$name2* respectively.

```
    $name1 = "John";
    $name2 = "Jane";
```

**4** **Step 4**: Call the **fwrite()** function with the correct number and sequence of arguments: the *file handle* and the string of data. Append a *line-feed* character to each name that we will append.

```
    fwrite($fp, $name1 . "\n");
    fwrite($fp, $name2 . "\n");
```

**5** **Step 5**: Go back to the call to **fopen()** and add the '**or die**' clause to warn the user if the file *names.txt* does not exist.

```
$fp = fopen($file, 'a') or die ("Can't
        Open The File");
```

**6** **Step 6**: Close the file pointer.

```php
fclose($fp);
```

**7** **Step 7**: Add an *echo* statement that will notify the user that the new data has been appended.

```php
echo("names.txt has been
overwritten!")
```

**8** **Step 8**: Close the PHP script and the HTML document and save your file again.

```php
?>
</body>
</html>
```

**9** **Step 9**: The complete code listing should now look like this:

## CODE LISTING: APPENDFILE.PHP

```php
<!DOCTYPE html>

<html>
<head>
    <title>Appending and Deleting Files
from the Server</title>
</head>

<body>

<?php
    $file = "names.txt";
    $fp = fopen($file, 'a') or die ("Can't
Open The File");
    $name1 = "John";
    $name2 = "Jane";
    fwrite($fp, $name1 . "\n");
    fwrite($fp, $name2 . "\n");
    fclose($fp);
    echo("New Data Has Been Added!")
```

```
?>
</body>
</html>
```

**10** Step 10: Run your script.

You should see the message "New Data Has Been Added," but let's access the file *names.txt* directly and see if the names "John" and "Jane" have indeed been added. Use Komodo Edit or any text editor to open the file *names.txt*.

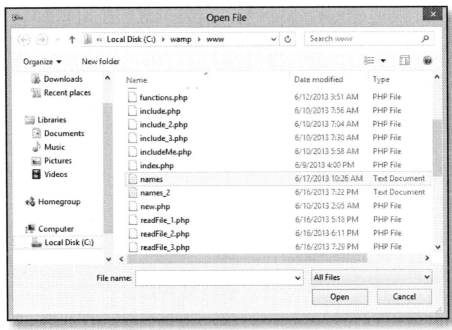

Figure 7.26: Verifying *names.txt* for the newly appended names "John" and "Jane".

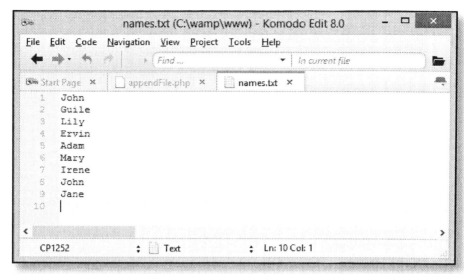

Figure 7.27: Viewing content of *names.txt* file from Komodo Edit.

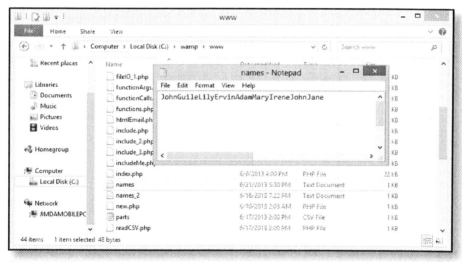

Figure 7.28: Viewing content of *names.txt* file from Notepad.

Now the two names "John" and "Jane" have been added into the *names.txt* file.

unlink()

Now let's delete a file from the server using the **unlink()** function, which accepts the complete filename of the file we intend to delete as its required first argument. For example:

```
unlink("filename.ext");
```

It's that simple. There is no need for a *file handle,* hence no need to use **fopen()** and **fclose()**.

But first, let's create the file that we will delete. It will be a simple text file, named *deletedMessage.txt,* containing the text "This file will be deleted from the server." We will create and save it in the www or htdocs folder.

**Step 1:** Using your text editor, click on New File and select *Text.* Choose the directory *C:\wamp\www* and type in the filename *deletedMessage.txt.* Click *Open.*

**Step 2:** In the text editor, type "This file will be deleted from the server." Save the file.

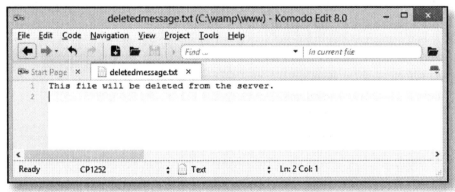

Figure 7.29: Content of *deletedMessage* as seen in Komodo Edit.

Now the file *deletedMessage* is saved on the server.

Look through the www or htdocs folder to check if the text file was successfully saved.

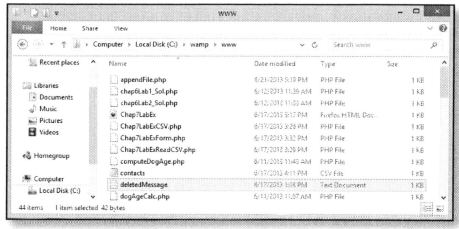

Figure 7.30: Viewing the file *deletedMessage.txt* from the local browser.

The text file can also be saved using Notepad.

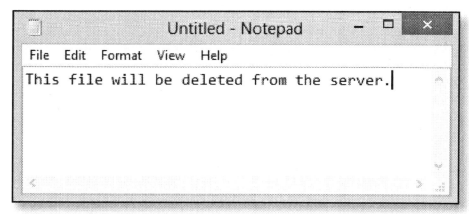

Figure 7.31: Creating the file *deletedMessage.txt* using Notepad.

Make sure you save this file inside the www or htdocs folder.

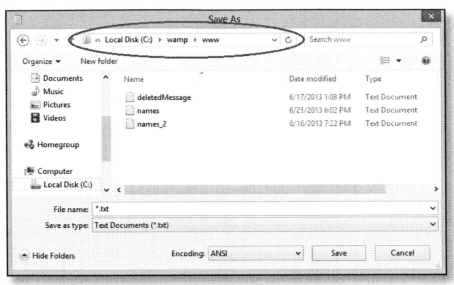

Figure 7.32: Local Disk (C:) > wamp > www folder.

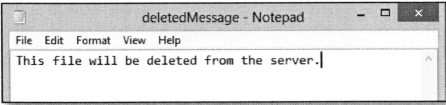

Figure 7.33: The file deletedMessage.txt was saved using Notepad.

**Step 3:** Create a new HTML5 document template and type the following code exactly as it appears here:

### CODE LISTING: VIEWDELETEFILE.PHP

```
<!DOCTYPE html>

<html>
<head>
    <title>Deleting Files from the
Server</title>
</head>

<body>
```

```php
<?php
    unlink("deletedMessage.txt");
    echo("</br> deletedMessage.txt has
been deleted!")
?>
</body>
</html>
```

**4** **Step 4**: Save the script with the filename *viewDeleteFile.php* and run it:

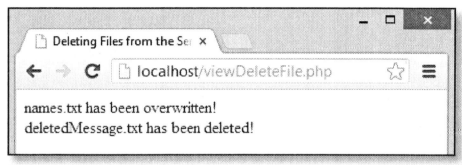

Figure 7.34: Output of *viewDeleteFile.php* when ran.

Now, check the www or htdocs folder and see if the file *deletedMessage. txt* is still there. Here is the view of c:\wamp\www folder—as you can see, the file is no longer there.

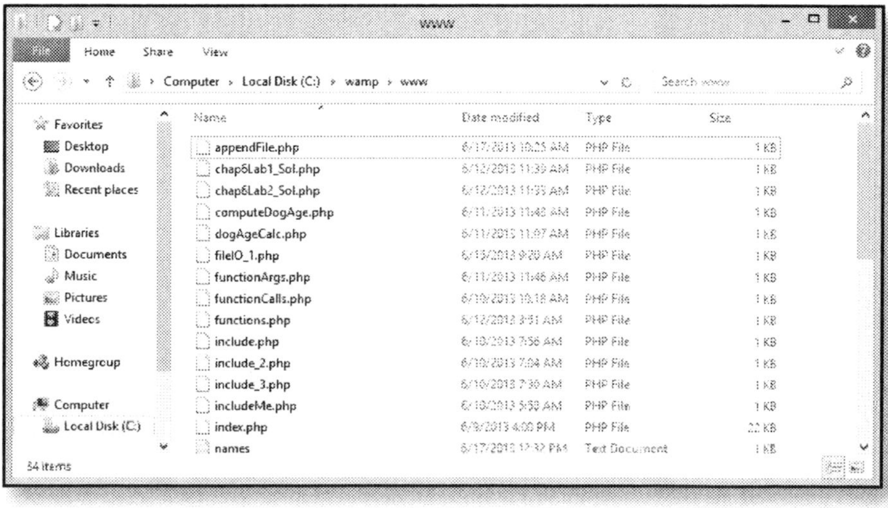

Figure 7.35: View of c:\wamp\www folder, *deletedMessage.txt* is no longer there.

# 7.4 CSV FILES

CSV files, or Comma-Separated Value files, are text files consisting of strings or values separated by commas. This is an example of a CSV file (which we will use in our sample PHP scripts later) named *deliveredItems.csv* :

> **CSV files**
>
> Comma-Separated Value files

```
m-000, meat, $12.00, 10
v-000, veggies, $2.50, 12
d-000, dairy, $1.50, 3
c-000, condiments, $1.00, 9
f-000, packaged mixed fruit, $3.00, 7
s-000, spices,$1.75, 1
```

CSV files are a very common and popular text document structure and are mainly used in converting data from one software format to another, for example, converting data from an Excel spreadsheet to a MySQL database or vice versa. In this situation, the data is first "exported" from either Excel or MySQL into a CSV file which is then "imported" into either MySQL or Excel.

In a CSV file, one line of text (terminated by a *line-feed* character) corresponds to one data record. Each comma-separated string corresponds to a field or column in that data record. If the contents of *deliveredItems.csv* were to be imported into a database table, it would look something like this:

| Category Number | Description | Unit Price | Quantity (boxes) |
|---|---|---|---|
| m-000 | meat | $12.00 | 10 |
| v-000 | veggies | $2.50 | 12 |
| d-000 | dairy | $1.50 | 3 |
| c-000 | condiments | $1.00 | 9 |
| f-000 | packaged mixed fruit | $3.00 | 7 |
| s-000 | spices | $1.75 | 1 |

Table 7.4: Listing for *deliveredItems.csv*.

PHP has a special function, **fgetcsv()**, which reads a line from a **CSV** file and then parses the comma-separated string values into an array. That is, each comma-separated string becomes an element of the array.

But first, let's use Komodo Edit to create the **CSV** file *deliveredItems.csv*. This is the file we will read using the **fgetcsv()** function.

**fgetcsv()**

CSV files are easily created by simply separating each field record string by commas and terminating each line by putting the next set of elements on a new line—or by pressing the *return* key after the last element in the line. We then save the file with the extension name .csv.

**1** **Step 1**: Using Komodo Edit, open a new text file in the c:\ wamp\www or c:\wamp\htdocs folder.

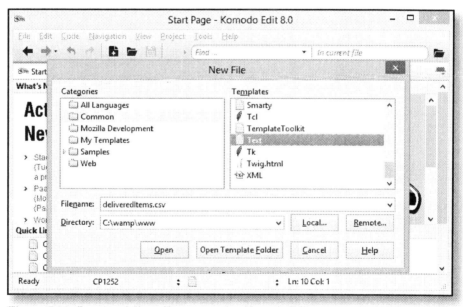

Figure 7.36: Creating *deliveredItems.csv* using Komodo Edit.

**2** **Step 2:** Type in the previously shown contents of *deliveredItems. csv*, as in the following screenshot, and save the file.

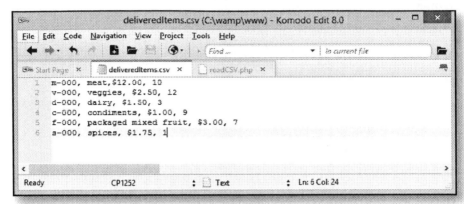

Figure 7.37: *deliveredItems.csv* just created.

The new column shown to the right side of the code listing area is called a Minimap. You can keep it from being displayed by clicking on "View" from the file menu then unchecking "View Minimap."

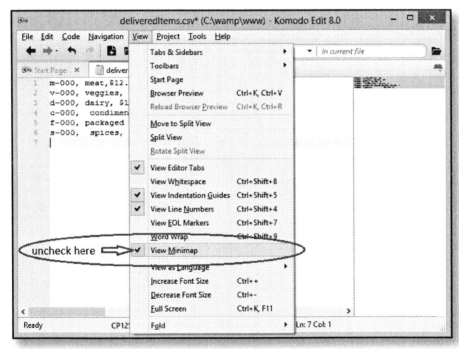

Figure 7.38: Where to uncheck "View Minimap" in Komodo Edit.

You get this final view of your file.

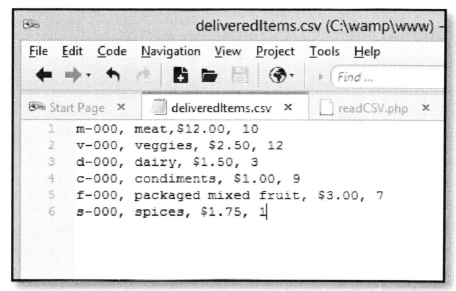

Figure 7.39: Plain view of deliveredItems.csv in Komodo Edit.

You may resize your window if you want, as has been done here, to see the images more clearly.

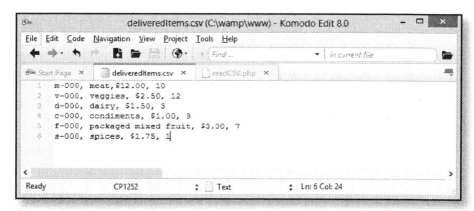

Figure 7.40: Resized view of Komodo Edit window.

Now, we are going to write a script that will read the entire contents of *deliveredItems.csv* and display each line as a row in a table and display each comma-separated value in a line as a cell in a table.

**Step 3:** Create a new PHP file using the HTML5 template. Save the file as *readCSV.php*. Embed the PHP opening script tags.

```
<!DOCTYPE html>

<html>
<head>
    <title>Reading CSV files</title>
</head>

<body>

    <?php
```

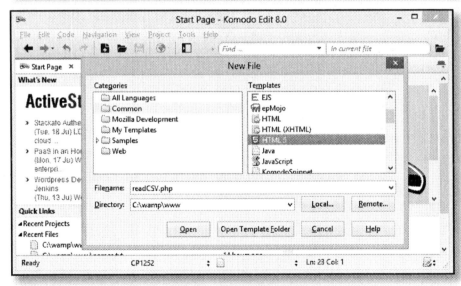

Figure 7.41: Creating a new HTML5 template for *readCSV.php*.

**Step 4:** Store the string "deliveredItems.csv" in the variable *$fileName*.

```
$fileName = "deliveredItems.csv";
```

**5** **Step 5:** Call the **fopen()** function to access *deliveredItems.csv* in 'r' mode. Store the returned *file handle* in the variable *$fp*.

```
$fp = fopen($fileName, 'r');
```

At this point, this is how your code should look:

```
<!DOCTYPE html>

<html>
<head>
    <title>Reading CSV files</title>
</head>

<body>

<?php
    $file = "deliveredItems.csv";
    $fp = fopen($file, 'r');

?>
</body>
</html>
```

Now, we are going to read *deliveredItems.csv* one line at a time by utilizing a *while-loop*. As we read a line, we will format the comma-separated values in that line into a row of a table and then append that row into the variable *$output*, which will eventually contain all the rows we have constructed.

 **Step 6:** Initialize the variable *$output* to the empty string "" just before the *while-loop*.

```
$output = "";
```

**7** **Step 7**: Now declare the *while-loop* with the conditional
expression !feof($fp)).

```
while(!feof($fp))
```

**8** **Step 8:** The first statement in the *while-loop* is a call to the
function **fgetcsv()** which will read one line from *deliveredItems.
csv* and then store each comma-separated value in that line as an
element in the array *$inventory*.

```
$inventory = fgetcsv($fp, 1024);
```

At this point, your code should look like this:

```
$output = "";
while(!feof($fp))
{
     $inventory = fgetcsv($fp, 1024);
```

After each call to **fgetcsv()**, *$inventory* will hold an array of four
elements. These four elements correspond to the four comma-separated
values in one line of *deliveredItems.csv*.

```
m-000, meat,    $12.00, 10
```

**9** **Step 9**: We will display the four elements of *$inventory* in a row
(consisting of four cells) of a table. The following code builds the
row of the table.

```
$line = "";
$line .= "<tr>";
$line .= "<td align='center'>" .
         $inventory[0] . "</td>";
$line .= "<td align='center'>" .
         $inventory[1] . "</td>";
$line .= "<td align='center'>" .
         $inventory[2] . "</td>";
```

```
$line .= "<td align='center'>" .
         $inventory[3] . "</td>";
$line .= "</tr>";
```

**10** **Step 10**: Once a row has been built, it is appended to the variable *$output* which will eventually contain all the rows of the table.

```
$output .= $line;
```

Note that we initialized *$output* to the empty string "" before we entered the loop.

**11** **Step 11**: When the *while-loop* terminates (because it has reached the *end-of-file* marker of *deliveredItems.csv*) we can display the output as a table.

```
print("<table border='1'
       cellpadding='1'>");
print($output);
print("</table>");
```

**12** **Step 12:** Close the script tag and the HTML document and save your file again.

Following is the complete code listing:

## CODE LISTING: READCSV.PHP

```
<!DOCTYPE html>

<html>
<head>
    <title>Reading CSV files</title>
</head>

<body>
<?php
```

```php
    $file = "deliveredItems.csv";
    $fp = fopen($file, 'r');

    $output = "";
    while(!feof($fp))
    {
        $inventory = fgetcsv($fp, 1024);
        $line = "";
        $line .= "<tr>";
        $line .= "<td align='center'>" .
$inventory[0] . "</td>";
        $line .= "<td align='center'>" .
$inventory[1] . "</td>";
        $line .= "<td align='center'>" .
$inventory[2] . "</td>";
        $line .= "<td align='center'>" .
$inventory[3] . "</td>";
        $line .= "</tr>";
        $output .= $line;
    }
    print("<table border='1'
cellpadding='1'>");
    print($output);
    print("</table>");
?>
</body>
</html>
```

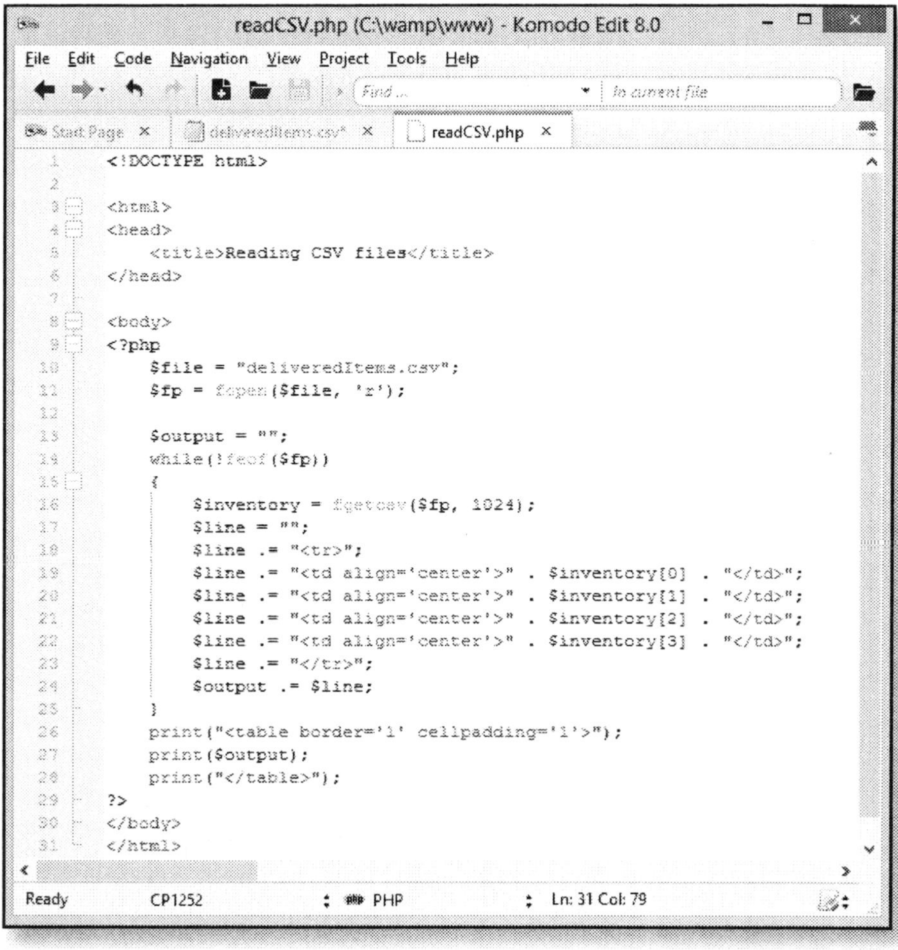
readCSV.php (C:\wamp\www) - Komodo Edit 8.0
File Edit Code Navigation View Project Tools Help
Find ...
In current file
Start Page
deliveredItems.csv*
readCSV.php
<!DOCTYPE html>
<html>
<head>
<title>Reading CSV files</title>
</head>
<body>
<?php
$file = "deliveredItems.csv";
$fp = fopen($file, 'r');
$output = "";
while(!feof($fp))
{
$inventory = fgetcsv($fp, 1024);
$line = "";
$line .= "<tr>";
$line .= "<td align='center'>" . $inventory[0] . "</td>";
$line .= "<td align='center'>" . $inventory[1] . "</td>";
$line .= "<td align='center'>" . $inventory[2] . "</td>";
$line .= "<td align='center'>" . $inventory[3] . "</td>";
$line .= "</tr>";
$output .= $line;
}
print("<table border='1' cellpadding='1'>");
print($output);
print("</table>");
?>
</body>
</html>
Ready
CP1252
PHP
Ln: 31 Col: 79

**Figure 7.42**: Complete code listing of *readCSV.php* in Komodo Edit.

**13** **Step 13**: Run your program and view your output.

Figure 7.43: Output of *readCSV.php* when ran.

> **Tip**: If you want the item description in the table to display as aligned to the left instead of centered, replace the table data <td> value from the *readCSV.php* code listing to 'left' instead of 'center'.

## QUESTIONS FOR REVIEW

1. What does File I/O mean?
   a. File Input and Output.
   b. File In and Out.
   c. File Into and Onto.
   d. File Inside and Outside.

2. What is the fastest method of retrieving the contents of text files in the server?
   a. file_get_contents
   b. fgets
   c. fread
   d. fopen

3. What mode does 'a' stand for?
   a. Affix.
   b. Append.
   c. Arbitrary.
   d. Apprehend.

4. What is usually required to append and delete files in the server?
   a. Access to the server.
   b. Permission from the server.
   c. command from the server.
   d. Favor from the server.

5. What does CSV mean?
   a. Comma-Saturated Values.
   b. Comma-Separated Variables.
   c. Comma-Secluded Variables.
   d. Comma-Separated Values.

# CHAPTER 7 LAB EXERCISE

1. Create an HTML form page that will contain the following entry fields and elements:

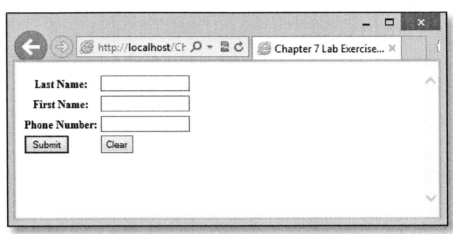

Figure 7.44: Prescribed 'Form Page 1' for Chapter 7 Lab Exercise.

2. As soon as the "submit" button is clicked, the form must redirect to a new form page confirming that the information entered has been saved. This confirmation page must include two buttons: "Add more" and "View all entries." The "Add more" button will be clicked if the user wishes to add more entries, while the "View all entries" is clicked if the user wants to view already saved data.

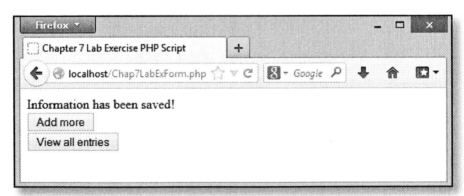

Figure 7.45: Prescribed 'Form Page 2' for Chapter 7 Lab Exercise.

3. Create a sub-program that will store the entered data in a CSV file.

4. Provide links in each of the pages to allow the user to easily navigate from one page to another.

5. Display the saved information in table form.

6. Apply the principles learned using forms, superglobals, server, and CSV files.

## CHAPTER LAB SOLUTION:

(1) HTML Entry Form Page:

## CODE LISTING: CHAP7LABEX.HTML

```
<!DOCTYPE html>

<html>
<head>
    <title> Chapter 7 Lab Exercise HTML</
title>
</head>

<body>
    <form action="Chap7LabExForm.php"
method="post">
    <table>
        <tr>
            <th>Last Name:</th>
            <td><input type="text"
name="lname" /></td>
        </tr>
        <tr>
            <th>First Name:</th>
            <td><input type="text"
name="fname" /></td>
        </tr>

        <tr>
            <th>Phone Number:</th>
            <td><input type="number"
name="pnumber" /></td>
```

```
            </tr>
            <tr>
                <td><input type="submit"
value="Submit" /></td>
                <td><input type="reset"
value="Clear"</td>
            </tr>
        </table>
</body>
</html>
```

(2)PHP Script- Data Entered Saved Confirmation Page

## CODE LISTING: CHAP7LABEXFORM.PHP

```
<!DOCTYPE html>

<html>
<head>
    <title>Chapter 7 Lab Exercise PHP</
title>
</head>

<body>
    <?php

        $lname = $_REQUEST['lname'];
        $fname = $_REQUEST['fname'];
        $pnumber = $_REQUEST['pnumber'];

        $file = "contacts.csv";
        $fp = fopen($file, 'a');

        fwrite($fp, $lname . ",");
        fwrite($fp, $fname . ",");
        fwrite($fp, $pnumber . "\n");
```

```
        fclose($fp);
        echo("Information has been
saved!</br>");


    ?>
    <form action="Chap7LabEx.html">
    <input type="submit" value="Add
more"/>
    </form>
    <form action="Chap7LabExForm.php">
    <input type="submit" value="View all
entries">
    </form>
</body>
</html>
```

(3)PHP Script View Saved CSV File in Table Form

## CODE LISTING: CHAP7LABEXREADCSV.PHP

```
<!DOCTYPE html>

<html>
<head>
    <title>Chapter 7 Lab Exercise Read
CSV</title>
</head>

<body>
    <?php
        $file = "contacts.csv";
        $fp = fopen($file, 'r');
        $table = "";

        while(!feof($fp))
        {
```

```php
            $list = fgetcsv($fp, 1024);
            $entry = "";
            $entry .= "<tr>";
            $entry .= "<td
align='center'>" . $list[0] . "</td>";
            $entry .= "<td
align='center'>" . $list[1] . "</td>";
            $entry .= "<td
align='center'>" . $list[2] . "</td>";
            $entry .= "</tr>";
            $table .= $entry;

        }

        print("<table border='1'>
                <tr>
                    <th>Last Name</th>
                    <th>First Name</th>
                    <th>Phone Number</th>
                </tr>");
        print($table);
        print("</table>")
    ?>
    <form action="Chap7LabEx.html">
        <input type="submit" value="Add
more"/>
    </form>
</body>
</html>
```

Output:

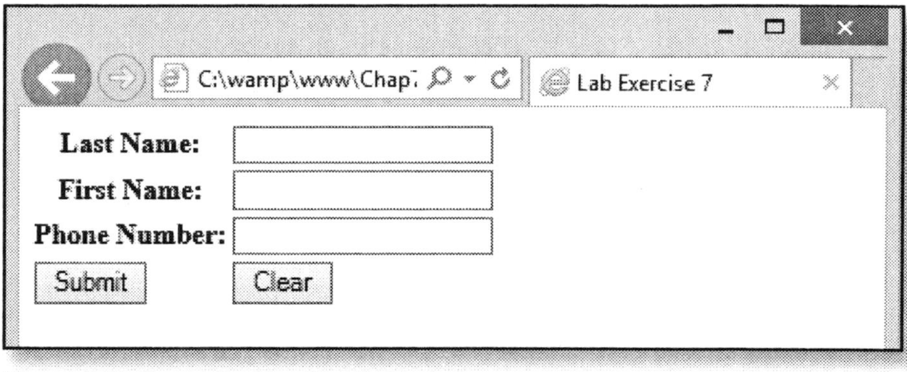

Figure 7.46: Output for *Chap7LabEx.html* when ran.

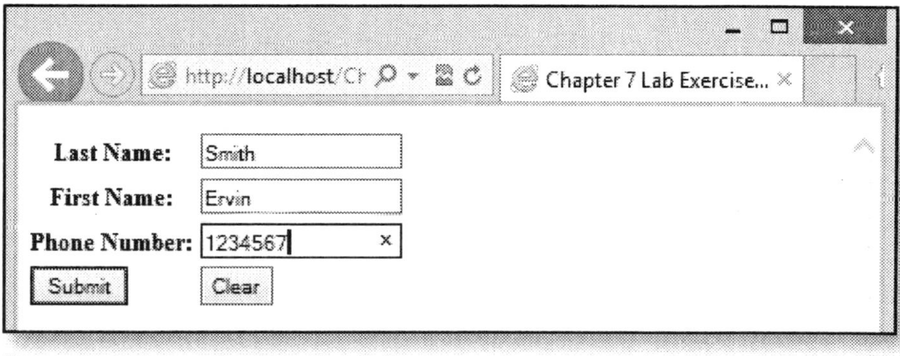

Figure 7.47: Output for *Chap7LabExForm.php* when ran.

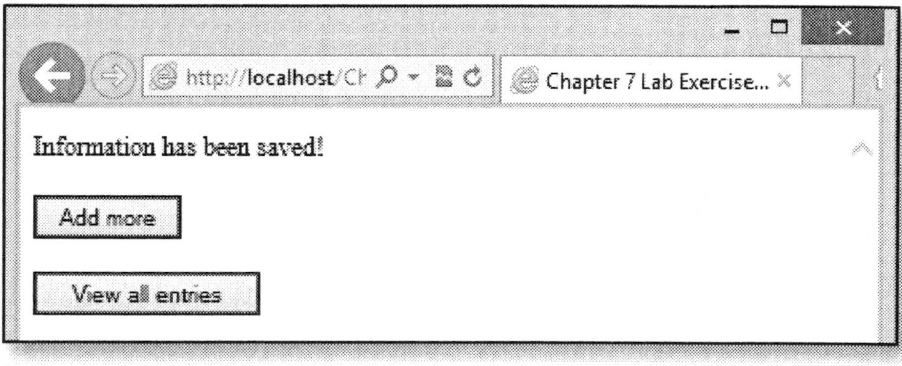

Figure 7.48: Output for *Chap7LabExReadCSV.php* when ran.

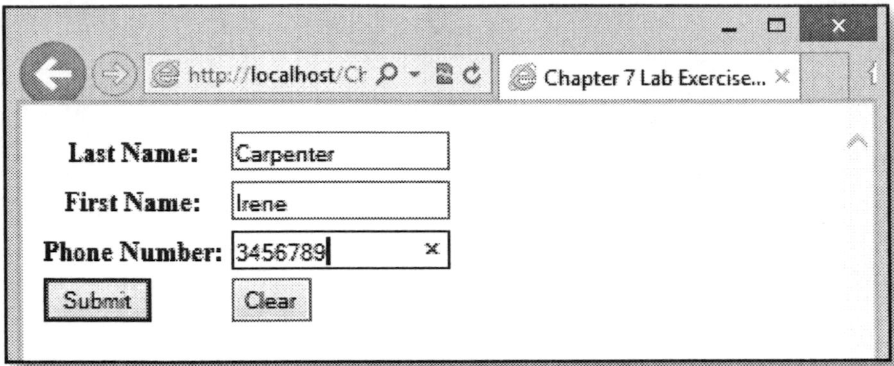

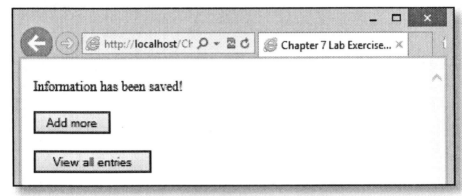

Figure 7.49: First user information being entered.

Figure 7.50: First user information submitted.

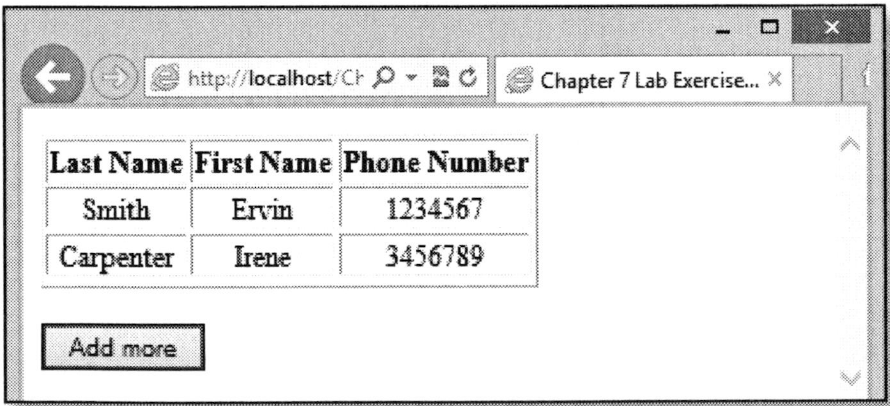

Figure 7.51: Saved user information viewed from localhost database.

# CHAPTER SUMMARY:

In this chapter you learned about PHP functions that perform file input/output operations: creating files, writing data to files, reading data from files, and deleting files.

As you worked through scripts that performed file input/output operations, you used forms that accepted data and retrieved that form data using superglobal arrays just before saving that data into text files. You also used arrays to display data retrieved from **csv** formatted files.

# CHAPTER 8

# SENDING EMAIL WITH PHP

## CHAPTER OBJECTIVES:

- You will learn the difference between text email and HTML email.
- You will learn how to download and install the **phpMailer** package.
- You will learn how to configure WAMPSERVER to work with the **phpMailer** package.
- You will write PHP scripts that will send text and HTML emails to a Gmail account using **phpMailer**.

# 8.1 SENDING TEXT EMAIL USING PHP

Have you ever wondered why you're receiving emails from a return address like noreply@domain.com? Or why someone would send you an email and imply by their email address that you are not supposed to respond? Actually, emails from such addresses are automatically generated and sent by a website that you recently visited. Sometimes they can be a confirmation of receipt, letting you know that an order you placed or an email you sent was received.

You could have registered on a certain website as a new member and opened an account. The website then sent you an email confirming your registration, requesting you to perform some activities verifying your identity and assigning your username and password. On other websites where you are already a registered, you will periodically receive email notifications of any activity affecting your account. For example, PayPal.com sends email notifications for every activity that its members conduct on their site: purchases, payments, funds transfers, and so on.

All these emails are automatically generated by the website application. They have to be automatically created and sent, otherwise a battalion-sized staff would be required to monitor all the activities of all the members of just one website.

**mail server**

Email sending and receiving requires a properly configured **mail server**. This is a computer program that functions as a virtual post office. It may run on its own dedicated hardware or share hardware resources with other server programs. It is designed to run automatically during normal operation without any manual intervention.

**SMTP**

**Simple Mail Transfer Protocol**

There are two types of mail servers: outgoing and incoming mail servers. Outgoing servers handle all sent emails and implement SMTP (*Simple Mail Transfer Protocol*) while incoming servers process all received emails and implement either POP3 (*Post Office Protocol, version 3*) or IMAP (*Internet Message Access Protocol*).

**POP3**

**Post Office Protocol Version3**

POP3 incoming servers store sent and received messages on the client's hard drive. This forces a user to access and process their emails from only one device or location. However, IMAP incoming servers store messages on servers, thus allowing users to access their emails from any location or any device.

**IMAP**

**Internet Message Access Protocol**

Sending and receiving emails entails several levels of communication between incoming and outgoing mail servers, a process that ensures that emails get to the right recipients.

---

**TIP**: To learn more about the nuts and bolts of how email servers transmit and accept email, you can access "How Email Works" at http://computer.howstuffworks.com/e-mail-messaging/email. htm and "How Does Email Work?" at http://www.howtogeek. com/56002/htg-explains-how-does-email-work/.

---

PHP allows you to create and send emails directly from a PHP script. This is done through the PHP **mail()** function. It has six possible arguments, all of the string data type. The first four are mandatory but the last two are optional. This is its syntax:

**mail()**

```
bool = mail(string $to, string $subject,
        string $message, string $from,
        [string $headers, string
$parameters] )
```

The following table provides details for each of the six arguments.

| Argument | Variable Designation | Description or Function |
|---|---|---|
| to | $to | Required. The receiver/receivers of the email. This could be an email address or another domain within a local server. |
| subject | $subject | Required. This is the main header of the email and a brief description of the contents of the email. It may consist of numbers, strings or a combination of both. It cannot contain any newline characters. |
| message | $message | Required. This is the actual message. Each line of the message should be separated with a LF (\n). Lines should not exceed 70 characters. |
| from | $from | Required. This is the email address of the sender. |
| headers | $headers | Optional. This specifies additional headers, like Cc, and Bcc. The additional headers should be separated by CRLF (\r\n) characters. |
| parameters | $parameters | Optional. This specifies any additional parameters. |

Table 8.1: Arguments for the PHP mail() function.

The PHP **mail()** function returns a boolean value of TRUE if the email was successfully sent, FALSE if otherwise.

Let's send a simple text email.

**1** **Step 1:** Open a blank HTML5 document template in Komodo Edit and save it as *simpleE-mail.php*.

**2** **Step 2**: Inside the <body> section, add the PHP script opening and closing tags.

```
<body>
   <?php

   ?>
</body>
```

**3** **Step 3**: From the table below, encode assignment statements assigning the string values in the second column to the corresponding variables in the first column. For example, for the first row in the table, the line of code should be:

```
$to = "someone@e-mail.com";
```

| Variable Argument | String Value |
|---|---|
| $to | someone@e-mail.com |
| $subject | Feedback for you. |
| $message | This is a test email created using PHP. |
| $from | test@learntoprogram.tv |
| $headers | "From:" . $from |
| Confirmation text | "Mail has been sent!" |

Table 8.2: Arguments list for *simplemail.php* PHP code list.

This is how the complete code listing will look:

### CODE LISTING: SIMPLEEMAIL.PHP

```php
<!DOCTYPE html>

<html>
<head>
    <title>A Simple Text e-mail</title>
</head>

<body>
    <?php
    $to = "someone@e-mail.com";
    $subject = "Feedback for you.";
    $message = "This is a test e-mail
created using php";
    $message .= "from LearnToProgram.tv";
    $from = "test@learntoprogram.tv";
```

```
    $headers = "From:" . $from;
    $retval = mail ($to, $subject,
$message, $headers);
    if ( $retval ) {
       echo ("Mail has been sent!");
    } else {
       echo ("Mail has not been sent!");
    }
  ?>
</body>
</html>
```

**4**   **Step 4**: Save your file and attempt to view your output.

Now, when you run this script, you will get the following error message shown in figure 8.1.

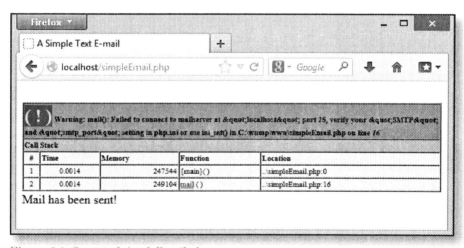

Figure 8.1: Output of *simpleEmail.php*.

The reason you get this error is because WAMPSERVER does not have a configured mail server as one of its components. So how does an aspiring PHP programmer, with WAMPSERVER installed, get to test PHP scripts that send email?

Not surprisingly, solutions abound! If you type "How to send email from WAMPSERVER using PHP" into Google you will find several work-arounds presented by enterprising web programmers. Some of these solutions date back to more than two years ago while one or two are just from this year. (Some of these different solutions even have the same name, "sendmail," which can cause a little confusion!)

Intuitively, we want to pick not only the latest solution but also a solution easy to implement. Fortunately, we have this in the very popular **PHPMailer**. Here is a succinct description taken from *PHPMailer Tutorial* at https://code. google.com/a/apache-extras.org/p/phpmailer/wiki/ UsefulTutorial.

**PHPMailer**

> "PHPMailer is a PHP class for PHP (www.php.net) that provides a package of functions to send email. The two primary features are sending HTML email and emails with attachments. PHPMailer supports nearly all possiblities to send email: mail(), Sendmail, qmail & direct to SMTP server. You can use any feature of SMTP-based email, multiple recipients via to, CC, BCC, etc. In short: PHPMailer is an efficient way to send email within PHP."

As you can see from the description, **PHPMailer** is a complete, feature-laden package for sending emails from PHP scripts. As much as we would like to examine and test all of **PHPMailer**'s features and capabilities, that would be impractical given the limitations of this book.

Now we will show you how to use **PHPMailer** to send a text email and an HTML email to a Gmail address.

The following steps will guide you in downloading and installing **PHPMailer**, configuring WAMPSERVER to work with **PHPMailer,** and coding the scripts.

**1** **Step 1:** Download *PHPMailer/SMTP* from https://github. com/PHPMailer/PHPMailer. The following screens show the GitHub page for PHPMailer and where the Download button can be located. You will obtain a zip file named *PHPMailer-master.zip* of approximately 200kb in size.

Figure 8.2: The upper left portion of the GitHub PHPMailer download page at https://github.com/PHPMailer/PHPMailer.

Figure 8.3: The download button on the lower right portion of the GitHub PHPMailer download page at https://github.com/PHPMailer/PHPMailer.

**2** **Step 2:** Unzip *PHPMailer-master.zip* into a folder.

**3** **Step 3:** In the folder where you unzipped *PHPMailer-master.zip*, locate the following three scripts and copy them to your c:/wamp/ www folder in Windows (or the corresponding folders on Mac and Linux systems).

      1. PHPMailerAutoload.php
      2. class.phpmailer.php
      3. class.smtp.php

**4** **Step 4:** In the WAMPSERVER Menu, enable the Apache ssl_ module by accessing the httpd.conf file as shown in the following screenshots.

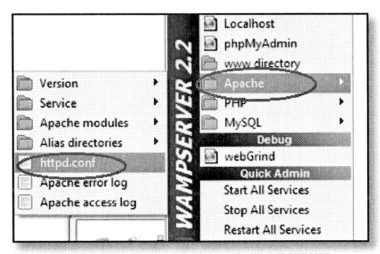

Figure 8.4: Accessing the httpd.conf file in the WAMPSERVER menu.

**5** **Step 5:** In the httpd.conf file uncomment the following line. (To uncomment remove the "#" sign at the beginning of the line.)

```
#LoadModule ssl_module modules/mod_ssl.so
```

The uncommented line is shown in figure 8.5.

```
#LoadModule speling_module modules/mod_speling.so
#LoadModule status_module modules/mod_status.so
#LoadModule unique_id_module modules/mod_unique_id.so
LoadModule userdir_module modules/mod_userdir.so
#LoadModule usertrack_module modules/mod_usertrack.so
#LoadModule vhost_alias_module modules/mod_vhost_alias.so
LoadModule ssl_module modules/mod_ssl.so
LoadFile "D:/wamp/bin/postgresql/9.2/bin/libpq.dll"
LoadModule php5_module "D:/wamp/bin/php/php5.2.8/php5apache2_2.dll"

# 'Main' server configuration
#
```

Figure 8.5: Uncommenting to enable the *ssl_module*

Alternatively, you can also enable the *ssl_module* through the WAMPSERVER menu choices *Apache -> Apache Modules -> ssl_module* as shown in the following figure.

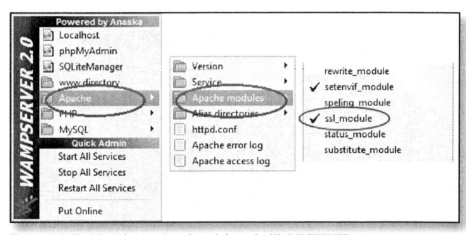

Figure 8.6: Enabling the Apache ssl_module in the WAMPSERVER menu.

**6** **Step 6:** In the WAMPSERVER menu, enable the *php_openssl*, *php_smtp* and *php_sockets* extensions for PHP as shown in figure 8.7.

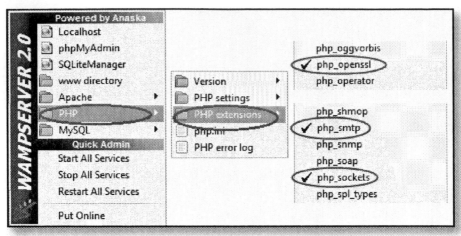

Figure 8.7: In the WAMPSERVER menu, enabling the *php_openssl*, *php_smtp* and *php_sockets* extensions for PHP.

 **Step 7**: Restart WAMPSERVER for your changes to take effect.

Figure 8.8: Restarting WAMPSERVER

You can test that PHPMailer was installed correctly by executing this code which should simply produce an empty browser page.

```php
<?php
    require("class.phpmailer.php");
    $mail = new PHPMailer();
?>
```

**8** **Step 8:** Copy and paste the following lines of code into Komodo Edit and save it as *sendEMailText.php*.

## CODE LISTING: SENDEMAILTEXT.PHP

```php
<?php
  require('class.phpmailer.php');
  $mail = new PHPMailer();
  $mail->IsSMTP();
  $mail->Mailer = 'smtp';
  $mail->SMTPAuth = true;
  $mail->Host = 'smtp.gmail.com';
  $mail->Port = 465;
  $mail->SMTPSecure = 'ssl';

  $mail->Username = "username@gmail.com";
  $mail->Password = "password";

  $mail->IsHTML(false);
  $mail->SingleTo = false;
  $mail->From = "email address of sender";
  $mail->FromName = "username of sender";

  $mail->addAddress("added email
address","added username");
  $mail->Subject = "Testing PHPMailer with
localhost";
  $mail->Body = "Hi,<br /><br />This
system is working perfectly.";

  If (!$mail->Send())
    echo "Message was not sent <br
/>PHPMailer Error: " . $mail->ErrorInfo;
  else
    echo "Message has been sent";
?>
```

**9** **Step 9:** Adjust the *Username* and *Password* values in the following lines.

```
$mail->Username = "username@gmail.com";
$mail->Password = "password";
```

For *Username*, enter your Gmail address and for *Password*, enter your Gmail password.

**10** **Step 10:** In the following lines, adjust the *From* and *FromName* strings to suitable values for you, as well as in the *addAddress* function.

```
$mail->From = "email address of sender";
$mail->FromName = "username of sender";

$mail->addAddress("added email
address","added username");
```

**11** **Step 11:** Run the script. In the browser, you should see:

```
Message has been sent.
```

You can now access your Gmail account to check for new mail.

# 8.2 SENDING HTML EMAIL

HTML emails contain a very small subset of HTML tags but there is no standard as to what HTML tags comprise this subset. Thus, different email clients vary in what HTML tags they can process in emails. Some email clients don't process HTML emails at all.

When HTML email appeared intially, there was some varied opposition to it for many reasons. One reason was security, as it would be possible to incorporate malicious code into HTML emails. Email attachments could also be malicious. Still, the use of HTML email has proliferated and email attachments are still being sent, and so opposition to HTML email has become silent resignation.

HTML email format and structure is similar to standard text email, except for additional header attributes. To code our script to send an HTML email, we will simply modify our script to send plain text email by adding a few lines to create the two headers required to send HTML email. These two headers are:

> **$headers = "MIME-Version : 1.0\r\n";**

This heading is used when sending an email that contains one of the following:

1. text character sets other than ASCII,
2. non-text attachments (pictures, music files, video files, etc),
3. message bodies with multiple parts, or
4. header information in non-ASCII character sets

> **$headers = "Content-Type text/html; charset=ISO-8859-1\r\n"**

This header defines which character encoding your HTML email will use. This is because a program must first choose a character encoding in order to validate or display an HTML document. For documents in English and most other Western European languages, the widely supported **ISO-8859-1** encoding is typically used.

These two new headers will be new additions in your PHP scripts and the HTML tags embedded in the message section of your email.

Now, here is the good news! With **phpMailer**, you don't have to bother with the additional headers that were just explained!

**1** **Step 1:** Retrieve *sendEmailText.php* and save it as *sendEmailHtml.php*.

**2** **Step 2**: Set the *IsHTML* function's parameter to TRUE or add the following line:

```
$mail->IsHTML(true);
```

**3** **Step 3**: Set *Body* and *AltBody* to the following string values.

```
$mail->Body = "Hello, <b>my friend</b>!
\n\n This message uses HTML entities!";

$mail->AltBody="Hello, my friend! \n\n
This message uses HTML entities, but you
prefer plain text !";
```

This is how the complete code listing should look:

### CODE LISTING: SENDEMAILHTML.PHP

```
<!DOCTYPE html>

<html>
<head>
    <title>HTML E-mail</title>
</head>

<body>

  <?php
    require('class.phpmailer.php');
    $mail = new PHPMailer();
```

```php
    $mail->IsSMTP();
    $mail->Mailer = 'smtp';
    $mail->SMTPAuth = true;
    $mail->Host = 'smtp.gmail.com';
    $mail->Port = 465;
    $mail->SMTPSecure = 'ssl';

    $mail->Username = "username@gmail.
com";
    $mail->Password = "password";

    $mail->IsHTML(true);
    $mail->SingleTo = false;
    $mail->From = "email address of
sender";
    $mail->FromName = "username of
sender";

    $mail->addAddress("added email
address","added username");
    $mail->Subject = "An HTML Message";
    $mail->Body = "Hello, <b>my friend</
b>! \n\n This message uses HTML
entities!";
    $mail->AltBody="Hello, my friend! \n\n
This message uses HTML entities, but you
prefer plain text !";

    if(!$mail->Send())
       echo "Message was not sent <br
/>PHPMailer Error: " . $mail->ErrorInfo;
    else
       echo "Message has been sent";
?>

</body>
</html>
```

1. Which corresponds to the recipient of the email in PHP?
   a. $to
   b. $from
   c. $header
   d. $message

2. What does the mail() function do?
   a. It sends and receives email using PHP through the server.
   b. It reads mail and notifies the user of their email.
   c. It sends a PDF file of a letter to a desired recipient.
   d. It sends a copy of an email to all addresses in a user's address book.

3. What does SMTP mean?
   a. Simple Mail Transfer Protocol.
   b. Simple Mommy Tailoring Protocol.
   c. Super Mail Transfer Protocol.
   d. Single Mail Transmit Parity.

4. What is an HTML email?
   a. A type of email that has HTML tags embedded in it.
   b. A type of email that is created using HTML.
   c. An email that is sent through HTML pages.
   d. A purely Javascript-generated email embedded in an HTML document.

5. What does the header MIME Version do?
   a. This heading indicates that the email contains characters other than ASCII text characters.
   b. Describes content type in general, including for the web and as storage for rich content in some commercial products.
   c. Mimes the email for the server.
   d. Copies the content of the email and saves it on the server.

6. What is the use of the content type text/HTML header?
   a. It declares that the email will contain both HTML and plain text in the message body.
   b. It allows the use of PHP scripts in the email.
   c. It allows the usage of Javascript in the email.
   d. It defines the character encoding the HTML email will use.

## CHAPTER 8 LAB EXERCISE

**PROBLEM:** Create an HTML email using PHP that will send the following HTML email. Use and assign the following values to its appropriate variable argument.

```
<html>
<body>
  <h1>This is Chapter 8 Lab Exercise HTML
test e-mail</h1>
  <p><strong>Such an easy Lab Exercise! </
strong></p>
</body>
</html>
```

SOLUTION:

### CODE LISTING: CHAP8LAB.PHP LAB SOLUTION

```php
<?php
  require('class.phpmailer.php');
  $mail = new PHPMailer();
  $mail->IsSMTP();
  $mail->Mailer = 'smtp';
  $mail->SMTPAuth = true;
  $mail->Host = 'smtp.gmail.com';
  $mail->Port = 465;
  $mail->SMTPSecure = 'ssl';

  $mail->Username = "username@gmail.
com";
  $mail->Password = "password";

  $mail->IsHTML(true);
  $mail->SingleTo = false;
```

```php
    $mail->From = "email address of
sender";
    $mail->FromName = "username of
sender";

    $mail->addAddress("added email
address","added username");
    $mail->Subject = "Chapter 8 Lab
EXercise";

    $message = "<html><body>";
    $message .= "</body></html>";
    $message .= "<h1>This is Chapter 8 Lab
Exercise HTML test e-mail</h1>";
    $message .= "<p><strong>Such an easy
Lab Exercise! </strong></p>";
    $message .= "</body></html>";

    $mail->Body = $message;
    $mail->AltBody= $message;

    if(!$mail->Send())
      echo "Message was not sent <br
/>PHPMailer Error: " . $mail->ErrorInfo;
    else
      echo "Message has been sent";
?>

</body>
</html>
```

# CHAPTER SUMMARY:

In this chapter you learned the difference between plain text email and HTML email.

You learned how to write basic PHP scripts that would send those two types of emails.

To be able to test those scripts, you learned how to download and install a powerful and popular PHP email package called **phpMailer**.

You also learned how to configure WAMPSERVER to work with **phpMailer** by adjusting a few of the numerous WAMPSERVER parameters.

With **phpMailer** installed and WAMPSERVER configured, you used PHP to send email to a Gmail account.

In the next chapter, we will discuss how to use PHP scripts to access MySQL Databases. MySQL is the most widely used open source relational database management system.

# CHAPTER 9

# WORKING WITH THE MySQL DATABASE

## CHAPTER OBJECTIVES:

* You will learn how to create a MySQL database using the phpMyAdmin web application.
* Using phpMyAdmin, you will learn how to create tables in a MySQL database and input data into those tables.
* You will learn to write PHP scripts to develop a simple and basic CRUD (Create, Retrieve, Update and Delete) application.
* You will learn how to use a combination of HTML forms and PHP scripts to input and update data in a MySQL database.
* You will learn how to construct SQL Insert, Retrieve, Update and Delete Query Statements and how to use PHP scripts to execute those statements on a MySQL database.
* You will learn how to use an application programming interface called **MySQLi** that will allow your PHP script to access a MySQL database.

Databases are the backbone of computers. The primary task of computer systems is to preserve and manage data, specifically to store data, organize it, update it, protect it, preserve its integrity and retrieve it in many more ways than one. Computer systems store data in *databases*.

**Database**

There are many classifications of *databases*: hierarchical, flat-file, network, distributed, and so on. Their differences are based on how they work and what they are used for. In business applications, the most commonly used type is the *relational* database. It is called as such because the tables of a *relational* database store not only data, but the relationships among the data.

> **TIP:** You will encounter the term *database management system,* or *dbms* which includes the software tools and utilities that are provided to manage the data in the *database.* Nowadays, both terms are used interchageably.

First, let's lay the groundwork with a crash course on some basic database terms and simplified concepts.

>> **Databases** – A database is an organized collection of related data. It is primarily made up of **tables**. It is in these tables that data is stored.

>> **Table** – A collection of closely related data or **columns** (or **fields**). For example, an accounting database would have a table of *Customers* (for monitoring receivables) and another table of *Suppliers* (for monitoring payables) as well as a table of *Employees* (for monitoring payroll and benefits).

>> **Column** – A table consists of **columns** or **fields** which are types of data you are storing in your table. For example, the *Employees* table would consist of the **columns**, *empID, lastName, firstName, department, position* and *salary*.

>> **Row** – This is a set of related data. For example, in the *Employees* table, a **row** would be the data for one employee.

>> **Fields** – This is another term for a **column**. Sometimes, a field refers to a specific **row's** column.

>> **Record** - This is another term for a **row**.

>> **Value** – A value is the data in a given **row** and **column**.

At this point, to help you visualize and understand the terms **table**, **columns**, **rows**, **fields**, **records**, and **values** we show a schematic representation of two tables – *Employee* and *Department*. (We will be creating these tables later in our code examples.)

| empId | lastName | firstName | depart-ment | position | salary |
|-------|----------|-----------|-------------|----------|--------|
| 001 | Smith | George | 1 | S Acct | 84000 |
| 002 | Valera | Linda | 2 | J Sales | 55000 |

Table 9.1: The *Employee* Table

The *Employee* table has six **columns** or **fields** and two **rows** of data. (The first row gives the names of the **columns** as a pictorial aid and is not part of the table.)

| departmentId | departmentName |
|---|---|
| 1 | Accounting |
| 2 | Sales |
| 3 | Operations |
| 4 | Management |

Table 9.2: The *Department* Table

The *Department* table has two **columns** or **fields** and four **rows** of data.

> ≫ **Relationship** – A relationship is a link between two tables. It is a powerful method for organizing your data. You define the relationship by establishing a link between the fields of two tables (where one or both fields is a **primary key** field). For example, we can establish a relationship between the two previous tables, *Employee* and *Department*, by linking the fields *department* of *Employee* and *deparmentId* of *Department*. This relationship makes the data of both tables available as one.

A table can have as many relationships as it has fields with other tables. For example, it is possible but impractical to link each of the six fields of *Employee* to other tables in the database.

> ≫ **Join** – This is another term for **relationship.**

> ≫ **Key** – This is a **column** or **columns** on which an **index** is constructed to allow rapid and/or sorted access to a table's data.

> ≫ **Index** – This is an internal system that a database system uses to locate data more quickly. In a table, you can specify that certain columns, usually keys, are indeces. Like **relationships** or **joins**, it is possible but impractical to create an index for every **column** of a table.

> ≫ **Primary key** – This is a **column** or group of columns in a given table that uniquely identifies each **row** of the table. To uniquely identify a **row**, no two **primary keys** can have the same value. In our example tables, the field *empId* is the **primary key** of the *Employee* table and the primary key of the *Department* table is *departmentId*.

> ≫ **Foreign key** – This is one or more **columns** in a table intended

to contain only values that match the related primary/unique key column(s) in the referenced table. **Foreign** and **primary keys** explicitly define the direct **relationships** between tables. In our example tables, the **primary key** column *departmentId* of *Department* establishes a relationship to the foreign key column *department* of *Employee*.

> **TIP:** For more database-related terms, you can check out *Database Terminology – A Dictionary of the Top 145 Database Terms* at http://raima.com/database-terminology/.

In this chapter, we will introduce you to the *open source, relational* type of database called MySQL. (It's pronounced either My S-Q-L or My Sequel.) It is a popular standard for many shared hosting services and it runs on many platforms – various Unix/Linux versions, Windows, and Mac OS X. It can be used with many programming languages – PHP, Java, C#, ASP, Visual Basic, and more.

Access to the data stored in a MySQL database is done through SQL (Structured Query Language) which was developed in the 1970s and is now the standard used in all databases, although slight differences exist in various implementations.

Access to MySQL can also be achieved through PHP with the use of APIs (Application Programming Interfaces) or extensions.

# 9.1 SETTING UP THE DATABASE

In this section, we will create a database. Then we will create two tables in that database (the two tables we illustrated previously – *Employee* and *Department*) and then store some sample data in those two tables. To do all of those, we have two tools provided by WAMPSERVER – *MySQL Console* and *PhpAdmin*. We will use the latter, but first let's cover some introductory details about *MySQL Console*.

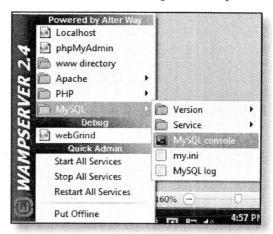

To start *MySQL Console* from the WAMPSERVER menu, click on *MySQL* and then click on *MySQL console* as shown in figure 9.1.

This will open a command line window as shown in figure 9.2.

Figure 9.1: MySQL Console at WAMPServer

```
c:\wamp\bin\mysql\mysql5.6.12\bin\mysql.exe
Enter password:
Welcome to the MySQL monitor.  Commands end with ; or \g.
Your MySQL connection id is 1
Server version: 5.6.12-log MySQL Community Server (GPL)

Copyright (c) 2000, 2013, Oracle and/or its affiliates. All rights reserved.

Oracle is a registered trademark of Oracle Corporation and/or its
affiliates. Other names may be trademarks of their respective
owners.

Type 'help;' or '\h' for help. Type '\c' to clear the current input statement.

mysql>
```

Figure 9.2: MySQL command line window.

If you type 'HELP' (without the quotation marks), you will get a display of all the possible commands you can type in the console as shown in the following help screen.

Figure 9.3: List of MySQL commands than can be used in the command line.

As you can see, it's not a user-friendly interface, as it favors the keyboard rather than the mouse and it's all white text on a black background. So, we can forget about *MySQL Console* and move on to *phpMyAdmin*.

To start *phpMyAdmin* from the WAMPSERVER menu, click on *phpMyAdmin* as shown in figure 9.4. Ideally, *phpMyAdmin* will require a *username* and a *password,* but to simplify testing, a default *username* of *root* and a blank *password* is automatically provided.

Figure 9.4: phpMyAdmin at WAMPServer

This will bring up the following *phpMyAdmin* main or opening screen.
Take a while to familiarize yourself with the panels and windows.
Look at the horizontal menu at the top of the screen which has the
choices: *Databases, SQL, Status, Users, Export,* and *More.* This last
choice, *More,* will open up another menu of additional options, namely:
*Settings, Synchronize, Binary Log, Replication, Variables, Charsets,* and
*Engines.*

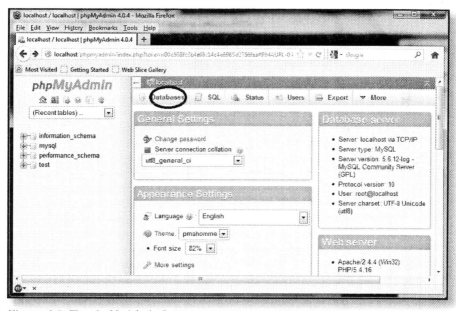

Figure 9.5: The phpMyAdmin Screen

Now, click on the option *Databases* in the top horizontal menu. This will bring up the Databases screen as shown in the following screenshot.

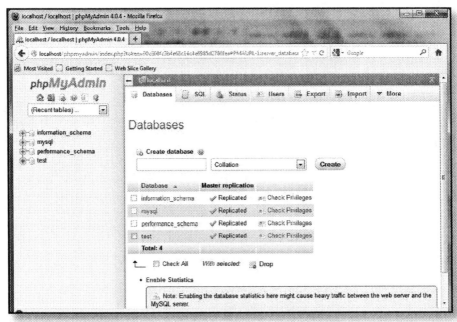

Figure 9.6: The screen for creating the database.

Look for the Create Database box (just below the large title 'Databases') and type 'Employees' (without the quotes).

In the Collation drop-down box, select 'utf8_general_ci'

Then, click the Create icon.

A message will then pop up, saying *The database employees has been created*. You will see this name of the database on the left panel, as shown here:

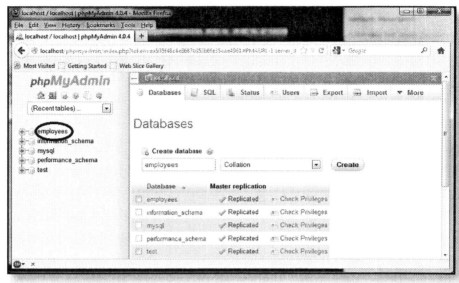

Figure 9.7: The database *employees* has been created.

If you click on the *employees* icon in the left panel of the screen, you will see the following:

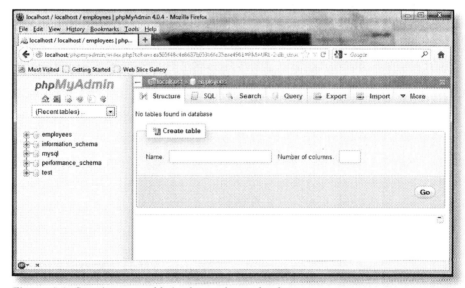

Figure 9.8: Creating new table in the *employees* database.

Now, we will create the *employee* table for the *employees* database.

Input 'Employee' in the Name box.

Input '6' in the Number of Fields box.

Click *Go*. This will bring you to the following screen:

Figure 9.9: The screen for creating the fields of the table *employee*.

Now, we can create the fields of the *employee* table, where each field will occupy a single column. You can start inputting data into the various fields using the following table as a guide.

| FIELD NAME | TYPE | LENGTH/ VALUE | Notes |
|---|---|---|---|
| empid | Int | 11 | Primary Key Auto-Increment |
| lastname | varchar | 40 | |
| firstname | varchar | 20 | |
| department | Int | 2 | |
| position | varchar | 20 | |
| salary | Int | 10 | |

Table 9. 3: Input data into the various fields for the *employee* table using this table as a guide.

Note that for the *empid* field, you have to specify the Index as *primary* (select *primary* from the dropdown box) and check the A_I checkbox (for Auto_Increment).

After specifying the names, types and length/values of each field, click the icon *save,* which will complete the process of creating the table *employee.*

Now, click the icon named *employee,* and then click *structure,* which will bring the following screen.

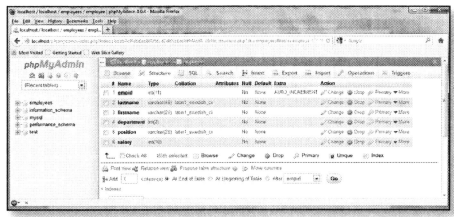

Figure 9.10: The *employee* table.

Let's move on to create our second table, *department.* Click on the Create Table icon on the left pane of the screen. This will bring up the following screen where you can define the fields or columns of the *department* table.

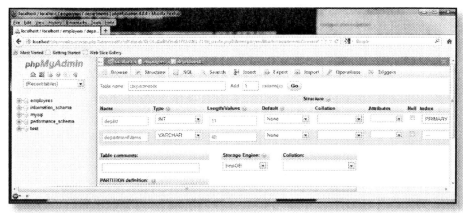

Figure 9.11: Specifying the fields in the table *department.*

You can start inputting data into the various fields using the following table as a guide.

| FIELD NAME | TYPE | LENGTH/ VALUE | Notes |
|---|---|---|---|
| deptId | int | 11 | Primary Key Auto-Increment |
| departName | varchar | 40 | |

Table 9. 4: Specifying the fields in the *department* table guide.

You also have to set up the field *deptid* as a primary key. Specify the Index as *primary* (select *primary* from the dropdown box) and check the A_I checkbox (for Auto_Increment).

Now, as we have set up the database with two tables, we should now add some data in the tables. To add data in the first table, click *employee,* and then click *insert.* After that, add some fictional data, as shown here:

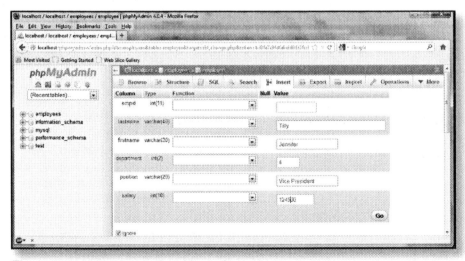

Figure 9.12: Adding data to the table *employee.*

*PHP and MySQL for Beginners*

Here, you can see that the *empid* field is left blank, as data in this field will be added automatically. After inserting, click *Go*. If you check the corresponding SQL code, you will see this:

```
INSERT INTO 'employees'.'employee'
('empid', 'lastname', 'firstname',
'department', 'position', 'salary')

VALUES (NULL, 'Tilly', 'Jennifer', '4',
'Vice President', '124500');
```

This is a nice feature of *phpmyAdmin*. As you perform various database operations, it will display the SQL statements that carry out that operation – a nice way to appreciate and master SQL code.

You need to add data for 10 employees here. After doing that, you will see something like this (by clicking browse>>profiling):

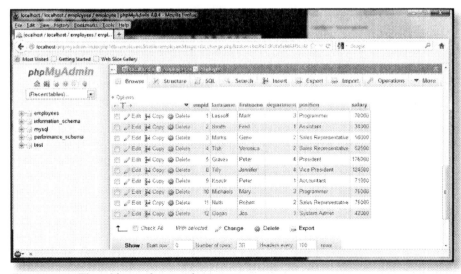

Figure 9.13: The table *employee* with 10 rows.

Here, you can easily edit and delete a row by clicking the corresponding icons. Now, add some rows in the *departments* table by following the same procedure:

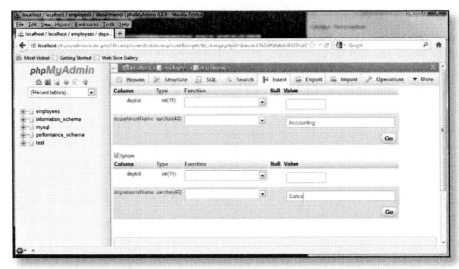

Figure 9.14: Adding data to the table *departments*.

The *departments* table will look like this:

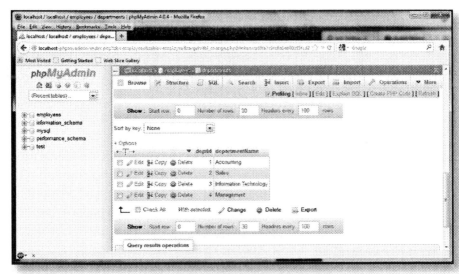

Figure 9.15: The table *departments* with four rows.

Now, your database is completely set up! In the next chapter, we will make a PHP application that will interact with this database.

## QUESTIONS FOR REVIEW

1. What should we type in order to get a list of commands in the MySQL command prompt?
   a. mysql>Help
   b. mysql>command
   c. mysql>list
   d. None of the above.

2. In order to make sure that each entry in a column will be unique, what do we use?
   a. Foreign key.
   b. Candidate key.
   c. Primary key.
   d. None of the above.

# 9.2 RETRIEVING A QUERY FROM THE DATABASE

In the previous section, using phpMyAdmin, we created the database *employees* and then, within that database, we created the tables *employee* and *department*. Still using phpMyAdmin, we inputted sample data into those two tables. Now, we are going to retrieve those data by writing PHP scripts that perform database operations on a MySQL database.

To enable PHP to access and manipulate the rows and columns of tables in a MySQL database, we use a MySQL *API Extension*. PHP provides three such extensions:

**API Extensions**

- The deprecated, orginal *MySQL API*
- The *MySQL PDO* functions
- The *MySQL Improved* extension, **MySQLi**.

We will be using the third *API extension*, **MySQLi**, which is also the latest. API means *application programming interface*. This interface defines the classes, methods, functions, and variables that your PHP script will need in order to interface with MySQL.

**MySQLi**

---

> **TIP:** To learn everything about the three PHP MySQL *API Extensions,* you can look up the document *PHP MYSQL API (2014-03-14 Revision 38079)*. This manual describes the PHP extensions and interfaces that can be used with MySQL. One site that hosts this document is downloads.mysql.com/docs/apis-php-en.a4.pdf. You can search for other sites by typing "php mysqli api" in your search engine.

---

Before we go into detail about **MySQLi**, let's first clarify what we mean by "to access and manipulate the rows and columns of tables in a MySQL database." We are going to write a very simple and basic PHP CRUD application. CRUD is an acronym for **C**reate, **R**etrieve, **U**pdate and **D**elete. A CRUD application:

**CRUD**

**Create**
**Retrieve**
**Update**
**Delete**

a. Adds new rows to the tables of a database (Create),
b. **R**etrieves data from the tables of a database,
c. Modifies the data in a table's columns (Update), and

d. **D**eletes rows from the tables of a database.

Each of those four previous functionalities is specifically carried out by a specific SQL statement

| INSERT | Adds new rows of data to a table in a database. |
| --- | --- |
| SELECT | Retrieves data from one or several tables. |
| UPDATE | Modifies existing data. |
| DELETE | Removes a row of data from a table. |

Our PHP scripts will construct the exact SQL statement needed and then use **MySQLi** to have the MySQL database execute the SQL statement.

**MySQLi** provides an object-oriented interface and a procedural interface. We will be using the former.

**OOP**

**Object-Oriented Programming**

You don't have to fully understand OOP (object-oriented programming) concepts to understand and appreciate **MySQLi**'s object-oriented interface. Except for some unfamiliar keywords and notations (like "new" and "->"), using an object-oriented interface is similar to calling functions and manipulating variables.

OOP, as the name implies, deals with objects. Objects are just program code and program data bundled up as one isolated package with clear boundaries and definite rules on how to access that object's program code and data.

For our CRUD application we will be using two objects: a *connection* object and a *resultset* object.

A **class** contains the blueprint for an object. A **class** specifies in detail what an object's program code and data are. We create objects from classes or in OOP-speak, we *instantiate* an object from its class. For example, the following line of code creates or *instantiates* a *connection* object from the *mysqli* class. (Note the use of the keyword *new*.) The *connection* object is stored or, more exactly, is referenced by the variable *$conn*.

```
$conn = new mysqli(HOSTNAME, USERNAME,
PASSWORD, DB_NAME);
```

An object's code can be accessed by calling its **methods. Methods** are just like functions but **methods** can only operate on an object's data. Like functions, an object's **methods** can receive arguments and return a value. Let's look at this line of code.

**Methods**

```
$rs = $conn->query($sql);
```

Here, we are calling the **query** method of the connection object. (Note the "–>" notation when referencing an object's methods.) We are providing one argument to the **query** method, the variable *$sql* which contains an SQL statement. The query method returns an object, a **resultset** object. (The **query** method *instantiates* a **resultset** object and returns a reference to that object.) The variable *$rs* references the **resultset** object.

**query()**

An object's data can be accessed by retrieving its **properties.** Properties are just like variables. However, some properties are *read-only*, you can only access their values, not change them. Other properties are *read-write*. In our CRUD application, all the properties we will be handling are *read-write*. Let's look at this line of code:

```
$rows_returned = $rs->num_rows;
```

Here, we are accessing the *read-only* property, **num_rows**, of the **resultset** object, *$rs,* and storing its value in the variable *$rows_ returned*. (Again, please note the use of the "–>" notation when referencing an object's properties as well as methods.)

That's it. That's all you need to understand and appreciate the object-oriented interface of **MySQLi.** Now, let's establish the general flow of logic of each of our four main scripts.

a. We establish a link to the MySQL database by creating a connection object, *$conn,* from the **mysqli** class.

b. We check if the connection object was successfully created and the link established. If not, we display an error message and exit the program.

c. If the connection object was successfully created, we construct an

SQL query (either INSERT, SELECT, UPDATE or DELETE).

d. We use the **query** method of the connection object, *$conn*, to execute the query we constructed to obtain a **resultset** object, *$rs*.

e. We check if the query was successful. If it was successful, we display certain parameters regarding the execution of the query. If not, we display an error message and exit the program.

f. In the case of the Retrieve functionality, if the query was successful, we obtain a resultset object. We then use the **fetch_array** method of the resultset to transfer the data of the resultset object to either an associative or indexed array.

g. When all database operations are completed (added, retrieved, updated and deleted), close the connection by calling the **close** method of the connection object, *$conn*.

close()

Let's start with a simple script, *connect.php*, which will create a connection object to our database *employees*. (This is step a and b from the previous paragraphs.) Type the following code and save it as *connect.php*.

```php
<?php
  define( "HOSTNAME", "localhost");
  define( "USERNAME", "root");
  define( "PASSWORD", "");
  define( "DB_NAME", "employees");

  $conn = new mysqli(HOSTNAME, USERNAME,
PASSWORD, DB_NAME);

  if ($conn->connect_errno) {
     echo( "<br/>Failed to connect to MySQL:
(" .
     $conn->connect_errno . ") " . $conn-
>connect_error );
  } else {
     echo( "<br/>Connected to database " .
DB_NAME);
     echo( "<br/>" . $conn->host_info );
  }
?>
```

Let's analyze the code. First, we define four constants – HOSTNAME, USERNAME, PASSWORD, and DB_NAME. These four constants will be provided as arguments to the class **mysqli()** which creates a connection object, referenced by the variable *$conn*. The methods of this connection object will allow us to access the database *employees*.

**mysqli()**

Note that to simplify procedures we have used "root" as our username and an empty string as our password, but in reality we should provide a real username and a strong password. These actual usernames and passwords should have been defined and set beforehand in our database *employees*.

Also remember that the use of constants should become one of your programming best practices. You should have a location in your code where you can place parameters that could vary frequently, such as usernames and passwords.

Now, if we run this script on a PC running Windows 7, we will see this:

```
Connected to database employees
localhost via TCP/IP
```

The second or last line will vary depending on your operating system. Some systems will generate:

```
127.0.0.1 via TCP/IP
```

Now, let's test our code by changing the line:

```
define( "DB_NAME", "employees");
```

to:

```
define( "DB_NAME", "competitors");
```

In effect, we are deliberately creating an error condition by providing the name of a non-existent database. If we run this modified *connect. php,* we should get the following screenshot.

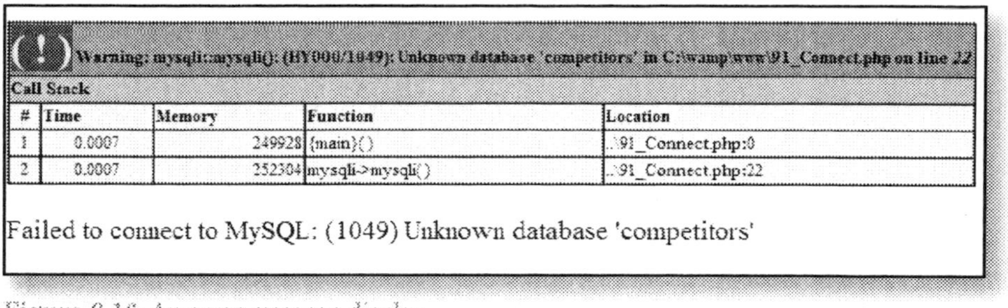

| # | Time | Memory | Function | Location |
|---|------|--------|----------|----------|
| 1 | 0.0007 | 249928 | {main}( ) | ..\91_Connect.php:0 |
| 2 | 0.0007 | 252304 | mysqli->mysqli( ) | ..\91_Connect.php:22 |

**Warning: mysqli::mysqli(): (HY000/1049): Unknown database 'competitors' in C:\wamp\www\91_Connect.php on line 22**

Call Stack

Failed to connect to MySQL: (1049) Unknown database 'competitors'

Figure 9.16: An error message display.

The last line of the display is generated by our line of code which reads:

```
echo( "<br/>Failed to connect to MySQL:
(" . $conn->connect_errno . ") " . $conn-
>connect_error );
```

The rest of the display is generated by the browser Google Chrome.

As you can see, our *connect.php* script is fully debugged and running nicely. Now, we will make some slight changes and save the modified script as *connectInc.php*. This is its code:

```
<?php

define( "HOSTNAME", "localhost");
define( "USERNAME", "root");
define( "PASSWORD", "");
define( "DB_NAME", "employees");

$conn = new mysqli(HOSTNAME, USERNAME,
PASSWORD, DB_NAME);

if ($conn->connect_errno) {
    echo( "<br/>Failed to connect to MySQL:
(" . $conn-
        >connect_errno . ") " . $conn-
>connect_error );
    die( '<br/>Program Terminated');
}
?>
```

We made these changes because *connectInc.php* is a script which we will include into our next scripts with the **require_once()** function, as shown in the following snippet of code.

**require_once()**

```php
<?php
    require_once("connectInc.php");
?>
```

Now, we are going to build a script which will construct a SQL Select statement to retrieve records from the table *employee*. Let's input the following code and save it in the file *Retrieve1.php*:

```php
<?php

require_once("connectInc.php");

$sql = "SELECT * FROM employee";
$rs = $conn->query($sql);
if ( $rs === false ) {
    trigger_error('Wrong SQL: ' . $sql . '
Error: ' . $conn->error, E_USER_ERROR);
} else {
    $arr = $rs->fetch_array( MYSQLI_ASSOC);
// MYSQLI_NUM
    $rows_returned = $rs->num_rows;
    echo( "<br>Rows: " . $rows_returned);
    echo("<br/>" . $arr['empid'] . ' ' .
            $arr['lastname'] . ' ' .
            $arr['firstname'] . ' ' .
            $arr['department'] . ' ' .
            $arr['position'] . ' ' .
            $arr['salary']);
}

?>
```

Let's analyze this code. Since we already know what the function **require_once()** does and we know the contents of *connectInc.php,* let's start with the line:

```
$sql = "SELECT * FROM employee";
```

Here we construct a SQL query statement (adhering to the SQL syntax and grammar rules) and store that query statement, which is an instruction to obtain all records in the table *employee,* in the variable *$sql*. Then, in the next line, we provide *$sql* as an argument of the *query* method of the connection object *$conn*.

```
$rs = $conn->query($sql);
```

The *query* method of the connection object, *$conn*, will execute the SQL statement in *$sql* and will obtain all the records in table *employee* and store those records as a resultset object referenced by the variable *$rs*.

A *resultset* (also known as *recordset)* is a memory image in the client's browser of the rows of a table of a database in the server. A *resultset* is the result of executing a query. In our previous query, we requested all the rows of the table *employee*. We could also have requested only those employees in a certain department. Whatever our query, the rows that match our query now exist as a resultset referenced by the variable *$rs*. We can perform operations on the resultset as if we were performing them on the actual table. The database engine will take care of updating the table as we update the resultset.

(Of course, if a table contained thousands of rows and we requested all those rows, the client's machine may not have enough memory to hold all those rows. So the server will have to use pagination techniques to serve up rows that can be handled by the memory capacity of the browser client.)

Now, back to the *query* method of the connection object referenced by *$conn* which executed the SQL statement in *$sql* and returned a resultset object referenced by the variable *$rs*.

If the query fails to execute, the variable *$rs* will contain the boolean value *false* and this line of code will display a specific error message.

```
trigger_error('Wrong SQL: ' . $sql . '
Error: ' . $conn->error, E_USER_ERROR);
```

To execute this **trigger_error()** function, change this line of code:

**trigger_error()**

```
$sql = "SELECT * FROM employee";
```

to:

```
$sql = "OBTAIN * FROM employee";
```

You will get this error message specifically pointing out that "OBTAIN" was the error in our SQL statement:

Fatal error: Wrong SQL: OBTAIN * FROM employee Error: You have an error in your SQL syntax; check the manual that corresponds to your MySQL server version for the right syntax to use near 'OBTAIN * FROM employee' at line . . .

If our query was successful, then all the records of the table *employee* are in the resultset object referenced by the variable *$rs*. We then execute the **fetch_array** method of the resultset object, *$rs*:

```
$arr = $rs->fetch_array(MYSQLI_ASSOC);
```

The **fetch_array** method will store the fields of the current row of the resultset *$rs* in an associative array *$arr* using the field names as keys because we provided the constant MYSQLI_ASSOC. If we change this constant to MYSQLI_NUM, then *$arr* will be a numerically indexed array.

**fetch_array()**

We said "store the fields of the current row of *$rs*." What will be the "current row of *$rs*"? Since we will be accessing *$rs* immediately after *$rs* was created (by the *query* method of the connection object *$conn*) in the line of code,

```
$rs = $conn->query($sql);
```

then the current row of *$rs* will be its first row. The fields of this first row will be stored in the associative array *$arr*. We now display those fields with the line:

```
echo( $arr['empid'] . ' ' .
      $arr['lastname'] . ' ' .
      $arr['firstname'] , ' ' .
      $arr['department'] , ' ' .
      $arr['position'] , ' ' .
      $arr['salary'] );
```

In your browser, you should see something similar to this:

```
101 Escudero, Ernesto 3 Utility Supervisor
10000
```

These are the fields of the first row of the table *employee*. Check that the values you get match the actual values of the fields of your first record in the correct order – *empid, lastname, firstname, department, position* and *salary*.

We also have these two lines of code:

```
$rows_returned = $rs->num_rows;
echo( "<br>Rows: " . $rows_returned);
```

which will produce the following output:

```
Rows: 9
```

**num_rows** is a property of the resultset object referenced by *$rs*, which stores the number of rows in *$rs*, which is also the number of rows in the table *employee*. Check that the value displayed in your browser matches the number of records in your *employee* table. You can use phpMyAdmin to accomplish this.

Now, we have two scripts that are running properly. One script, *connectInc.php,* establishes a connection to the MySQL database *employees.* The second script *retrieve1.php* executes a Select query on the database and retrieves all the records of the table *employee* into the resultset object *$rs.* But, it only displays the first record! How do we display all the rows of the resultset *$rs*? (In effect, how do we display all the rows of the table *employee?).* The answer: we use a *while-loop.*

When we call the **fetch_array** method for the first time, it will extract the fields of the first row of *$rs* (the current row) into the elements of array *$arr.* **Fetch_array** then makes the second row the current row.

If we call **fetch_array** again, it is the fields of this second row which will be extracted and then the third row becomes the current row. So if we keep calling **fetch_array** repeatedly, we are able to consecutively process all the rows of the resultset *$rs.*

So, to make repeated calls to **fetch_array** within a *while-loop,* we modify the code of *retrieve1.php* and save it as *retrieve2.php.* This is its code:

```php
<?php

require_once ("connectInc.php");

$sql = "SELECT * FROM employee";
$rs = $conn->query ($sql);

if ( $rs === false ) {
    trigger_error ('Wrong SQL: ' . $sql . '
Error: ' . $conn->error, E_USER_ERROR);
} else {
    $rows_returned = $rs->num_rows;
    echo ( "<br>Rows: " . $rows_returned);
    while ( $arr = $rs->fetch_array (MYSQLI_
ASSOC) ) {
        echo ("<br/>");
        echo ($arr['empid'] . ' ' .
```

```
                    $arr['lastname'].' '.
                    $arr['firstname'] . ' ' .
                    $arr['department'] . ' ' .
                    $arr['position'].' '.
                    $arr['salary']);
        }
    }
?>
```

When we execute this script, we will see all the rows of the *employee* table displayed in the following manner.

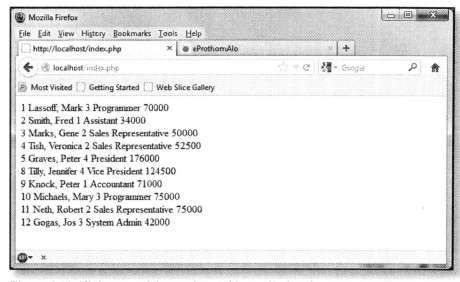

1 Lassoff, Mark 3 Programmer 70000
2 Smith, Fred 1 Assistant 34000
3 Marks, Gene 2 Sales Representative 50000
4 Tish, Veronica 2 Sales Representative 52500
5 Graves, Peter 4 President 176000
8 Tilly, Jennifer 4 Vice President 124500
9 Knock, Peter 1 Accountant 71000
10 Michaels, Mary 3 Programmer 75000
11 Neth, Robert 2 Sales Representative 75000
12 Gogas, Jos 3 System Admin 42000

Figure 9.17: All the rows of the *employee* table are displayed.

To present this information in a table, replace the else block with the following code, and save the script as *retrieve3.php*:

```
    {
        $rows_returned = $rs->num_rows;
        echo( "<br>Rows: " . $rows_returned);
        echo("<table>");
        while ($arr = $rs->fetch_array( MYSQLI_
ASSOC)) {
            echo("<tr>");
```

```
      echo "<td>" . $arr['empid'] . "</
td>"
        ."<td>" . $arr['lastname'] . "</
td>"
        ."<td>" . $arr['firstname'] . "</
td>"
        ."<td>" . $arr['department'] .
"</td>"
        . "<td>" . $arr['position']. "</
td>"
        . "<td>" . $arr['salary'] . "</
td>";
    echo '</tr>';
    }
  echo("</table>");
}
```

When we execute *retrieve3. php*, we will get a display similar to the following, where the columns are neatly aligned.

In this chapter, we are able to query the database using a SQL command, get a *$result* object by sending the query to the database itself, and then loop through the rows of the *$result* object and create a table out of that data.

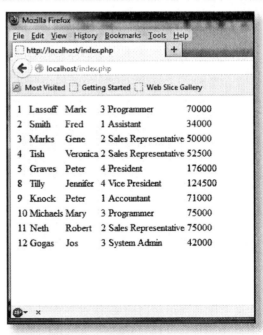

Figure 9.18: The information is represented in a table form.

## CODE LISTING *RETRIEVE3.PHP*

```php
<?php

  require_once("connectInc.php");

  $sql = "SELECT * FROM employee";
  $rs = $conn->query($sql);

  if ( $rs === false ) {
    trigger_error('Wrong SQL: ' . $sql . '
Error: ' . $conn->error, E_USER_ERROR);
  } else {
    echo("<table>");
    while($arr = mysqli_fetch_array($rs,
MYSQLI_ASSOC)) {
                echo("<tr>");
                echo "<td>" .
$arr['empid'] . "</td>"
                      ."<td>" .
$arr['lastname'] . "</td>"
                      ."<td>" .
$arr['firstname'] . "</td>"
                      ."<td>" .
$arr['department'] . "</td>"
                      . "<td>" .
$arr['position']. "</td>"
                      . "<td>" .
$arr['salary'] . "</td>";
                echo '</tr>';
        }
        echo("</table>");
    }
  ?>
```

1. Which class serves as a blueprint to a connection object which enables PHP scripts to access a MySQL database?
   a. connection class
   b. mysqli class
   c. physics class
   d. recordset class.

2. Which command indicates that if *mysql_connect* does not work, it will go ahead and provide a MySQL error that occurred?
   a. or end
   b. or die
   c. or finish
   d. or error

# 9.3 STORING INFORMATION IN THE DATABASE

Let's review our past efforts. We used phpMyAdmin to create our database, *employees,* and its two tables – *employee* and *department.* We also used phpMyAdmin to input test data into our two tables. Then, we wrote several PHP scripts to carry out the Retrieve functionality of our CRUD application. Now, we are going to code PHP scripts to handle the Create functionality.

The first thing we need to do is create a form where the user will type the information that will directly go into the database. Here, we are not going to include *empid,* as it will be generated automatically. We will open a new file called *insert.php,* where we will use the HTML *form* tag, and write the following code there:

```
<!doctype html>
<html lang="en">
<head>
    <meta charset="UTF-8">
    <title>Insert Employee</title>
</head>
<body>
    <form action="insertProcess.php"
method="post">
        <p>Last Name<br/>
        <input type="text" name="last"/></
p>

        <p>First Name<br/>
        <input type="text" name="first"/></
p>

        <p>Department<br/>
        <input type="text"
name="department"/></p>

        <p>Position<br/>
        <input type="text"
name="position"/></p>
```

```
        <p>Salary<br/>
        <input type="text"
name="salary"/></p>

        <input type="submit" value="Save
Information" />
    </form>
</body>
</html>
```

Let's take a look at this line of HTML code:

```
<form action="insertProcess.php"
method="post">
```

This form tag sets the action attribute to the file *insertProcess.php*
which will receive and process the data input into this form. We also
use the *post* method, which passes the information as an array instead
of creating a *query string* which appears in the URL.

If we run the script *insert.php* in our browser, we will see this:

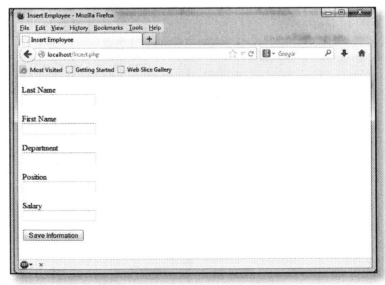

Figure 9.19: The form through which new data will be inserted.

Now we have a form that can be used to put data into the database.
However, you can see that you can type anything in the box under
*Department,* which is not what we want.

We want the user to select the department name, but it is not
the department name that will be saved in the database, but the
corresponding Department ID which can only have a value between 1
and 4. To do this, we modify our HTML code in this way.

```
<p>Department<br/>
    <select name="department">
        <option value="1">Accounting</
option>
        <option value="2">Sales</option>
        <option value="3">Information
Technology</option>
        <option
value="4">Management</
option>
    </select>
</p>
```

Here, it is the value attribute of the
option tag that is going to be posted
when its corresponding literal—
either Accounting, Sales, Information
Technology, or Management—is selected
by the user.

Now, before actually inserting data
into this form, let's code the script
*insertProcess.php.* The first task of
this script is to extract the data input
in the form displayed by *insert.php.*
We thus access the superglobal array
*$_REQUEST* with the following lines
of code and then display it with an echo
function:

Figure 9.20: The dropdown box
for the Department field.

```
<?php
    $last = $_REQUEST['last'];
```

```
$first= $_REQUEST['first'];
$department= $_REQUEST['department'];
$position= $_REQUEST['position'];
$salary= $_REQUEST['salary'];
echo($last . ' ' .
     $first . ' ' .
     $department . ' ' .
     $position . ' ' .
     $salary);
?>
```

Now, let's test if the data input in *insert.php* was actually passed to *insertProcess.php*. Run the script *insert.php* and input the data as shown in figure 9.21.

When we click the *Save Information* button, you should see this on the screen:

```
Smith  Fred  3
Programmer  65000
```

First, you may see some slight discrepancies with the code for Information Technology. We show a '3', but you might get a '2' or '4'. No matter, the data displayed should be in the order *lastname, firstname, departmentID, position,* and *salary*. If the data you input in the form of *insert.php* is displayed correctly in this order, then the inputted data was passed correctly to this script *insertProcess.php*.

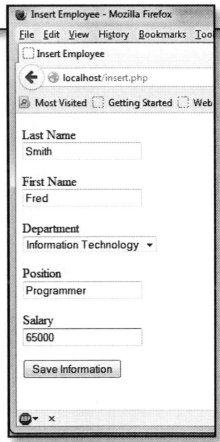

Figure 9.21: Passing information to the database.

Now, before we complete the rest of the code of *insertProcess.php* that will store this data in the table *employee*, please go back to somewhere near the beginning of Section 9.2 (Retrieving a Query from the Database) where we outline "the general flow of logic of each of our four main scripts." Here is a brief summary of that flow of logic.

    a. Establish a link to the database with a connection object *$conn*.
    b. Check if *$conn* was successfully created.
    c. Construct either an INSERT, SELECT, UPDATE or DELETE query.
    d. Use the **query** method of *$conn* to execute the query.
    e. Check if the query executed successfully. In the case of the Retrieve functionality, obtain a resultset object and transfer its contents to an array.
    f. Close the connection.

Now we complete the code of the script *insertProcess.php*. First, we extract the data posted by *insert.php* from the super global array *$_REQUEST* and store it in the variables *$last, $first, $department, $position* and *$salary*.

```
$last = $_REQUEST['last'];
$first= $_REQUEST['first'];
$department= $_REQUEST['department'];
$position= $_REQUEST['position'];
$salary= $_REQUEST['salary'];
```

The data that we will store in the table *employee* is now in the five variables - *$last, $first, $department, $position, $salary*. As an aid to debugging, we display in the browser the values of those five variables with the line:

```
echo($last . ' ' .
     $first . ' ' .
     $department . ' ' .
     $position . ' ' .
     $salary);
```

Later on, in the production version of our application, we can remove this line.

Next, we establish a connection with our database and check if this connection was successful. This is steps a and b of our "general flow of logic." This is carried out by the code in the script *connectInc.php* which we include into our *insertProcess.php* script:

```
require_once("connectInc.php");
```

Next, (step c) we build our SQL Insert statement and store this statement in the variable *$sql*.

```
$sql= "INSERT INTO employee VALUES ('',"  .
"'"  . $last . "',"  .
"'"  . $first . "',"  .
"'"  . $department . "',"  .
"'"  . $position . "',"  .
"'"  . $salary . "')";
```

Next, (step d) we call the **query** method of the *connection* object *$conn*. We provide *$sql* as an argument to the **query** method. We make this call in the **if** clause of an **if-else** statement as in the following code:

```
if ($conn->query($sql) == false ) {
    $errmsg = 'Wrong SQL: ' . $sql . '
Error: ' . $conn->error;
    trigger_error( $errmsg, E_USER_ERROR);
} else {
    . . .
}
```

Now, (step e) we check if the **query** method was successful. The call to the **query** method will return the boolean value FALSE if the **query** method failed to carry out the INSERT statement stored in *$sql*. The **trigger_error()** function will then be executed and the script terminated.

If the **query** method succeeded in writing our data to the table *employee* as a new row, then we can access two properties of the *connection* object, *$conn*, and display those two properties for debugging purposes.

```
$last_inserted_id = $conn->insert_id;
$affected_rows = $conn->affected_rows;
echo( "<br/>Last Inserted Id: " . $last_
inserted_id );
   echo( "<br/>Affected rows:    " .
$affected_rows );
```

Notice also that in the preceeding code we have added a link that the user can click if he needs to enter more new employees.

Next, we need to close the SQL connection (step f) with a call to the **close** method of the *connection* object, *$conn:*

```
$conn->close;
```

Now, let's test our two scripts by executing *insert.php* and then inputting the data shown on the following screen.

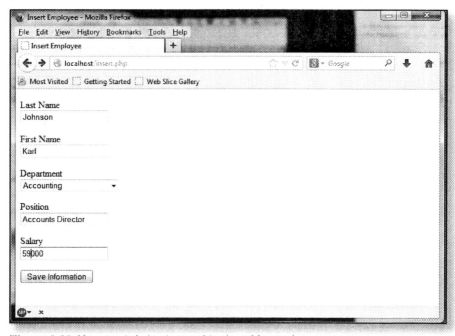

Figure 9.22. New row is being inserted in the table *employee*.

If we click *Save Information*, we will see this:

```
Johnson Karl 1 Accounts Director 59000
INSERT INTO employee VALUES
('','Johnson','Karl','1','Accounts
Director,'59000')
Last Inserted Id: 114
Affected rows: 1
Johnson successfully added to the
database.
```

We can use phpMyAdmin to check if our data was actually added
If we check the actual database in our *phpMyAdmin* application, we
will find that a new row is successfully added at the bottom, as shown
here:

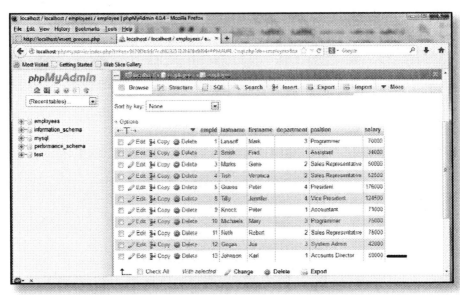

Figure 9.23: A new row is added in the table *employee*.

This shows that our attempt to add new information into the database
was successful.

In the sections that follow, we are going to call the script *insert.php*
from a dashboard script that we will name *index.php*. A dashboard
script is a central or main script that provides links to other scripts of
the system. In our CRUD application, the dashboard script *index.php*

will have links to the Create, Update and Delete functionalities of our application.

Now, once our dashboard script *index.php* calls the Create script *insert.php,* which in turn executes *insertProcess.php,* we should be able to return to the dashboard from *insertProcess.php.* Therefore, in *insertProcess.php* our last line of code will be:

```
echo( "<br/>Go back to <a href='index.
php'>Add-Upd-Del Page</a>" );
```

## CODE LISTING: *INSERTPROCESS.PHP*

```php
<?php

   $last = $_REQUEST['last'];
   $first= $_REQUEST['first'];
   $department= $_REQUEST['department'];
   $position= $_REQUEST['position'];
   $salary= $_REQUEST['salary'];
   echo( $last . ' ' .
     $first . ' ' .
     $department . ' ' .
     $position . ' ' .
     $salary);

   require_once("ConnectInc.php");
   $sql= "INSERT INTO employee VALUES ('',"

     "'" . $last . "'," .
     "'" . $first . "'," .
     "'" . $department . "'," .
     "'" . $position . "'," .
     "'" . $salary . "')";

   if ($conn->query($sql) == false ) {
     trigger_error('Wrong SQL: ' . $sql . '
Error: ' . $conn->error, E_USER_ERROR);
```

```
    } else {
      $last_inserted_id = $conn->insert_id;
      $affected_rows = $conn->affected_rows;
      echo( "<br/>Last Inserted Id: " .
$last_inserted_id );
      echo( "<br/>Affected rows:    " .
$affected_rows );
      echo( "<br/>" . $last . " successfully
added to the database." );
    }

    $conn->close();
    echo( "<br/>Go back to <a href='index.
php'>Add-Upd-DelPage</a>" );

?>
```

## QUESTIONS FOR REVIEW

1. What is the data type of the information that the *post* method uses?
   a. an array.
   b. a linked list.
   c. a single data.
   d. None of the above.

2. Which method of the *connection* object is used to close itself?
   a. exit
   b. end
   c. close
   d. none of the above.

# 9.4 DELETING AND UPDATING DATABASE RECORDS

Now that we have scripts for the Create and Retrieve functionalities of our very simple and basic *CRUD* application, we are going to write the scripts for the Update and Delete functionalities.

First, we will modify the script *retrieve3.php* and save it as *index.php*. We want this script's page display to act as a dashboard—a central control point of the application. *Index.php* will also be the opening script of our CRUD application and from its dashboard page display, we can access the Create, Update and Delete scripts of our application. This is the modified code for *index.php*.

```php
<?php

require_once("connectINC.php");
$sql = "SELECT * FROM employee";
$rs = $conn->query($sql);
if ( $rs === false ) {
    $errmsg = 'Wrong SQL: ' . $sql . '
Error: ' . $conn->error;
    trigger_error( $errmsg, E_USER_ERROR);
} else {
    echo("<table>");
    while ($arr = $rs->fetch_array( MYSQLI_
ASSOC )) {
        echo("<tr>");
        echo( "<td>" . $arr['empid'] . "</
td>"
        . "<td>" . $arr['lastname'] . "</
td>"
        . "<td>" . $arr['firstname'] . "</
td>"
        . "<td>" . $arr['department'] . "</
td>"
        . "<td>" . $arr['position']. "</
td>"
```

```
           .  "<td>" . $arr['salary'] . "</td>"
           .  "<td><a href='delete.php?id=" .
$arr['empid'] .
           "'>Delete</a></td>"
           .  "<td><a href='updateForm.php?id="
. $arr['empid'] .
           "'>Update</a></td>" );
      echo '</tr>';
    }
   echo("<tr>
      <td></td> <td></td> <td></td> <td></
td>
      <td></td><td></td><td><a href=insert.
php>Add New</a></td>");
   echo("</tr>");
   echo("</table>");
}
$conn->close();
?>
```

When we run this script, all the sample data that you entered in table
*employee* should appear on the screen in orderly rows and columns as
this screenshot shows.

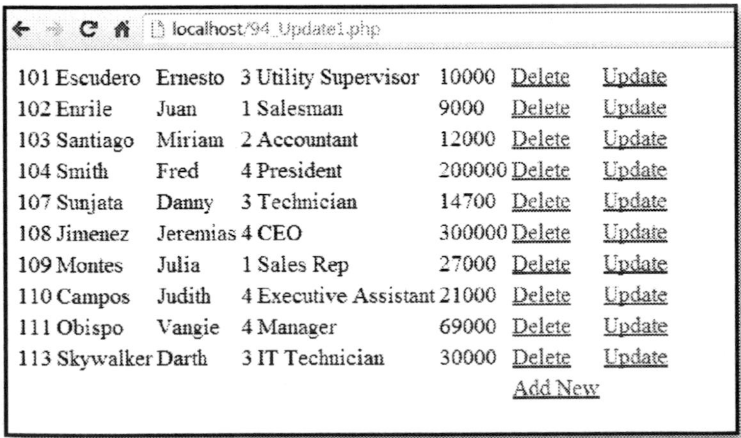

| ← → C ⋔ | localhost/94_Update1.php | | | | | |
|---|---|---|---|---|---|---|
| 101 Escudero | Ernesto | 3 Utility Supervisor | 10000 | Delete | Update |
| 102 Enrile | Juan | 1 Salesman | 9000 | Delete | Update |
| 103 Santiago | Miriam | 2 Accountant | 12000 | Delete | Update |
| 104 Smith | Fred | 4 President | 200000 | Delete | Update |
| 107 Sunjata | Danny | 3 Technician | 14700 | Delete | Update |
| 108 Jimenez | Jeremias | 4 CEO | 300000 | Delete | Update |
| 109 Montes | Julia | 1 Sales Rep | 27000 | Delete | Update |
| 110 Campos | Judith | 4 Executive Assistant | 21000 | Delete | Update |
| 111 Obispo | Vangie | 4 Manager | 69000 | Delete | Update |
| 113 Skywalker | Darth | 3 IT Technician | 30000 | Delete | Update |
| | | | | Add New | |

Figure 9.24: The screen display generated by the script *index*.php which shows the rows
of the *employee* table with *Delete* and *Update* buttons for each employee. There is also an
*Add New* button at the bottom of the table to create a record for a new employee.

> **TIP:** To align the *Add New* button with the column of Delete buttons, add or remove the table cell tags <td></td> just before the link which defines the *Add New* button.

If you compare the code of *index.php* with the code of *retrieve3.php*, you will see that we added lines of code that create *Delete* and *Update* buttons for each employee record displayed. With these two buttons, we can remove an employee's record or modify their data. We also created an *Add New* button at the bottom of the screen to allow us to add new employees to the database. The *Add New*, *Delete* and *Update* buttons are also links to the *insert.php*, *delete.php* and *updateForm.php* scripts, respectively. Clicking on any of these three buttons will execute their respective PHP script.

This is the function of the script *index.php* as a dashboard. Its screen display allows us to access the *Create*, *Update* and *Delete* functionalities of our CRUD application.

When we link to the *delete.php* and *updateForm.php* scripts, we also have to pass the ID of the individual record that we want to either delete or update. For that, we use a **query string**. This is a part of a URL that contains data to be passed to web applications. You may have seen a **query string** before, where there is a question mark (?) at the end of a URL, and then a set of key phrases, like the following:

**query string**

```
http://program/path/?query_string
```

The following line of sample code creates the *Delete* button and links it to the *delete.php* script. It also builds the **query string** that will be passed to the *delete.php* script.

```
><td><a href='delete.php?id=" .
$arr['empid'] . "'>Delete</a></td>
```

There is an almost identical line for the *Update* button.

```
><td><a href='updateForm.php?id=" .
$arr['empid'] . "'>Update</a></td>
```

The line to build the *Add New* button initially looks different and more complicated than the two previous lines but it is essentially the same. It has been pre-padded with <td></td> tags to align the *Add New* button with the column of *Delete* buttons.

```
<td></td> <td></td> <td></td> <td></td>
<td></td> <td></td>
        <td><a href='insert.php'>Add New</
a></td>");
```

When you run the *index.php* script and hover your mouse over any of the *Update* and *Delete* buttons, the full **query string** showing a corresponding employee ID is displayed at the bottom of the screen. For example:

```
localhost/
delete.php?id=3
```

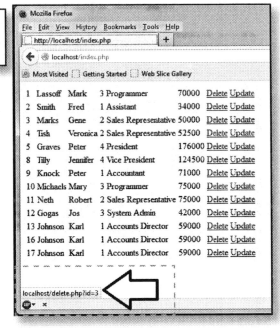

In figure 9.25, you can see the complete **query string** at the lower left corner, as indicated by the big white arrow.

Now, we are going to write the script *delete.php*. This is the script that will be executed when we click on a *Delete* button and it will also receive the **query string** from the *index.php* script.

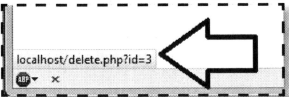

Figure 9.25: The *Delete* and *Update* buttons are represented as links and a complete query string is displayed at the lower left of this screenshot.

This is the complete code of *delete.php*.

## CODE LISTING *DELETE.PHP*

```php
<?php
   require_once("connectInc.php");
   $id = $_REQUEST['id'];
   $sql = "DELETE FROM employee WHERE
empid= '" . $id . "';";

   if ($conn->query($sql) === false) {
       trigger_error('Wrong SQL: ' . $sql .
' Error: ' . $conn->error, E_USER_ERROR);
   } else {
       $affected_rows = $conn->affected_
rows;
       echo( "<br/>" . $sql);
       echo( "<br/>Affected rows:    " .
$affected_rows );
       echo( "<br/>User " . $id . " deleted
from the database.");
   }
   $conn->close();
   echo("<br/>Return to <a href='index.
php'>Add-Upd-Del Page</a>");
?>
```

Before we analyze this code, let's summarize the the general flow of logic of each of our four main scripts.

a. Establish a link to the database with a connection object *$conn*.
b. Check if *$conn* was successfully created.
c. Construct either an INSERT, SELECT, UPDATE or DELETE query.
d. Use the **query** method of *$conn* to execute the query.
e. Check if the query executed successfully. In the case of the Retrieve functionality, obtain a resultset object and transfer its contents to an array.
f. Close the connection.

Now, let's look at the code of *delete.php*.

Steps a and b are carried out by the code in the script *connectInc.php* which we include into our *delete.php* script:

```php
require_once("connectInc.php");
```

We obtain the *empid* of the employee whose record we are going to delete with:

```php
$id = $_REQUEST['id'];
```

We use the value of *$id* in building our SQL Delete query. Here's step c.

```php
$sql = "DELETE FROM employee WHERE empid= '" . $id . "';";
```

We execute the query and check for its successful execution. (steps d and e).

```php
if ($conn->query($sql) === false) {
    trigger_error('Wrong SQL: ' . $sql .
' Error: ' . $conn->error, E_USER_ERROR);
    } else {
. . .
```

If the query is successful, we display parameters related to the query's operation.

```php
$affected_rows = $conn->affected_rows;
echo( "<br/>" . $sql);
echo( "<br/>Affected rows:    " .
$affected_rows );
echo( "<br/>User " . $id . " deleted
from the database.");
```

We close the connection (step f).

```php
$conn->close();
```

We display a link to allow our user to return to the dashboard, the script *index.php*.

```
echo("<br/>Return to <a href='index.
php'>Add-Upd-Del Page</a>");
```

Now, run the script *index.php* and select an employee to delete. (Note the *empid* of the employee.) When you click the Delete button, you should then get a display similar to the following.

```
DELETE FROM employee WHERE empid= '112';
Affected rows: 1
User 112 deleted from the database.
Return to Add-Upd-Del Page
```

This shows the result of deleting an employee who *empid* is 112. (Replace 112 with the *empid* of the employee you deleted.)

You can see that the first record is not there, which indicates that our *delete* operation is successful.

Now, let's look at the complete code of *updateForm.php* which is actually a full HTML document.

## CODE LISTING: UPDATEFORM.PHP

```
<!doctype html>
<html lang="en">
<head>
  <meta charset="UTF-8">
  <title>Update Form</title>
</head>

<body>
  <?php
    require_once("connectInc.php");

    $id=$_REQUEST['id'];
    $sql = "SELECT * FROM employee WHERE
```

```php
empid = '" . $id . "';";
    $rs = $conn->query($sql);

    if ( $rs === false ) {
        trigger_error('Wrong SQL: ' . $sql
. ' Error: ' . $conn->error, E_USER_
ERROR);
        die( "Select Error: " . $sql);
    } else {
        $arr = $rs->fetch_array( MYSQLI_
ASSOC);
    }
    $conn->close();

?>
<form action="updateProcess.php"
method="post">
    <input type="hidden" name="id"
value="<?php print($id); ?>" />
    <p>Last Name<br/>
<input type="text" value="<?php
print($arr['lastname']) ?>"
name="last"/></p>

    <p>First Name<br/>
    <input type="text" value="<?php
print($arr['firstname']) ?>"
name="first"/></p>

    <p>Department<br/>
    <select name="department">
      <option <?php
if($arr['department']==1)
{ print('selected'); } ?>
value="1">Accounting</option>
      <option <?php
if($arr['department']==2) {
```

```
print('selected'); } ?> value="2">Sales</
option>
      <option <?php
if($arr['department']==3)
{ print('selected'); } ?>
value="3">Information Technology</option>
      <option <?php
if($arr['department']==4)
{ print('selected'); } ?>
value="4">Management</option>
    </select></p>

    <p>Position<br/>
    <input type="text" value="<?php
print($arr['position']) ?>"
name="position"/></p>

    <p>Salary<br/>
    <input type="text" value="<?php
print($arr['salary']) ?>" name="salary"
/></p>

    <input type="submit" value="Update
Information" />
  </form>

</body>

</html>
```

The function of this form is to display the data of one employee. The following lines of PHP script, placed in the <head></head> section of our HTML document, perform the necessary database operations to retrieve the data of one employee.

```
require_once("connectInc.php");
$id=$_REQUEST['id'];
$sql = "SELECT * FROM employee WHERE
```

```
empid = '" . $id . "';";
   $rs = $conn->query($sql);
   if ( $rs === false ) {
       trigger_error('Wrong SQL: ' . $sql .
' Error: ' . $conn->error, E_USER_ERROR);
       die( "Select Error: " . $sql);
   } else {
       $arr = $rs->fetch_array( MYSQLI_
ASSOC);
   }
   $conn->close();
```

As you read and analyze this code, note that it also follows the pattern of steps a-f which we just recently detailed as we analyzed the code of *delete.php*.)

  a. Create a *connection* object, *$conn*.
  b. Check if *$conn* was successfully created.
  c. Construct SQL query.
  d. Execute query with **query** method of connection object.
  e. Check if query executed successfully. (For **SELECT** queries, process the *resultset* object, *$rs*.)
  f. Close connection.

The reason we keep repeating these six steps is that this will be the basic pattern of any PHP script that accesses a MySQL database. Understanding and mastering the logic of those six steps will spare you any future headaches when accessing MySQL databases!

Now, the retrieved data of one employee is stored in the associative array, *$arr,* by the line:

```
$arr = $rs->fetch_array( MYSQLI_ASSOC );
```

The data in this array is then used by the form elements to display the data.

Let's analyze the following HTML and PHP code which displays the data in the associative array, *$arr*:

```
<input type="text" value="<?php
```

```
print($arr['lastname']) ?>" name="last"
/></p>
```

Here, we set the value attribute of the <input> element to the value of an element of the array *$arr*, specifically the element indexed by the key *lastname*. We use PHP code to do this. In typing this line, you really have to be careful to place every character where they belong, otherwise you get all kinds of errors.

In the case of the *Department* field, it is a different process. We have to test individually for each of the *departmentId* values (1-4) before we can display the corresponding *departmentName*. Again, you really have to be careful in typing this line, misplace any character, especially a comma, quotation mark, forward slash, opening or closing braces, brackets or parentheses, and you get all kinds of errors.

```
<option <?php if($arr['department']==1)
{ print('selected'); } ?>
value="1">Accounting</option>
```

Lastly, we have to deal with the *empid* field. Remember, this field is a primary key and is auto-generated by the MySQL database. Once it is assigned to an employee, it can never be modified. But we need to retrieve the value of *empid* from the database and securely preserve this value during our Update procedures, because it will have to be passed back to the MySQL database to identify the exact record of the *employee* table that has to be updated with our changes.

Thus, we will use a hidden field as this line of code shows.

```
<input type="hidden" name="id"
value="<?php print($id); ?>" />
```

Storing the *empid* field in a hidden <input> element ensures that this value will also be included in the post method. Now, consider the action attribute of the <form> element. This attribute is set to the script *updateProcess.php*.

```
<form action="updateProcess.php"
method="post">
```

In order to ensure that the updated information is saved in the database, we are going to create the file *updateProcess.php*, with the following code:

```php
<?php

   require_once("ConnectInc.php");

   $id = $_REQUEST['id'];
   $last = $_REQUEST['last'];
   $first= $_REQUEST['first'];
   $department= $_REQUEST['department'];
   $position= $_REQUEST['position'];
   $salary= $_REQUEST['salary'];
   echo( $last . ' ' .
       $first . ' ' .
       $department . ' ' .
       $position . ' ' .
       $salary);

   $sql= "UPDATE employee SET " .
       "lastname = '" . $last . "', " .
       "firstname = '" . $first . "', " .
       "department = '" . $department .
"', " .
       "position = '" . $position . "', "
.
       "salary = '" . $salary . "' WHERE
empid = '" . $id . "';";

   if ($conn->query($sql) == false ) {
       trigger_error('Wrong SQL: ' . $sql .
' Error: ' . $conn->error, E_USER_ERROR);
   } else {
       $affected_rows = $conn->affected_
rows;
       echo( "<br/>" . $sql);
       echo( "<br/>Affected rows:      " .
```

```
$affected_rows );
   }
   $conn->close();
    echo( "<br/>User " . $id . " has been
updated. <br/>Back to <a href='index.
php'>Add-Upd-Del Page</a>.");

?>
```

Here, we have used the SQL query for an *update* operation, where we have set the fields to their new values, and used the *where* clause to indicate the record that we are actually updating.

Now, run the script *index.php*, select an employee and then click the *Update* button for that employee's record. You should get the following page (with your corresponding test data).

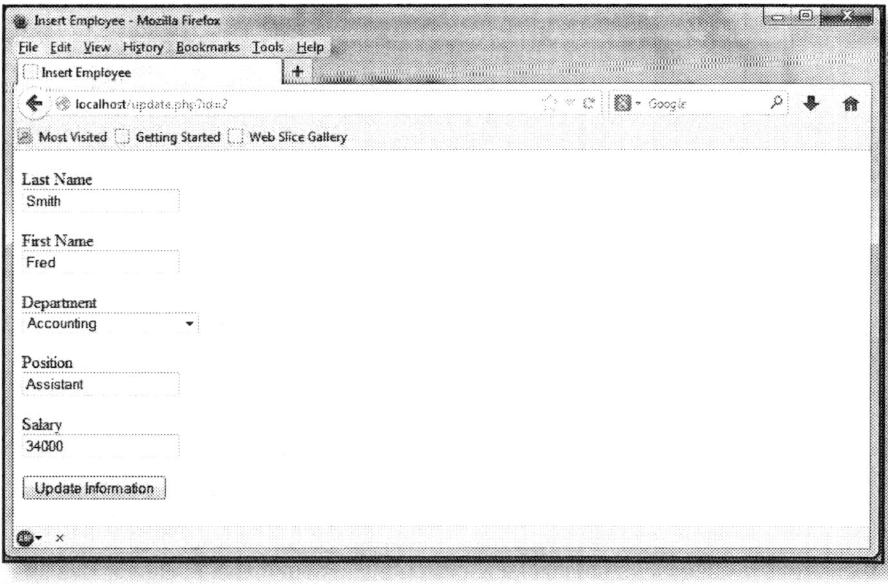

Figure 9.26: Updating the data of one employee.

Make whatever changes you want to any of the fields. In fact, to completely test the *update.php* and *updateProcess.php* scripts, make changes to all the fields! Then click the *Update Information* button. You should get a display similar to the following (with your corresponding test data).

```
Obispo Vangie 4 Manager 69000
UPDATE employee SET lastname = 'Obispo',
firstname = 'Vangie', department = '4',
position = 'Manager', salary = '69000'
WHERE empid = '111';
Affected rows: 1
User 111 has been updated.
Back to Add-Upd-Del Page.
```

When you click the *Add-Upd-Del Page* link, you will be returned to the
screen display of *index.php*. Check if the data you updated was actually
modified.

You could also use *phpMyAdmin* to make changes to any field of any
table in the database, but for now, just use *phpMyAdmin* to verify the
changes we make using our CRUD application.

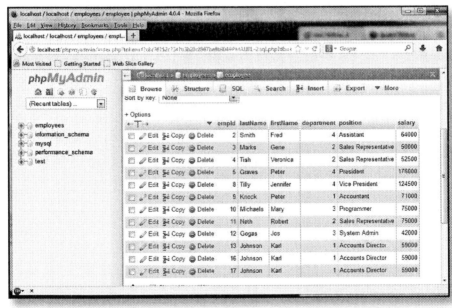

Figure 9.27: Using phpMyAdmin to edit fields of tables in a database.

Our simple and basic CRUD application is complete.

1. Which symbol is used in a query string?
   a. #        c. &
   b. $        d. ?

2. What is *$_REQUEST[]* ?
   a. A function
   b. A command
   c. An array
   d. A super global array

# CHAPTER 9 LAB EXERCISE

1. Ensure that your MAMP or WAMP server stack is downloaded, installed and running. You can download the WAMP server for Windows at www.wampserver.com/en/. You can download the MAMP server for Mac at www.mamp.info.

2. Set up an HTML document and embed an opening and closing PHP tag in the <body> section of the document. Save that document in your www folder (Windows) or htdocs folder (Macintosh) as described.

3. Create a database to track students and grades in a Computer Science Class. Create a database in mySQL as follows:

Database Name: CSClassData
Number of Tables: 1

4. In the CSClassData, create a table called students. The table should have the following fields:

studentID int(5)
lastName varchar(40)
firstName varchar(20)
test1Grade int(3)
test2Grade int(3)
test3Grade int(3)

test4Grade int(3)
finalExamGrade int(3)

5. Enter fictional data for 10 students including a first name, last name, and grades for all 5 tests. (Grade on the standard scale of 0-100).

6. Create a database connection script that connects to your MySQL database and the CSCLassData Database you created.

7. Create a page called *grade_list.php*. On this page, output all of the grades from the database by student. You should use a table for this.

8. Once you have output all of the grades, add two columns in the table. The first column should contain the numerical average the student received by averaging the five grades.

The second new column should display their final grade in A-F form according to the following:

A ➜ 90-100
B ➜ 80-89
C ➜ 70-79
D ➜ 60-69
F ➜ Below 60

You should be able to add the final two columns without altering anything in the database—these will be calculated fields and not stored database fields.

9. Use CSS to make your output table more readable.

10. To the right of the calculated average and letter grade field, add links to delete and edit pages. Call the delete page *grades_delete.php* and the update page *grades_updateForm.php*. At the bottom of the table, add a link to call the Add New Student page, *grade_insert.php*.

11. Write PHP code to make the *update, delete* and *create* functional as demonstrated in this chapter.

12. Make sure that pages are linked to each other so that the user may easily navigate between functions in your completed PHP application.

# CHAPTER 9 LAB SOLUTIONS

## *FILE: GRADESCONNECT.PHP*

```php
<?php
  define( "HOSTNAME", "localhost");
  define( "USERNAME", "root");
  define( "PASSWORD", "");
  define( "DB_NAME", "CSClassData");

  $conn = new mysqli(HOSTNAME, USERNAME,
PASSWORD, DB_NAME);

  if ($conn->connect_errno) {
    echo( "<br/>Failed to connect to
MySQL: (" . $conn->connect_errno . ") " .
$conn->connect_error );
    die( '<br/>Program Terminated');
}
?>
```

## *FILE: GRADES_DELETE.PHP*

```php
<?php

  require_once("gradesConnect.php");

  $id = $_REQUEST['id'];
  $sql = "DELETE FROM students WHERE
studentID= '" . $id . "';";

  if ($conn->query($sql) === false) {
    trigger_error('Wrong SQL: ' . $sql . '
Error: ' . $conn->error, E_USER_ERROR);
  } else {
    echo( "<br/>" . $sql);
    $affected_rows = $conn->affected_rows;
```

```php
    echo( "<br/>Affected rows:      " .
$affected_rows );
    echo( "<br/>User " . $id . " deleted
from the database.");
  }

  $conn->close();
  echo( "<br/>Return to <a href='grades_
list.php'>Add-Upd-Del Page</a>");

?>
```

## FILE: GRADES_LIST.PHP

```php
<!doctype html>
<html lang="en">

<head>
    <title>Grade List</title>
    <style>
        table, th, td, tr  {
            border: 1px solid black;
            border-collapse: collapse;
        }
    </style>
    <?php
      require_once("gradesConnect.php");
      $sql = "SELECT * FROM students";
      $rs = $conn->query($sql);

      if ( $rs === false ) {
         trigger_error('Wrong SQL: ' . $sql
. ' Error: ' . $conn->error, E_USER_ERROR);
         die();
      }
      $conn->close();
    ?>
```

```
</head>
<body>
  <table>
    <tr>
      <th>Student ID</th>
      <th>Last Name</th>
      <th>First Name</th>
      <th>Test 1</th>
      <th>Test 2</th>
      <th>Test 3</th>
      <th>Test 4</th>
      <th>Final Exam</th>
      <th>Average</th>
      <th>Letter Grade</th>
    </tr>
    <?php
    while ($arr = $rs->fetch_array(
MYSQLI_ASSOC )) {
        $average = ($arr['test1Grade'] +
$arr['test2Grade'] + $arr['test3Grade']
+ $arr['test4Grade'] +
$arr['finalExamGrade'])/5;
        if ($average > 89) {
          $letterGrade = 'A';
        } elseif ($average > 79) {
          $letterGrade = 'B';
        } elseif ($average > 69) {
          $letterGrade = 'C';
        } elseif ($average > 59) {
          $letterGrade = 'D';
        } else {
          $letterGrade = 'F';
        }
        echo("<tr id='" .
$arr['studentID'] . "'>");
        echo("<td>" . $arr['studentID'] .
"</td>");
        echo("<td>" . $arr['lastName'] .
```

```php
"</td>");
            echo("<td>" . $arr['firstName'] .
"</td>");
            echo("<td>" . $arr['test1Grade']
. "</td>");
            echo("<td>" . $arr['test2Grade']
. "</td>");
            echo("<td>" . $arr['test3Grade']
. "</td>");
            echo("<td>" . $arr['test4Grade']
. "</td>");
            echo("<td>" .
$arr['finalExamGrade'] . "</td>");
            echo("<td>" . $average . "</
td>");
            echo("<td>" . $letterGrade . "</
td>");
        echo("<td><a href='grades_updateForm.
php?id=" . $arr['studentID'] . "'>Update</
a></td>");
        echo("<td><a href='grades_delete.
php?id=" . $arr['studentID'] . "'>Delete</
a></td>");
        echo("</tr>");
    }
    echo("<tr>
        <td></td> <td></td> <td></td> <td></
td> <td></td>
        <td></td> <td></td> <td></td> <td></
td> <td></td>
        <td><a href='grades_insert.php'>Add
New</a></td>");
    echo("</tr>");
  ?>
  </table>
</body>
</html>
```

# FILE: GRADES_UPDATEFORM.PHP

```php
<?php
  require_once("gradesConnect.php");

  $id = $_REQUEST['id'];
  $sql = "SELECT * FROM students WHERE
studentID = '" . $id . "';";
  $rs = $conn->query($sql);

  if ( $rs === false ) {
    trigger_error('Wrong SQL: ' . $sql . '
Error: ' . $conn->error, E_USER_ERROR);
    die("Select Error: " . $sql);
  } else {
    $arr = $rs->fetch_array( MYSQLI_
ASSOC);
  }
  $conn->close();
?>

<html lang="en">
<head>
    <title>Update Student</title>
</head>
<body>
    <form action="grades_updateProcess.
php" method="post">
        <input type="hidden" value="<?php
print($arr['studentID']) ?>" name="id" />
        <p>Last Name<br/>
<input type="text" value="<?php
print($row['lastName']) ?>"
name="last"/></p>

        <p>First Name<br/> <input
type="text" value="<?php print(
```

```
$arr['firstName']) ?>" name="first"/></p>

        <p>Test 1 Grade<br/>
<input type="text" value="<?php
print( $arr['test1Grade']) ?>"
name="test1Grade"/></p>

        <p>Test 2 Grade<br/>
<input type="text" value="<?php
print( $arr['test2Grade']) ?>"
name="test2Grade"/></p>

        <p>Test 3 Grade<br/>
<input type="text" value="<?php
print( $arr['test3Grade']) ?>"
name="test3Grade"/></p>

        <p>Test 4 Grade<br/>
<input type="text" value="<?php
print( $arr['test4Grade']) ?>"
name="test4Grade"/></p>

        <p>Final Exam Grade<br/>
<input type="text" value="<?php
print( $arr['finalExamGrade']) ?>"
name="finalExamGrade"/></p>

        <input type="submit" value="Update
Information" />
    </form>
</body>
</html>
```

**FILE: GRADES_INSERT.PHP**

```
<!doctype html>
<html lang="en">
```

```html
<head>
    <title>Insert Student</title>
</head>
<body>
    <form action="grades_insertProcess.php"
method="post">
        <p>Last Name<br/>
        <input type="text" name="last"/></
p>

        <p>First Name<br/>
        <input type="text" name="first"/></
p>

        <p>Test 1 Grade<br/>
        <input type="text"
name="test1Grade" /></p>

        <p>Test 2 Grade<br/>
        <input type="text"
name="test2Grade" /></p>

        <p>Test 3 Grade<br/>
        <input type="text"
name="test3Grade" /></p>

        <p>Test 4 Grade<br/>
        <input type="text"
name="test4Grade" /></p>

        <p>Final Exam Grade<br/>
        <input type="text"
name="finalExamGrade" /></p>

        <input type="submit" value="Save
Information" />
    </form>
</body>
</html>
```

```php
<?php

  require_once("gradesConnect.php");

  $last = $_REQUEST['last'];
  $first= $_REQUEST['first'];
  $grade1 = $_REQUEST['test1Grade'];
  $grade2 = $_REQUEST['test2Grade'];
  $grade3 = $_REQUEST['test3Grade'];
  $grade4 = $_REQUEST['test4Grade'];
  $final = $_REQUEST['finalExamGrade'];

  $sql= "INSERT INTO students VALUES ('',"

    "'" . $last . "'," .
    "'" . $first . "'," .
    "'" . $grade1 . "'," .
    "'" . $grade2 . "'," .
    "'" . $grade3 . "'," .
    "'" . $grade4 . "'," .
    "'" . $final . "')";

  if ($conn->query($sql) == false ) {
      trigger_error('Wrong SQL: ' . $sql .
' Error: ' . $conn->error, E_USER_ERROR);
  } else {
      $last_inserted_id = $conn->insert_id;
      $affected_rows = $conn->affected_
rows;
      echo( "<br/>Last Inserted Id: " .
$last_inserted_id );
      echo( "<br/>Affected rows:     " .
$affected_rows );
      echo( "<br/>" . $last . "
successfully added to the database." );
  }
```

```php
  $conn->close();
  echo( "<br/>Go back to <a href='grades_
list.php'>Add-Upd-Del Page</a>" );
?>
```

## FILE: GRADES_UPDATEPROCESS.PHP

```php
<?php
  require_once("gradesConnect.php");

  $id = $_REQUEST['id'];
  $last = $_REQUEST['last'];
  $first = $_REQUEST['first'];
  $grade1 = $_REQUEST['test1Grade'];
  $grade2 = $_REQUEST['test2Grade'];
  $grade3 = $_REQUEST['test3Grade'];
  $grade4 = $_REQUEST['test4Grade'];
  $final = $_REQUEST['finalExamGrade'];

  $sql= "UPDATE students SET " .
     "lastName = '" . $last . "', " .
     "firstName = '" . $first . "', " .
     "test1Grade = '" . $grade1 . "', " .
     "test2Grade = '" . $grade2 . "', " .
     "test3Grade = '" . $grade3 . "', " .
     "test4Grade = '" . $grade4 . "', " .
     "finalExamGrade = '" . $final . "'"
WHERE studentID =  '" . $id . "';";

  if ($conn->query($sql) == false ) {
     trigger_error('Wrong SQL: ' . $sql .
' Error: ' . $conn->error, E_USER_ERROR);
  } else {
     $affected_rows = $conn->affected_
rows;
```

```
        echo( "<br/>Affected rows:      "
. $affected_rows );
    }

    $conn->close();
    echo( "User " . $id . " has been
updated. Back to <a href='grades_list.
php'>Add-Upd-Del Page</a>.");

?>
```

# CHAPTER 9 SUMMARY

This has been a chapter heavy in concepts and techniques. Besides learning additional PHP code, you learned how to use a web application, *phpMyAdmin,* to perform database operations on a MySQL database. You learned how to build SQL statements to insert, retrieve, update and delete data in a MySQL database. You learned how to use an *application programming interface* so that your PHP code can access a MySQL database. Using all those, you built a simple and basic CRUD (Create, Retrieve, Update, Delete) application. There's still a lot to learn and master about using PHP to access databases, but if you understand and retain the concepts and techniques explained here, you're on your way to being an expert PHP and MySQL geek.

In the next chapter, we will discuss some useful PHP classes and objects. We will also learn how to access and manipulate date and time information using PHP.

# CHAPTER 10

# USEFUL PHP CLASSES AND OBJECTS

## CHAPTER OBJECTIVES:

- You will learn two important PHP date functions, **date()** and **time()**, and how to use these functions to access and manipulate date and time information.
- You will learn how to manipulate strings using some of the many string functions of PHP.
- You will understand how to use **sessions** and **cookies** to maintain state between browser requests in your PHP application.

## 10.1 THE DATE FUNCTION

All computer programs have to manipulate and work with dates and times. For example, web applications have to record the date and time a page was accessed and how long it was accessed. This is a relatively simple task that is made slightly more complicated by having to consider 24 different time zones. Accounting programs also have to calculate what date a reoccuring payment falls on, which is complicated further by the fact that each month of the year has a different number of days and leap years have to be considered. Besides those types of calculations, computer programs also have to take into account how to present dates and times. Does the user prefer *February 14, 2001* or *2001-02-14* or *02-14-2001*? Do you display time as military time, *17:45* or 12-hour time, *5:45p*?

Some programming systems have a specific date and time data type. PHP doesn't, but PHP does provide numerous date and time functions and objects (see http://php.net/datetime). In this section of this chapter, we will look at the **time()** and **date()** functions.

time()

date()

Every computer keeps track of the current date and time by using a built-in clock. You can obtain this built-in clock's date and time with the **time()** function. If you type the following code in your browser:

```php
<?php
    print("<br/>" . time());
?>
```

You may be surprised to see a 10-digit integer.

```
1395034340
```

This is a **timestamp**. It is the number of seconds between midnight of January 1, 1970 and the current date and time. This is the format that computers use to monitor and store dates and times because in this integer format date and time calculations are much easier.

**timestamp**

If you execute the above script again, you may get something like:

```
1395034355
```

Notice that the last two digits have changed from 40 to 55, meaning that 15 seconds have elapsed between the first and second time you executed the script. The computer's built in clock is running and keeping track of time.

Now, we can easily convert this **timestamp** into a date and time format that we can understand by using the **date()** function. For example, the script:

```php
<?php
    date("D - F d, Y", 1314934340);
?>
```

will return

```
        Fri - September 02, 2011
```

The date function accepts two arguments. The first is a mandatory format string, "*D - F d, Y*", that specifies how the date and time will be formatted. The second argument is optional. It is the timestamp (1314934340) that we wish to format. If the second argument is omitted, the **date()** function will use the timestamp returned by the **time()** function.

The meaning of each character of the format string is summarized in the following table.

| Character | Description |
|-----------|-------------|
| d | The 2-digit day of the month with a leading zero if needed. |
| D | The day of the week as a three-letter string ( ex. "Mon"). |
| F | The month as a full word (ex. "January"). |
| Y | The year as a four-digit number. |

Table 10.1: A few of the character formats for the format string for the date() function.

Study the previous date format string carefully and note how it results in the displayed output. Now, let's make a slight change in the previous date format string so that it now reads:

```
date("l - F d, Y", 1314934340);
```

Did you spot the change? It is the "l" (lowercase "L") right after the opening double quotes. The display will now be:

```
Friday - September 02, 2011
```

This is the meaning of the "l" (lowercase "L") character in the date format string:

| Character | Description |
|-----------|-------------|
| l ( lowercase "L") | The day of the week as a full word (for example, "Monday"). |

Table 10.2: Lowercase "L" character format for the format string for the date() function.

There are many other character formats for formatting dates in the **date()** function. They can be found at http://php.net/date.

Now, let's modify our script to include character formats for formatting time:

```php
<?php
    print(date("D F d, Y h:i:s"));
?>
```

This script will yield:

```
Mon - March 17, 2014 11:47:58
```

We did not provide a second argument, so the **date()** function used the timestamp returned by the **time()** function and formatted the time according to our newly added format string for formatting time, "h:i:s". The meaning of each character for formatting time is summarized in the following table.

| Character | Description |
|-----------|-------------|
| h | The hour in 12 - hour format, with leading zeros (01 -- 12). |
| i | Minutes, with leading zeros (00 – 59). |
| s | Minutes, with leading zeros (00 – 59). |

Table 10.3: A few of the character formats for the format string for the **time()** function

At the start of this section, we stated that PHP stores the **timestamp**, its internal clock, as a 10-digit integer because date and time calculations are much easier in this format. So, now let's calculate what the date and time will be 30 days from now. Here is the code to execute in your browser:

## CODE LISTING: CALCULATE 30 DAYS FROM NOW

```php
<?php
    print(date("D F d, Y h:i:s"));
    print("<br/>");
    print(time());
```

```
    $thirtyDays = 60 * 60 * 24 * 30;

    print("<br/>30 days from right now: " .
 (time()+ $thirtyDays));
 ?>
```

You should get something like this (of course, the current date and time will depend on when you execute this code):

Tue April 15, 2014 09:13:51
1397596431
30 days from right now: 1400188431

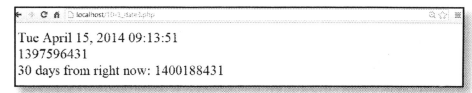

Figure 10.1: Various outputs of the **date()** function.

The 10-digit **timestamp** is of little use to us, so let's format it in a more readable and usable form. We use the **date()** function and this is the code to add:

```
print("<br/>30 days from right now:
" . (date("D F d, Y h:i:s",time()+
$thirtyDays)));
```

Viewing it in the browser, we will see something similar to this:

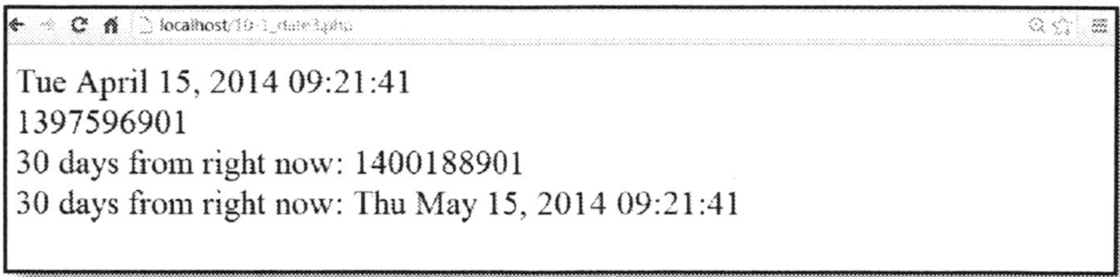

Tue April 15, 2014 09:21:41
1397596901
30 days from right now: 1400188901
30 days from right now: Thu May 15, 2014 09:21:41

Figure 10.2: The date and time, 30 days after the current date and time, is displayed more clearly.

We can also subtract days by simply replacing the plus sign (+) with a minus sign (-). Add the following code to the previous script and see the results in the browser.

```
print("<br/>30 days before: " . (time()-
$thirtyDays));
```

We can also get the exact time 18 hours from now. Here is the code to add:

```
$eighteenHours = 60 * 60 *18;

print("<br/>18 Hours from now: " .
(date("D F d, Y h:i:s", time() +
$eighteenHours)));
```

Notice that we are adding 18 hours by adding 60 * 60 * 18 or the number of seconds in 18 hours. In the browser, we will see this:

Figure 10.3: The exact time is displayed, 18 hours from the current time.

This has been a quick review of the **date()** and **time()** functions in PHP. Later in the section on cookies, we will use the **time()** function again specifically when we set the future expiration date and time of cookies. For a complete reference of all PHP date and time functions, please go to http://php.net/date.

## CODE LISTING: TIME AND DATE

```php
<?php
    print(date("D F d, Y h:i:s"));

    print("<br/>");

    print(time());

    $thirtyDays = 60 * 60 * 24 * 30;

    print("<br/>30 days from right now: "
. (time()+ $thirtyDays));

    print("<br/>30 days from right now:
" . (date("D F d, Y h:i:s",time()+
$thirtyDays)));

    $EighteenHours = 60 * 60 *18;

    print("<br/>18 Hours from now: "
. (date("D F d, Y h:i:s", time() +
$EighteenHours)));

?>
```

1. How many arguments does the **date()** function have?
   a. One
   b. Two
   c. Three
   d. Four

2. Which letter is used to obtain the full textual display of the month?
   a. F
   b. M
   c. m
   d. D

# 10.2 STRINGS IN PHP

In programming, a **string** is a series of characters. Here are examples of valid strings:

string

```
"Hi There!"
"How are you?"
"123456"
"!@#$%"
```

PHP has some unique features when working with strings.

The first concerns the use of single and double *quotes*. Let's consider the following PHP code:

quotes

```php
<?php
    $name = "Mark";
    echo("My name is $name");
    echo('<br/>My name is $name');
?>
```

In the browser, we will see this:

My name is Mark
My name is $name

Figure 10.4: The use of single and double quotation marks in PHP.

We can see that within the double quotation marks, expressions and variables are evaluated, while within the single quotation marks they are not.

*heredoc*

The second unique feature of PHP strings is the ability to define large blocks of strings by use of the *heredoc* syntax.

> **TIP:** In computer science, a **here document** is a file literal or input stream literal: it is a section of a source code file that is treated as if it were a separate file.

*Heredoc* lets you take a block of code, no matter how large, and make it into a string. The symbol that is used to display *heredoc* is <<<. This is an example.

### Heredoc Code Sample

```
$poem = <<< TEST
Roses are Red<br/>
Violets are Blue<br/>
I'm no fan of Heredocs<br/>
But I can teach you.<br/>
<br/>
TEST;

echo($poem);
```

Viewing in the browser, we will see this:

```
My name is Mark
My name is $name
Roses are Red
Violets are Blue
I'm no fan of Heredocs
But I can teach you.
```

Figure 10.5: The use of *heredoc* in PHP.

Using heredoc can be very tricky. Study this example carefully, as well as the explanations in the four lettered paragraphs **a**, **b**, **c** and **d**.

```
$string = <<< identifier
    Your string goes here. It can include
commas, quotes etc.
identifier;
```

**a**. *identifier* can be anything. In the previous example, TEST was used.

**b**. The leading tag, <<< *identifier,* tells the PHP parser that you're writing a heredoc. There must be a space between the "<<<" and the word "identifier". There should be nothing following this leading tag.

**c**. The closing tag, *identifier,* should be on a single line without anything else. Hit enter if you need to ensure it is on a single line.

**d**. Do not indent the closing tag.

Now, we are going to try out some of the many other PHP **string** functions. If you take a look at the PHP manual, you will find a number of available **string** functions as shown here:

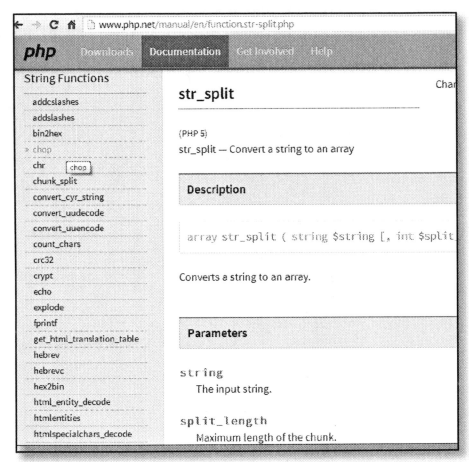

Figure 10.6: Some of the *string* functions used in PHP, taken from
http://www.php.net/manual/en/ref.strings.php.

*PHP and MySQL for Beginners*

Let's start with the **str_split()** function, which converts a string into an array. If you look at the syntax of this function in the PHP manual, you will see this:

**str_split()**

Figure 10.7. The syntax of the **str_split()** function taken from http://www.php.net/manual/en/function.str-split.php.

Let's use this **str_split()** function in our code:

```
$name = "Mark";
print_r(str_split($name));
```

The **print_r()** function displays an array in human readable form. In the browser, we will see this:

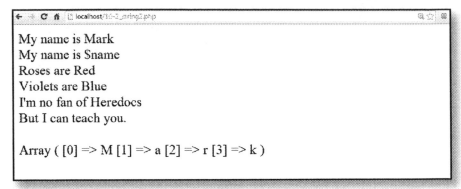

**print_r()**

Figure 10.8: The result of using the str_split() function.

Here you can see that the **str_split()** function took the letters of the name *Mark,* and split them into an array, where each letter occupies a single index of the array.

**strrev()**

Let's try the **strrev()** function which is used for reversing the characters of a string. If we use the following code:

```
print(strrev("Wheel of Fortune"));
```

In the browser, we will see:

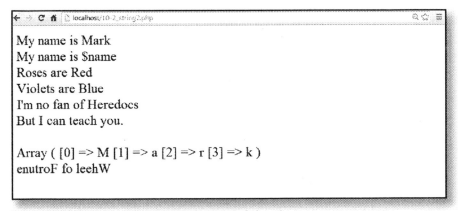

Figure 10.9: The result after using the strrev() function.

Here, you can see that the string "Wheel of Fortune" is perfectly reversed by using the **strrev()** function.

We can also get a part or portion of the string using the **substr()** function. This function has three arguments: the original string, the starting point,

**substr()**

and the length of the substring, that is, the number of characters of the original string that we want to display. Let's use the code in this way:

```
print(substr($poem, 0, 30));
```

In the browser we will get the following output, where the first 30 characters are displayed as a substring:

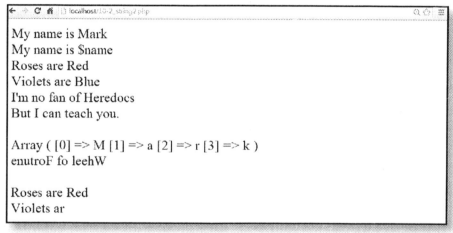

Figure 10.10: The first 30 characters of the string are displayed.

There are many other string functions (take a look at http://www.php.net/manual/en/ref.strings.php) that are available in PHP and you will have no problem finding a function or a combination of several functions to accomplish a specific programming task.

```php
<?php

$name = "Mark";

echo("My name is $name");
echo('<br/>My name is $name');
echo("<br/>");

$poem = <<<TEST
Roses are Red<br/>
Violets are Blue<br/>
I'm no fan of Heredocs<br/>
But I can teach you!<br/>
<br/>
TEST;

echo($poem);

print_r(str_split($name));
print("<br/>");

print(strrev("Wheel of Fortune"));

print("<br/>");
print("<br/>");

print(substr($poem, 0, 30));


?>
```

## QUESTIONS FOR REVIEW

1. The symbol that is used to display *heredoc* is:
   a. <<<
   b. >>>
   c. +++
   d. ---

2. What function converts a string into an array?
   a. strrev()
   b. str_split()
   c. str_con()
   d. str_arr()

# 10.3 SESSIONS

When you surf the Internet, you move from one webpage to another by clicking on links. When you click on a link, the web server interprets this as a request for the page pointed to by the link you clicked. It loads the page and executes that page's HTML and CSS commands as well as any PHP scripts.

PHP variables will be initialized, computations performed, text formatted, images resized and positioned, and then the fully rendered page is sent to your browser. The web server then erases that page from its memory. The values of any PHP variables are lost as well as the results of any computations. If for some reason you later click on that same link again, the web server will go through the same process again with no recollection that it had rendered this page before. This is what is meant by "stateless."

This was fine in the early, primitive days of the Internet when most of the time information was displayed in nicely formatted pages. But now, in the era of e-commerce and interactivity, some connection between webpages has to be maintained. As you move from one webpage to another and back, the values of variables in a webpage have to be preserved and passed on to the next webpages. This is what is meant by "maintaining state" or in more specific terms "preserving an application's state between browser requests."

For example, a shopping cart application has to remember what items you selected from the various webpages that you visited. In a massively multiplayer online role playing game (mmorpg), your character has to maintain its health status, weapons, spells, and so on. Not only as you move from level to level, but also as you log out on one day and log in on another day.

**Sessions**

PHP has several mechanisms for maintaining state between webpages, namely **hidden form fields, query strings**, **cookies** and **sessions**. We will survey only **sessions** (in this section) and **cookies** (in the next) which are the two most commonly used methods for maintaining state between browser requests.

**Short Session ID**

A PHP **session** is a temporary file on the server where you can store data. A short session ID (**SID**) is used to identify and protect that file. This **SID** is sent by the server to the browser as part of a cookie. The next time the browser makes a request to the server, it sends the **SID** cookie back to the server allowing the server to retrieve any **session** data it previously saved and makes this **session** data available in the superglobal array $_SESSION. (The **SID** generated by the server is unique, random and practically impossible to guess, making it—and your session data—secure from hackers.)

Although you can store a relatively adequate amount of data in a server session file (more data than you can store in a 4kb cookie), keep in mind that sessions are primarily used for storing temporary data to maintain state between webpages. Once you close your browser, the session data is no longer available. To store large amounts of data on a permanent basis, a database would be the appropriate tool.

When working with sessions, whether creating a session or retrieving data from a previous session, we always start our code with the **session_start()** function. This function creates a session or resumes one based on a **SID**.

When you call **session_start()**, this function will search for an existing **SID** in the client and if it finds one, it will send this **SID** to the server. The server then uses this **SID** to retrieve data from a previous session file. If no **SID** is found, **session_start()** won't send anything and the server, detecting this, will automatically create an **SID** and send it back to the browser and wait for any data to be saved in a session file it has created. All this takes place automatically just by calling the **session_start()**.

**session_start()**

There is one warning, though. The code that contains the call to **session_start()** should be placed in the <head></head> section of an HTML document. This is to make sure that the call to **session_start()** takes place before any output is sent to the browser. (This same warning also holds when we discuss cookies.)

Take a look at the following code and input it into a script named *sessions.php*.

## SESSIONS.PHP

```php
<?php
    session_start();
    $name="Mark";
    $_SESSION['name'] = $name;
    $_SESSION['password'] =
"lobsterchops";
    $_SESSION['age'] = "37";
?>
<a href="sessions2.php">Sessions 2</a>
```

As you can see, our first line of code is the call to the **session_start()** function. We then start saving data to a session file on the server by assigning that data as key-value pairs to the associative superglobal array $_SESSION. It's that simple. We just saved the values "Mark", "lobsterchops" and "37" to a session file on the server. Those saved values were assigned the respective keys "name", "password" and "age". It is by means of those keys that we retrieve their respective values. Note the last line which is a link to another script *sessions2.php*.

In *sessions2.php* we are going to retrieve the session data which we saved in *sessions.php*. This is the code for *sessions2.php*. Note that our first line of code is a call to **session_start()**.

## SESSIONS2.PHP

```php
<?php
    session_start();
    $name = $_SESSION['name'];
    $pw = $_SESSION['password'];
```

```
    $age = $_SESSION['age'];
    print("Stored in the session: $name
$pw $age");
?>
```

Now, let's run *sessions.php*. This is what you will see in the browser. Note that this is a hyperlink as evidenced by the different font color and the underscoring.

```
Session 2
```

When you click on this link you execute the script *sessions2.php* and get this display in your browser.

```
Stored in the session: Mark lobsterchops
37
```

Sessions are automatically deleted when you exit your browser but you may find it necessary to erase a session's data before it is automatically deleted. This is achieved with the **session_destroy()** function. Let's add the following two lines of code to the end of the script *sessions2.php*.

**session_destroy()**

```
session_destroy();
print("Session Destroyed. Please go to <a
href='sessions3.php'>Sessions 3</a>.")
```

*Sessions2.php* will now retrieve the session values saved by *sessions. php* and then destroy the session. Now, to verify that the session has indeed been destroyed, we will create the script *sessions3.php* which contains the following code.

### SESSIONS3.PHP

```
<?php
    session_start();
    if(isset($_SESSION['name']))
```

```
    {
    $name = $_SESSION['name'];
    $pw = $_SESSION['password'];
    $age = $_SESSION['age'];
    } else
    {
        print("Session appears to have
been terminated.");
    }
?>
<a href="sessions.php">Session 1</a>
```

The **isset()** function returns TRUE if a variable is not set to NULL. It returns FALSE if otherwise.

**isset()**

Let's now consecutively execute the scripts *sessions.php*, *sessions2.php* and *sessions3.php*. This will result in the following three respective screens.

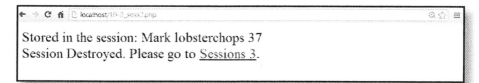

Figure 10.11: Screen output of script *sessions.php*

Figure 10.12: Screen output of script *sessions2.php*

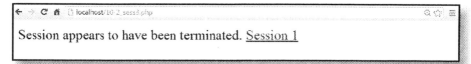

Figure 10.13: Screen output of script *sessions3.php*

## COMPLETE CODE LISTING: SESSIONS.PHP

```php
<?php
    session_start();

    $name="Mark";
    $_SESSION['name'] = $name;
    $_SESSION['password'] =
"lobsterchops";
    $_SESSION['age'] = "37";
?>
<a href="sessions2.php">Sessions 2</a>
```

## COMPLETE CODE LISTING: SESSIONS2.PHP

```php
<?php
    session_start();
    $name = $_SESSION['name'];
    $pw = $_SESSION['password'];
    $age = $_SESSION['age'];

    print("Stored in the session: $name
$pw $age");

    session_destroy();
    print(" <br> Session Destroyed.
Please go to <a href='sessions3.
php'>Sessions 3</a>. </br>")

?>
```

## COMPLETE CODE LISTING: SESSIONS3.PHP

```php
<?php
    session_start();
    if(isset($_SESSION['name']))
    {
    $name = $_SESSION['name'];
    $pw = $_SESSION['password'];
    $age = $_SESSION['age'];
    } else
    {
        print("Session appears to have
been terminated.");
    }
?>
<a href="sessions.php">Session 1</a>
```

### QUESTIONS FOR REVIEW

1. What function is used to begin each session?

   a. session_start()
   b. session_begin()
   c. session_initiate()
   d. None of the above

2. What function is used when we no longer want a session?
   a. session_end()
   b. session_finish()
   c. session_destroy()
   d. None of the above

# 10.4 COOKIES

In the previous section, we discussed **sessions,** which are temporary files on the server where the client's browser stores data to maintain state between browser requests. **Cookies**, on the other hand, are files no larger than 4kb which are left by the server on the client's computer.

Cookies

When a browser requests a page from the server, the server then sends one or more cookies to the browser in the headers of its response to the browser request.

The next time the browser makes a request to that same server that left the cookie, data in the cookie is automatically sent to the server within the request. By means of the cookie, the server "remembers" this particular browser client and can use the data in the cookie sent by this client to tailor responses uniquely to this particular client browser.

Cookies can only be retrieved by the servers that created them, thus providing a certain level of security. Still, they are vulnerable to hacker attacks and should be used only for non-critical data, such as user preferences. Browsers can also disable cookie support, cutting any access to cookies. Some clients may not support cookies at all. There is also a limit to how many cookies a client can hold. Only 20 cookies are allowed per domain and a client can hold only 300 cookies at any one time. Still, for non-security critical data such as user preferences, cookies can be an invaluable tool in maintaining state.

The data in a cookie should be arranged in the following sequential order of parameters:

| Cookie Field | Description |
|---|---|
| name | A unique name for a particular cookie. No whitespaces or semicolons are allowed. |
| value | The arbitrary string value attached to this cookie. |
| expire | The expiration date for this cookie. The expiration is specified as a timestamp or the number of seconds since midnight January 1, 1970 (GMT). |
| path | The browser will return the cookie only for URLs below this path. |

| domain | The browser will return the cookie only for URLs within this domain. |
|---|---|
| secure | The browser will transmit the cookie only over *https* connections. |

Table 10.4: Mandatory sequential order of cookie parameters.

Creating a cookie and sending it to the browser is easy with the **setcookie()** function. This function sends the appropriate HTTP header to create

**setcookie()**

the cookie in the browser. The arguments of the **setcookie()** function are the same parameters in the order shown in the previous table. Generally, though, you need to provide only the first three or first four parameters, (name, value, expire, and path) but you should provide six arguments whenever possible.

The **setcookie()** function should also be called before sending any output to the browser, because **setcookie()** sends the cookie within the server's HTTP response header. If you send output to the browser before calling **setcookie()**, PHP will automatically send the response headers first. **Setcookie()** thus loses its ability to send the cookie with the response header. It is for this reason that the code that contains the call to **setcookie()** is placed in the <head></head> section of the HTML document.

Here is the code to create two cookies named 'band' and 'food', respectively. The cookie 'band' will expire in one hour while 'food' will expire in 30 days. Save this code in a script named *cookies.php* and execute it.

**COOKIES.PHP**

```php
<?php

setcookie("band" , "Journey", time()+
3600); // Expires in One Hour

setcookie("food" , "pasta", time()+ (60 *
60 * 24 * 30) ); // 30 Day cookie

?>
```

We now have two cookies in the browser client and retrieving cookies is as easy as creating them. You use the superglobal associative array $_COOKIES which contains a list of all the cookie values sent by the browser in the current request. You provide the *name* parameter as a key to obtain the *value* parameter of the cookie.

Input this code in the PHP script *cookies2.php* and run the script.

### COOKIES2.PHP

```php
<?php
    $band = $_COOKIE['band'];
    $food = $_COOKIE['food'];
    print("Band: " . $band);
    print("<br/>Food: " . $food);
?>
```

The display should look like this:

```
Band: Journey
Food: pasta
```

Understand that a newly created cookie cannot be accessed via $_COOKIES until the next browser request is made. This is because the server first sends the cookie to the browser and at this point, the browser cannot send the cookie back to the server until the browser makes its next request.

Now, to delete or "expire" a cookie, you call **setcookie()** with the name of the cookie you want to delete as your first argument, an empty string (or any value) as your second argument, and a date and time in the past as your third argument. For example:

```php
setcookie("food" , "", (time()-1));
```

Need we explain why setting a time in the past deletes or expires our cookie? Now, add the previous call to **setcookie()** to the code in the script *cookies2.php*. Run the script again and you should get the same display as in Figure 10 - 16. But *cookies2.php*—because of our call to **setcookie()** with a previous timestamp as one argument—has no deleted the cookie 'food.' To verify that this cookie has been deleted, input the following code and save it as *cookies3.php*.

## COOKIES3.PHP

```php
<php
    $band = $_COOKIE['band'];
    print("Band: " . $band);

    if(isset($_COOKIE['food']))
    {
        print("<br/>Food cookie set");
    }
    else
    {
        print("<br/>No Food cookie
found.");
    }
?>
```

The **isset()** function returns TRUE if a variable is not set to NULL. Otherwise, it returns FALSE.

When you run *cookies3.php*, you will get the following result in the browser.

```
Band: Journey
No food cookie found.
```

The cookie 'food' has been deleted or expired.

## COMPLETE CODE LISTING: COOKIES.PHP

```php
<?php

    setcookie("band" , "Journey", time()+
36000); // Expires in One Hour
    setcookie("food" , "pasta", time()+ (60
* 60 * 24 * 30) ); // 30 Day cookie

?>
```

## COMPLETE CODE LISTING: COOKIES2.PHP

```php
<?php

    $band = $_COOKIE['band'];
    $food = $_COOKIE['food'];

    print("Band: " . $band);
    print("<br/>Food: " . $food);

    setcookie("food" , "", (time()-1));

?>
```

## COMPLETE CODE LISTING: COOKIES3.PHP

```php
<?php

    $band = $_COOKIE['band'];
    print("Band: " . $band);

    if(isset($_COOKIE['food']))
    {
        print("<br/>Food cookie set");
    }
    else
    {
        print("<br/>No food cookie
found.");
    }

?>
```

## QUESTIONS FOR REVIEW

1. What is a cookie?
   a. A file.
   b. A function.
   c. A command.
   d. None of the above.

2. What function is used to create a cookie?
   a. setcookie()
   b. startcookie()
   c. createcookie()
   d. None of the above.

# CHAPTER 10 LAB EXERCISE

1. Ensure that your MAMP or WAMP server stack is downloaded, installed, and running.

2. Set up an HTML document and embed an opening and closing PHP tag in the <body> section of the document. Save that document in your www folder (Windows) or htdocs folder (Mac) as described.

3. Create a short form in which the user enters a user name. Store the user name in a session variable.

4. Create a second page which reads the user name from the session variable. Output a greeting to the user.

5. After outputting the greeting, destroy the session and store the username in a cookie called username. Make the cookie expire in 30 minutes.

6. Create a new page and retrieve the cookie. Display the current date at the top of the page using the **date()** function.

7. Place the string "You have reached the end of PHP for Beginners." in the variable $message.

8. Output the number of characters in the string.

9. Using a string function and whatever code is necessary, replace all of the vowels with an X and output the string again.

10. Using a string function, convert the string into an array and output each element of the array using a loop. (Don't use print_r.)

# CHAPTER 10 LAB SOLUTIONS

## LAB.PHP:

```php
<!doctype html>
<head>
    <title>Lab 10</title>
    <?php
        $user;
        if(isset($_REQUEST['user']))
        {
            $user = $_REQUEST['user'];
            session_start();
            $_SESSION['username'] = $user;
            print("Session saved");
        }
    ?>
</head>
<body>
    <form action="lab.php" method="post">
        <label for="user">Username:</label><input type="text" id="user" name="user" />
        <br/><input type="submit" value="Save Session" />
        <br/><a href="lab2.php">Go to page 2</a>
    </form>
</body>
</html>
```

## LAB2.PHP

```php
<?php
    session_start();
    $username = $_SESSION['username'];
    print("Hello " . $username);
    session_destroy();
    setcookie("username", $username,
time() + 1800);
    print("<br/><a href='lab3.php'>Go to
page 3</a>");
?>
```

## LAB3.PHP

```php
<?php
    print(date("D F d, Y h:i:s"));
    $username = $_COOKIE["username"];
    print("<br/>From Cookie: " .
$username);

    $message = "You have reached the end
of PHP for Beginners.";
    print("<br/>");
    print("String length: " .
strlen($message));

    print("<br/>");
    print("<br/>");
    $vowels = array("a", "e", "i", "o",
"u", "A", "E", "I", "O", "U");
    $newMessage = str_replace($vowels,
"X", $message);
    print($newMessage);

    print("<br/>");
    print("<br/>");
```

```php
    $messageArray = explode(" ",
$message);
    for($i=0;$i<count($messageArray);$i++)
    {
        print($messageArray[$i] .
"<br/>");
    }
?>
```

Username: Alison

Save Session

Go to page 2

Hello Alison
Go to page 3

Figure 10.14: Screen output of script
*Lab.php.* 'Alison' has been entered in
the username field.

Figure 10.15: Screen output of
script *Lab2.php*

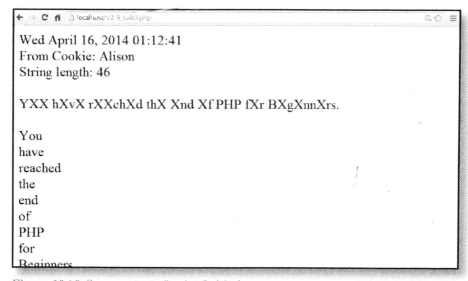

Wed April 16, 2014 01:12:41
From Cookie: Alison
String length: 46

YXX hXvX rXXchXd thX Xnd Xf PHP fXr BXgXnnXrs.

You
have
reached
the
end
of
PHP
for
Beginners

Figure 10.16: Screen output of script *Lab3.php*

# CHAPTER 10 SUMMARY

In this chapter you learned how to use PHP's **date()** and **time()** functions to access and manipulate date and time information. You have also been introduced to different ways of manipulating strings with PHP as well as two unique behaviors of PHP strings: the use of single and double quotes and the *heredoc* notation.

We have explored the use of sessions and cookies to maintain state between browser requests to the server.

As we close this last chapter, we salute and commend you for having persevered through the ten long chapters of this introductory book on PHP programming. You should be very proud of yourself—good job! Now, let me offer you a piece of advice: I'm sure you're famblar with the saying "use it or lose it", right? Well, that saying applies to your programming knowledge, too! Make sure you actively use your knowledge—practice and review key concepts now and again to keep everything fresh in your mind. Now get started programming your webpages with what you have learned! Good luck!

## ANSWER KEY: PHP AND MYSQL FOR BEGINNERS

### Chapter 1: Your First PHP Script

1. What does PHP stand for?
   Answer: b. Pre Hypertext Processor.

2. What does A in WAMP stand for?
   Answer: a. Apache.

3. What address do you use to check the homepage generated by the Apache server for Windows?
   Answer: a. http://localhost

4. What is the correct opening PHP tag?
   Answer: d. <?php

5. Which command can display a formatted string output?
   Answer: d. printf( " ");

### Chapter 2: Variables

1. What are variables?
   Answer: a. Variables are containers for strings and numbers.

2. What are the operations of the common arithmetic operators?
   Answer: b. Addition, subtraction, multiplication, division.

3. What is the correct syntax for the combined operation concatenate then return in PHP?
   Answer: c. .=

4. Instead of writing a routine that adds 1 to a certain variable, what operator can be used instead?
   Answer: a. increment

### Chapter 3: Arrays

1. What are arrays?
   Answer: b. Arrays are containers for multiple variables.

2. If a member of an array is to be assigned as the fourth member, what should the proper syntax be?
Answer: c. $arrayName[4]=data;

3. In the example,
$example = array( "Cooper" => 25000,    "Oswald" => 23500);
which is/are the key/s?
Answer: a. Cooper, Oswald

4. What is the simplest explanation for multidimensional arrays?
Answer: b. They are arrays within an array.

5. What is the difference between a simple array and a superglobal array?
Answer: b. Superglobal arrays come from the user inputs from the web server, URLs, cookies, and HTML files, while simple arrays are declared by the programmer.

## Chapter 4: Control Structures - Branching

1. What are conditionals?
Answer: d. Statements that evaluate an expression condition to be true or false and perform the corresponding action associated with either true or false value.

2. What conditional operator does the condition "<=" depict?
Answer: d. Less than or equal to.

3. What is an example of a complex conditional?
Answer: d. A series of if-else-if statements.

4. What are switch-case-break conditionals best defined as?
Answer: c. A conditional that has many cases.

5. Is switch-case-break case sensitive?
Answer: d. By default, yes, but it can be customized by adding multiple cases that would remove the case sensitivity.

6. What are ternary operators?
Answer: a. A one line if-else statement associated with a variable.

7. What do the symbols (?) and (:) in ternary statements mean, respectively?
Answer: a. If and else.

## Chapter 5: Control Structures - Looping

1. What are loops?
   Answer: c. Commands that repeat the process of a code segment depending on the condition set in the program.

2. What is the main difference between *while-loops* and *do-while-loops*?
   Answer: c. *Do-while-loops* iterate at least once even if the condition is initially set to FALSE; *while-loops* ignore the loop if the initial value is FALSE.

3. What is a *for-loop*?
   Answer: c. *For-loops* are a compact type of loops that contain the logic and parameters of the loop all in one line.

4. Which loop would be wise to use when dealing with complex arrays?
   Answer: d. *foreach-loop*

## Chapter 6: Custom PHP Functions

1. What are functions?
   Answer: a. Blocks of related code that are stored under a specific keyword that may be called and repeatedly used.

2. What are arguments?
   Answer: a. Values or strings that are passed into a function.

3. How does the return statement work?
   Answer: a. Return ends the execution of a function and returns a value to the caller of the function.

4. Which function will produce an error and terminate the script if the filename passed to that function as an argument cannot be found?
   Answer: c. require

## Chapter 7: Server File I/O

1. What does File I/O mean?
   Answer: a. File Input and Output.

2. Which is the fastest method of retrieving the contents of text files in the server?
   Answer: a. file_get_contents

3. What mode does 'a' stand for?
   Answer: b. Append.

4. What is usually required to append and delete files in the server?
   Answer: b. Permission from the server.

5. What does CSV mean?
   Answer: d. Comma-Separated Values.

## Chapter 8: Sending EMail with PHP

1. Which corresponds to the recipient of the email in PHP?
   Answer: a. $to

2. What does the mail() function do?
   Answer: a. It sends and receives email using PHP through the server.

3. What does SMTP mean?
   Answer: a. Simple Mail Transfer Protocol.

4. What is an HTML email?
   Answer: a. A type of e-mail that has HTML tags embedded in it.

5. What does the header MIME Version do?
   Answer: a. This heading indicates that the email contains characters other than ASCII text characters.

6. What is the use of the content type text/HTML header?
   Answer: d. It defines the character encoding the HTML email will use.

## Chapter 9.1 Setting up the Database

1. What should we type for getting a list of commands in the MySQL command prompt?
   Answer: a. mysql>Help

2. In order to make sure that each entry in a column will be unique, what do we use?
   Answer: c. Primary Key

## Chapter 9.2 Retrieving a Query from the Database

1. Which class serves as a blueprint to a connection object which enables php scripts to access a MySQL database?
   Answer: a. mysql_connect.

2. Which command indicates that if *mysql_connect* does not work, it will go ahead and provide a MySQL error that occcurred?
   Answer: b. or die

## Chapter 9.3 Storing Information in the Database

1. What is the data type of the information that the *post* method uses?
   Answer: a. array.

2. Which method of the *connection* object is used to close itself?
   Answer: c. close

## Chapter 9.4 Deleting and Updating Database Records

1. Which symbol is used in a query string?
   Answer: d. ?

2. What is *$_REQUEST[]* ?
   Answer: d. a super global array

## Chapter 10.1 Date Object

1. How many arguments does the **date()** function have?
   Answer: b. Two

2. Which letter is used to obtain the full textual display of the month?
   Answer: a. F

## Chapter 10.2 Strings in PHP

1. The symbol that is used to display *heredoc* is:
   Answer: a. <<<

2. What function converts a string into an array?
   Answer: b. str_split()

## Chapter 10.3 Sessions

1. What function is used to begin each session?
   Answer: a. session_start()

2. What function is used when we no longer want a session?
   Answer: c. session_destroy()

## Chapter 10.4 Cookies

1. What is a cookie?
   Answer: a. A file

2. What function is used to create a cookie?
   Answer: a. setcookie()

# Appendix

| Terms | Definitions and Descriptions |
|---|---|
| *api* | This is an acronym for application programming interface. It is a set of rules, routines, protocols and **function** calls that define how software components and packages can interact with each other. |
| *argument* | This is a value or **variable** that is passed to a function. |
| *array* | This is one of the eight data types of **PHP**. Arrays can store more than one value of any data type. Arrays can be **simple**, **associative** or **multi-dimensional**. |
| *associative array* | This is one of the two types of **arrays** in PHP that assigns a unique key value to each array member or element. It uses named keys to identify and distinguish its members or elements as opposed to the numeric keys (indexes) used for **simple** arrays. |
| *boolean* | This is one of the eight data types of **PHP**. It has only two Boolean values – TRUE and FALSE. |
| *branching control structure* | See '**control structure**' |
| *break* | This is a **PHP** keyword used to terminate the execution of either a **branching** or **looping** **control structure**. |
| *browser* | This is also known as a web browser which is a program with a graphical user interface (GUI) that retrieves, presents, and traverses information resources on the world wide web. |
| *class* | This is the blueprint for an object. A **class** specifies in detail what an object's program code and data are. Objects are created (instantiated) from classes. |

| Terms | Definitions and Descriptions |
|---|---|
| *client* | A **client** is a computer program that runs on a personal computer or workstation and accesses a **server** (for data and computer resources) to perform its tasks. For example, an email **client** is a computer program that sends and receives email. |
| *code block* | A group of contiguous lines of code usually but not always delimited by curly braces '{}'. |
| *cookies* | These are **files** no larger than 4kb which are left by the server on the client's computer. Along with **sessions**, cookies are used in "preserving an application's state between browser requests." |
| *column* | A **table** in a **database** consists of several **columns** or **fields** which store various types of data. |
| *concatenation* | The process of joining several distinct things or objects into one whole unit. |
| *comparison operator* | This is an operator that compares two **operands** in a **conditional expression**. Examples are the identical operators "===", and the less than operator, "<". |
| *conditional expression* | This is an expression that evaluates to either of the **Boolean** values true or false. |
| *conditional statement* | This is a line of programming code which abides by a strict syntax and grammar rule. It contains a **conditional expression** and is the beginning statement of a **branching control structure**. |
| *control structure* | In programming, this is a language construct or the specific way lines of code are written and arranged which allows the flow of execution to be altered. There are basically two types of programming control structures – **branching** and **looping (iteration).** |

| Terms | Definitions and Descriptions |
|---|---|
| *CRUD* | This is an acronym for Create, Retrieve, Update, and Delete. A CRUD application creates, retrieves, updates and deletes data from a **database**. |
| *csv file* | This is a comma-separated value (csv) text **file** consisting of values (numeric and text) separated by commas. |
| *database* | This is an organized collection of related data. It is primarily made up of **tables**. It is in these **tables** that data is stored. |
| *do-while* | This is one of the four **looping control structures** of **PHP**. The other three are: **while-loop**, **for-loop** and **foreach-loop**. |
| *dot operator* | The dot operator '.' is PHP's **concatenation operator**. For example, the **concatenation operator** between the two strings "Hello" . "There" will yield the string "HelloThere". |
| *email client* | This is the program a user (an individual) uses to send or receive emails such as Microsoft Outlook. Users who use Gmail use a webmail **client**. |
| *esmtp* | This is an acronym for Extended Simple Mail Transfer Protocol which is a slightly updated version of the **SMTP** protocol. ESTMP allows the transmission of multimedia through email. |
| *expression* | This is any valid combination of **variables**, constants, **literal values**, **operators**, objects and even **functions** that can be evaluated to produce a value. |
| *field* | In a database, a **field** is another term for a **column**. Sometimes, a **field** refers to a specific **row's** column. |

| Terms | Definitions and Descriptions |
|-------|------------------------------|
| *file* | This is a collective and generic term for data that is stored on a computer whether that data is in the form of text, binary, pictures, video, sound, webpages, etc. A file is assigned a unique filename to identify and distinguish it from other files |
| *file handle* | This is the return value of the **fopen()** function and is the primary means a **PHP** script accesses a **server** file. For every file a script accesses, a **file handle** is assigned. **File handles** are of the **PHP** data type **resource**. |
| *filename* | A **file** on a computer is given a unique **filename** to identify it. The **filename** consists of a name of a certain number of characters (in Windows the **filename** has a maximum of 255 characters) optionally followed by a dot a character extension. The character extension usually identifies the type of file. For example, the extension "avi" indicates a video file, "mp3" indicates a sound file, etc. |
| *file i/o* | This means file input-output or the creation and retrieval of files on a computer. In **PHP**, **file i/o** concerns only server files as **PHP** is forbidden from performing **file i/o** (except for the case of cookies) on a client's computer. |
| *floating-point* | This is one of the eight data types of **PHP**. It represents numeric values with decimal digits. |
| *foreach-loop* | This is one of the four **looping control structures** of PHP. The other three are: **while-loop, do-while-loop, for-loop.** |
| *for-loop* | This is one of the four **looping control structures** of PHP. The other three are: **while-loop, do-while-loop** and the **foreach-loop.** |
| *function* | This is a self-contained block of program statements, with well-defined boundaries, that performs a specific task. |

| Terms | Definitions and Descriptions |
|---|---|
| *here document* | In computer science, this is a file literal or input stream literal. It is a section of source code file that is treated as if it were a separate file. |
| *heredoc* | This is a block of code, no matter how large, that can be treated as a string. |
| *if-else / if-elseif statement* | This is one of three of **PHP**'s **conditional statements** that are used to create **branching control structures**. The other two are the **if-statement** and the **switch-statement**. |
| *if-statement* | This is one of three of **PHP**'s **conditional statements** that are used to create **branching control structures**. The other two are the **if-else/if-elseif-statement** and the **switch-statement**. |
| *imap* | This means Internet Mail Access Protocol. This is the protocol used by an incoming **mail server** that stores incoming and outgoing messages on the **server**. |
| *incoming mail server* | This processes all received emails and implements either POP3, *Post Office Protocol, version 3,* or IMAP, *Internet Message Access Protocol.* POP3 **incoming servers** store sent and received messages on the client's hard drive. This forces a user to access and process his emails from only one device or locations. However, IMAP **incoming servers** store messages on servers thus allowing users to access their emails from any location or any device. |
| *indexed array* | This is one of the two types of **arrays** in PHP that use numeric indexing to identify and distinguish its members or elements. |
| *integer* | This is one of the eight data types of **PHP**. It is a whole number whose range of values depends on the hardware. |

| Terms | Definitions and Descriptions |
|---|---|
| *ip address* | This is a unique number that is assigned to every computer that is connected to the internet. IP means "internet protocol". |
| *join* | In a database, this is another term for **relationship.** |
| *key* | In a database, this is a **column** or **columns** on which an **index** is constructed to allow rapid and/or sorted access to a table's data. |
| *keyword* | This is a word that is reserved by a programming language because it has a special meaning in the grammar and syntax rules of the language. Programmer's cannot use keywords to name their variables or for any other purpose. Examples are: 'break', 'else', 'if, 'function' and many more. |
| *linux* | This is an open source (free) cross-platform operating system based on UNIX. |
| *literal value* | This is an expression that consists of only one **operand** and no **operators**. It is a single scalar value expressed by its actual string value (i.e. not referenced by a variable). For example, 1, 1.414 and "string" are literal values. **Literal values** as expressions evaluate to themselves |
| *logical operator* | This combines **conditional expressions** to produce a **boolean** result of either TRUE or FALSE. For example, $age < 21. |
| *looping control structure* | See '**control structure**'. |
| *mail server* | This is a type of **server** that handles the sending and receiving of emails. It may run on its own dedicated hardware or share hardware resources with other server programs. It runs automatically during normal operations without any manual intervention. There are two types of **mail servers – outgoing** and **incoming mail servers.** |

| Terms | Definitions and Descriptions |
|---|---|
| *mode* | A mode specifically identifies a type of **file i/o** operation. Some **file i/o** functions require a mode as one of their arguments. Modes are identified by either a character and or a plus sign, '+'. For example, 'r' means 'read access only' while 'r+' means 'read and write access'. |
| *multi-dimensional array* | This is an **array** whose elements or members are **arrays**. It is one main **array** containing several **arrays** called "sub-arrays". |
| *mysql* | This is a popular, open source, relational database management system (RDBMS) that supports multiple administrative tools, programs and libraries, and application programming interfaces. As of March, 2014, it is the world's second most widely used open-source (RDBMS). |
| *null* | This is one of the eight data types of **PHP**. **Null** indicates that a **variable** has no valid value whatsoever stored in it. |
| *object* | This is a programming construct consisting of program code and program data bundled up as one isolated package with clear boundaries and definite rules on how to access that **object's** program code and data. |
| *or die()* | This is a PHP language construct equivalent to exit. |
| *open source software* | This is computer software with its source code made available and whose license states that the copyright holder provides the rights to study, change and distribute the software to anyone and for any purpose. |
| *operator* | This is a symbol that specifies a particular programming action to be performed. This action usually results in a new value. There are ten groups of **PHP operators** - arithmetic, array, assignment, bitwise, comparison, error control, execution, logical, string, and incrementing/decrementing. |

| Terms | Definitions and Descriptions |
|---|---|
| *operand* | This is what receives the action of an **operator**. Most of the time, an **operand** is a **variable** but it could also be a **literal**, an **object**, a **function** or anything that an **operator** can validly perform its action on. |
| *outgoing mail server* | This type of **server** handles all sent emails and implements SMTP – *Simple Mail Transfer Protocol.* |
| *parameter* | This is a **variable**, declared in a **function's** definition that accepts the values of the arguments passed to the **function**. |
| *PEAR* | This is an acronym for **PHP** Extension and Application Repository. It is a large collection of free, high-quality, source code packages that can be downloaded and used in any **PHP** application. |
| *pop3* | This means Post Office Protocol version 3. This is the protocol used by an incoming mail server that stores sent and received messages on the client's hard drives. |
| *post* | This method passes the information as an array instead of creating a *query string* which appears in the URL. |
| *PHP* | This is a recursive abbreviation where the first letter stands for the abbreviation itself and it means "**PHP**: Hypertext Processor. |
| *PHPMyAdmin* | This is a free and open source tool written in **PHP** and run from a **web browser**. It allows the user to create, modify or delete MySQL databases as well as any of the tables of the database or rows and fields of any table. **PHPMyAdmin** executes SQL statements on the database as well as manages users and permissions. |
| *primary key* | This is a **column** or **field** or several **columns** or **fields** whose values make sure that each **row** of a **table** will be unique. |

| Terms | Definitions and Descriptions |
|---|---|
| *query string* | It is the part of a **URL** that contains data to be passed to web applications. |
| *record* | In a database, this is another term for a **row**. |
| *relationship* | In a database, a relationship is a link between two **tables**. |
| *resource* | This is one of the eight data types of **PHP**. |
| *return value* | This is an optional value returned by a **function** to its caller. |
| *row* | In a database, this is a set of related data in a **table**. |
| *scope* | This is an important concept in programming and refers to the visibility or accessibility of a variable in a program. Specifically, it refers to the portions of code in a program where the variable can be accessed. **PHP** provides global and local scope. |
| *server* | This is a system (software and suitable computer hardware) that is designed to process requests and deliver data to other computers (**clients**) over a local network or the Internet. |
| *session* | This is a temporary file on the server where you can store data. The client browser stores data in a **session** to "maintain state between browser requests" or in more specific terms "preserving an application's state between browser requests." |
| *SID* | This is an acronym for **session** id. The SID is generated by the **server** and is used to identify and protect a **session**. |
| *SQL* | This means Structured Query Language (often pronounced as "see-qwell"). It is a programming language used to search, sort, add and extract data in relational databases. |
| *simple array* | See **indexed arrays**. |

| Terms | Definitions and Descriptions |
|---|---|
| *smtp* | This is an acronym for Simple Mail Transfer Protocol. This is the protocol used when email is delivered from an email **client**, such as Outlook Express, to an email **server** or when email is delivered from one email **server** to another. SMTP uses port 25. Nowadays, though, most mail servers use **ESMTP**, an updated version of SMTP. |
| *state* | This word is used in the context of the phrase "maintaining state" or in more specific terms "preserving an application's state between browser requests." When a **browser** requests a web page from a **server**, neither the **browser** nor the **server** has any memory of the **browser's** previous requests. Values of any **variables** in a web page are lost when a new page is loaded. Preserving those values is what is meant by "maintaining state". |
| *string* | This is one of the eight data types of **PHP**. It is a sequence of characters of arbitrary length. |
| *sub-array* | This is an **array** within a **multi-dimensional array.** |
| *superglobal* | This is a built-in (pre-defined) **associative array** variable in **PHP** that is automatically available to all **PHP** code especially within functions (global scope). Superglobals represent data coming from **URLs**, HTML forms, **cookies, sessions**, and the **web server** itself. |
| *switch-statement* | This is one of three of **PHP**'s conditional statements that are used to create branching control structures. The other two are the **if-statement** and the **if-else/if-elseif-statement.** |
| *table* | In a database, this is a collection of closely related data or **columns** (or **fields**). |
| *ternary operator* | This **operator** works on three **operands** and is a compact form of the **if-else statement**. |

| Terms | Definitions and Descriptions |
|---|---|
| *timestamp* | This is the number of seconds between midnight of January 1, 1970 and the current date and time. **PHP** internally stores the **timestamp** as a 10-digit integer. |
| *URL* | This means Universal Resource Locator. It is a specially formatted string of text used by web browsers and other network software. It identifies a *network resource* on the Internet. Network resources are files that can be plain Web pages, other text documents, graphics, or programs. An example of a URL is http://www.website.com/myfinename. |
| *value* | In a **table** in a MySQL **database**, a value is the data in a given **row** and **column**. |
| *variable* | This is a memory unit allocated to store a value which can be any of the eight **PHP** data types, namely: **integers, floating-point numbers, strings, booleans, arrays, objects, resources** (or **handles**) and **null**. |
| *web browser* | See **browser** |
| | This is one of the eight data types of **PHP**. |
| *while-loop* | This is one of the four **looping control structures** of PHP. The other three are: **do-while-loop, for-loop, foreach-loop**. |